RELIABLE DATA STRUCTURES IN C

Thomas Plum

Plum Hall Inc
1 Spruce Avenue
Cardiff New Jersey 08232

Library of Congress Cataloging in Publication Data

Plum, Thomas, 1943-
  Reliable Data Structures in C.

  Bibliography: p. 10-1.
  Includes index.
  1. C(Computer program language) 2. Data
structures (Computer science) I. Title.
QA76.73.C15P59 1985   005.13'3   85-45156
ISBN 0-911537-04-X

Acknowledgement of trademarks: UNIX is a trademark of AT&T Bell Laboratories; PDP-11 and VAX are trademarks of Digital Equipment Corporation; CP/M is a trademark of Digital Research Corporation; Venix is a trademark of VenturCom, Inc.; Xenix and MS-DOS are trademarks of Microsoft Corporation; Lattice is a trademark of Lattice, Inc.; Idris is a trademark of Whitesmiths, Ltd.; Tplus is a trademark of Textware International; Safe C is a trademark of Catalytix Corporation; MC68000 is a trademark of Motorola Inc. C is not a trademark, nor are the names of the software development commands such as cc.

This book was set by the author, using a Hewlett-Packard LaserJet controlled by the Textware Tplus output driver, formatted by troff under the Venix version of the UNIX operating system on a PDP-11/23.

For Joan

PREFACE

This book is meant to follow an introductory book on C. It assumes that you have successfully written some programs in C and that you are familiar with the basics of variables, operators, functions, pointers, and structures. It does not assume that you know the more advanced features such as pointers to functions, pointers to structures, dynamic allocation, enumerations, typedef, bit-fields, union's, FILE I/O, or dynamic data structures; these will be covered herein.

Also covered are rules for reliable programming, programming with no surprises.

The book also introduces the important topics of data structures: arrays, strings, pointers, records, stacks, queues, double-ended queues ("deques"), trees, record files, and hashed files. Besides discussing the formal aspects of each data structure, we also present working general-purpose C functions that implement the technique.

From its conception in the early 1970's, the design of C allowed for small compilers that could run on small hardware. Extra checking was available from tools like lint, the "extended syntax checker" distributed with UNIX systems. Now, some of the checking that lint does has been incorporated into recent C compilers.

A new level of reliability checking has been introduced by run-time checking environments such as Safe C from Catalytix and bcc from Delft, such as enforcing strict bounds for arrays and pointers, catching overflow errors, use of uninitialized variables, etc. The trend toward greater automated assistance in programming has my support, and I hope the book is useful in this area.

In the future we expect to see greater use of the computer's reasoning ability to assist in the production of software for new devices. The existing techniques go by the names "artificial intelligence" and "expert systems." And just as a growing number of existing language translators produce C language as their intermediate output, I expect that we will see a growing interest in C as the output from "expert program writer" systems. In order to achieve the reliability that is needed for this level of automation, the properties needed in the generated code must be strictly verifiable. One of my intentions in this book is to prepare the way for new levels of expressive power in programming.

One of the central tenets of my approach to programming instruction is that there is an important difference between *project* code and *publication* code. Project code is written to achieve a programming purpose. It tends to make extensive use of software resources developed by the project team, especially headers and libraries. Appropriate use is made of defined types and defined constants for the usages that are typical in the project.

Publication code is written for journals, articles, and some textbooks. It uses only the standard headers and libraries.

I have chosen to present C in a "project code" style, because I think that this style comes closer to the realistic programming environment. Indeed, many of you will be working in an environment that has adopted our *C Programming Guidelines* as a local standard. But even if your local project standard is different, it will probably resemble the "project" style more than the "publication" style.

Working in "project" style means that more effort is needed at the start to create an environment of headers, but the effort pays off in readability and portability.

At the beginning of some sections you will find the notation *"Topics assumed from previous book."* Then a number of topics are listed, with page references to *Learning to Program in C* [Plum, 1983]. These assumed topics are covered in most of the introductory books on C. If you find that you are not familiar with one of the assumed topics, consult one of the introductory books first for further details. I have tried to make this book reasonably self-contained without recapitulating C language from the ground up.

This book's approach to reliable programming attempts to be a codifying of successful practice, building upon a growing number of successful applications in C. Rules for reliable use of C are presented which are based upon the experience of numerous working programmers.

One of the most frequent questions regarding a readable style for C is "where should code be commented and what should be in the comments." My approach to "properties of data" is meant to provide an important part of the answer to this question: the comment appearing on a variable's declaration should describe the defining property of the data, and anywhere in the code that this property is not true, there should be a succinct comment that documents this warning.

The C language and its library have been the subject of several standardization efforts during the middle 1980's. One effort was organized by /usr/group, an organization of commercially-oriented users of UNIX operating systems and similar other systems. In 1984, /usr/group published a "standard for computer operating systems that are functionally compatible with UNIX Operating Systems developed by AT&T Bell Laboratories." In particular, the function library associated with C was standardized in this document. Those who served as officers of the /usr/group Standards Committee include Heinz Lycklama, David Buck, Donald Kretsch, Michael Tilson, John Bass, Thomas Hoffman, and Eric Peterson.

In 1983, a committee was organized under the auspices of ANSI (the American National Standards Institute) to begin the standardization of C. This committee is under the administrative control of ANSI X3, the group responsible for computer systems, and is known as X3J11. Those who have served as officers of X3J11 and its subcommittees include Jim Brodie, P. J. Plauger, Ralph Phraner, Larry Rosler, Ralph Ryan, and myself.

One of the early decisions of X3J11 was to adopt the /usr/group library standard as the starting point ("base document") for the standardization of the C library. Careful attention was paid to eliminating the system-specific aspects of this library; the eventual library specification for ANSI C is meant to be portable to all operating systems which provide support for C compilation and execution. As of the writing of this book (mid-1985), the current draft of X3J11 has been forwarded to ANSI X3 for publication as an Information Bulletin, one step short of a formal Draft Proposed Standard. Current expectations are for an ANSI standard for C to be adopted during the year 1986. Many vendors are already incorporating many of the features of this evolving standard, so you are likely to encounter these features with the next releases of your compilers.

This book attempts to provide a style of writing C which will allow compilation of programs both with current compilers and with new compilers that adopt features of the evolving standard. I have attempted throughout the book to inform you of the likely future direction of C. Still, there will be changes to the X3J11 draft before it becomes an official standard, so it must be understood throughout that none of this book is an official statement of the X3J11 committee. I especially ask reviewers not to cite my observations about the ANSI draft as representations of the final decisions of X3J11.

This book describes a style of programming that is compatible both with the (June 1985) draft of ANSI C and with a broad spectrum of existing compilers. The approach has been specifically verified against the compiler and library of UNIX System V (Release 2), Whitesmiths 2.3 and 3.0, Lattice 2.15, and Catalytix Safe C, as well as the library standardized by /usr/group. This level of C will be referred to as "recent C" in the book. But where it is specifically necessary to refer to the (draft) ANSI C standard, I have done so.

The official ANSI standard for C is expected during 1986, but the reliability advantages of recent C compilers are available now. The rules described in this book represent techniques that can be used now, with existing compilers, for maximum reliability in both the current and the future (ANSI C) environments.

There are a number of people whom I would like to acknowledge for their important contributions to this book. Yoram Bar-Am and Steve Bennett wrote the original version of the menu processor which I adapted for Chapter 6. Jim Brodie, Jim Ginn, Jim D'Ottavi, David Graham, Steve Hersee, Andrew Johnson, Bob Racko, Roland Racko, Christopher Skelly, and my mother, Ruby Schunior, read several drafts and made many helpful suggestions. Dave Brown, Dennis Cook, Debbie Fullam, Jim Griffin, Tom Hoffman, Paul Kleppner, Bill Koenig, Neil Ludlam, Mike Meissner, Ed Rathje, and Larry Rosler provided numerous helpful ideas during various stages of the book. Many thanks go to Joe Lochel for his clams and his friendship. Tim Cwik provided tireless assistance with the programming examples and the final production work. I am especially grateful to Roland Racko for writing the ev editor, which provides an identical screen-editing interface on the four different machine environments in our office. My thanks also to Whitesmiths, Ltd., for the reliability of the Idris systems, on which I did my development work up to the typesetting stage. Alan Feuer and Jonathan Lettvin advanced the state-of-the-art in C reliability with the Safe C environments and made numerous helpful suggestions, especially regarding the ranges of pointers. Brent Byers, the author of the Tplus formatter, provided valuable assistance with the typesetting. I am indebted to P. J. Plauger for many contributions: for pioneering the development of C compilers for a wide range of popular operating systems, for innumerable discussions of the subject matter across several continents, and for his careful reading of a preliminary draft of the book. My thanks should in no way imply that each of these people agrees with every one of my conclusions.

I also wish to thank Dennis Ritchie for designing a language of unique elegance, power, and utility.

There are some other people who made important contributions to the work which has culminated in this book. They include John Colligan, Paul Davis, Kee Dewdney, Dennis Geller, John Holland, G. M. Weinberg, Steve Robertshaw, J. A. Robinson, Gil Roeder, Steve Schustack, Barbara Smyly, Glenn Smyly, and Ed Yourdon. My sincere thanks to each of them.

My heartfelt thanks to all the staff of Plum Hall Inc — Linda Deutsch, Suzanne Battista, Cathy Bertino, and Anne Hall — for everything that they did to bring this book into existence. I am profoundly grateful to my late father, George E. Schunior, for his love and direction. And to my family, the Halls, McEvoys, Pritchetts, Richters, Schuniors, Schanzes, and Whynmans, goes my deepest gratitude for their steadfast support. To them, and especially to Joan Hall, my thanks for everything.

CONTENTS

INTRODUCTION

A programmer needs to know several things, in order to write reliable programs using C data structures (simple and complex):

1. The exact meaning of "data types of variables and expressions": Type mismatches are usually accompanied by a bug; the code is likely to be either erroneous, or hard-to-modify, or non-portable.

2. What is available in the C library: Libary knowledge is required for correct use of the functions and avoidance of potentially buggy "re-inventing the wheel."

3. The meaning of "properties of data": Starting with the simple distinction between "defined" and "undefined," a grasp of data properties is essential to producing correct programs.

4. Relevant algorithms, including static structures, dynamic structures, and files.

5. How to create re-useable libraries of functions and macros.

Here is what a programmer needs to *do* to create reliable programs:

1. Follow a design discipline that ensures that data objects and program control structures have clear invariants.

2. Wherever possible, make use of re-useable code (headers and libraries) to avoid "re-inventing."

3. Write in a style that would allow all possible automated checking assistance. Whether or not automated assistance is used, the discipline means fewer reliability problems.

4. As much as possible, preserve the defining properties of data objects, and give warning in the transitional regions of code.

5. Use executable assertions wherever practical.

There is an important relationship between reliability and portability. A successful C program is very likely to be ported to new environments. If it was not written with due regard for portability, reliability problems pop up when the code is ported. Thus, in most cases it is not adequate for the program to work in only one environment.

There is, of course, an important role for code which is intentionally targeted to just one environment. C can be used to replace assembler code for low-level applications where one controls the special resources of a particular machine. What reliability demands in these cases is that the environment-dependent nature of the code be clearly documented, preferably with explicit mention of the environment-dependent features.

To give you now a brief overview of the book's contents, Chapter 1 describes the definition capabilities of C, describing both the preprocessor and the use of typedef. Header files are presented both for the standard library and for the functions that will be presented in the book.

Chapter 2 covers the reliable use of the scalar data types of C: floating-point numbers, integers, and characters. The relevant libaries are discussed, along with suggestions for the handling of errors.

Chapter 3 describes arrays. The use of loop invariants and assertions is described in the context of two algorithms for sorting an array. Strings, and other arrays of characters, are covered, along with the library functions that use them.

Chapter 4 deals with pointers, their types and their properties.

Chapter 5 discusses the standard I/O facilities of the C library, as well as methods for direct control of screen-oriented I/O.

Chapter 6 covers structures, unions, bit-fields, and the use of structures to create a handler for "menu" interactions.

Chapter 7 describes dynamic data structures, the malloc and free functions, and the macros and functions needed to create stacks, queues, double-ended queues ("deques"), and trees.

Chapter 8 covers file I/O of both the "stream" and "record" varieties. Binary I/O, direct access, and "hashed" files are used to implement a simple database.

An appendix summarizes the reliability rules presented in the text, along with notes on the state of the ANSI C draft.

One consistent focus of this book is precision of speaking and of documentation. To this end, I have made use of several abbreviations borrowed from various sources. Each will be explained in its proper context, but it will be useful to provide a brief preview here:

nul	means the char value '\0'
{lo:hi}	means the range of values from lo to hi
a[i:j]	means the subarray a[i] through a[j]
a[*]	means the entire array a (for emphasis)
p[*]	means the array to which pointer p provides access
a[*] => sorted	means that a[*] is now sorted
a[*] : string	means that a[*] must be a string

None of these notations are part of C syntax. They just provide a concise way to describe the behavior of a program. You could replace each of them with a verbal phrase, if you prefer.

In this book, the use of the word "reliable" as applied to programs is meant to have very practical connotations: Reliable programs produce no surprises. The actual behavior of the code is readily determined by a reading of the program. The program does what it appears to do. This is easy to say, and not quite so easy to do.

Our quest for reliable C programs begins with the definition capabilities of C, which is the subject of the first chapter.

CHAPTER 1: PREPROCESSING

The "definition" capabilities of C provide techniques for writing programs that are more portable, more readable and easier to modify reliably. For a simple example,

```
#define SCR_CLR_ALL "\33[2J"
```

defines a string which will clear the entire screen (on "ANSI" terminals). A program that contained numerous instances of `printf(SRC_CLR_ALL)` would be considerably more readable than one containing lots of `printf("\33[2J")` uses.

In addition, definitions can aid in modifiability. Using the `SCR_CLR_ALL` example, the program that uses the defined name can be more easily modified than the one which contains instances of the actual string sprinkled throughout the program.

In this chapter, we will see a variety of uses of definitions and header files which are helpful in achieving reliable programs.

1.1 Defined Constants

Topics assumed from previous book: `#include` [2.10], `#define` [2.10], `ctype.h` [3.5], `stdio.h` [3.21], defined constant [3.21].

A file of definitions to be `#include`'d is known (in ANSI C terminology) as a *header*. (In other Plum Hall books, it is also referred to as an *include-file*.) In the standard header `stdio.h` are found some definitions such as

```
#define EOF (-1)
```

This definition causes any subsequent appearance of the name EOF to be replaced by the characters (-1). Since the definition contains an operator (the "minus"), we enclose the definition in parentheses. If we left the parentheses off the definition, as in

```
#define EOF -1
```

it is possible that the name could generate an expression that would be misunderstood by the compiler. For example, this erroneous code

```
if (c EOF)
```
WRONG - should be   `(c != EOF)`

would be interpreted as

```
if (c - 1)
```
syntactically correct, but unintended

which would not generate any compile errors, even though it is certainly not what the programmer intended. This suggests a rule for reliable programming (the first of many that will be presented):

Rule 1-1: Any macro definition containing operators needs parentheses around the entire definition. Each appearance of a macro argument in the definition also needs to be parenthesized if an embedded operator in the argument could cause a precedence problem.

All the reliability rules are summarized in the appendix [1-1].

There are two main reasons for creating defined constants. The first is readability: the defined constant clarifies the meaning of the constant. The name EOF tells the reader that it is a special indication for "end-of-file." For another example from <stdio.h>, consider

```
#define BUFSIZ 512
```

Again, the name clarifies the meaning: BUFSIZ is the "buffer size" used in efficient I/O transfers.

The second reason for defined constants is modifiability: the defined constant shows how the program can be modified for a different value. Thus, on systems where 1024 is a better value for the size of disk I/O transfers, the standard header stdio.h could specify the value 1024 for BUFSIZ.

Rule 1-2: Reliable modification of defined constants requires an environmental capability: there must be a means for ensuring that all files comprising a program have been compiled using the same set of headers. (The UNIX make command is one such capability.)

EOF, however, exemplifies a defined constant which cannot be modified arbitrarily: many implementations of the character-type tests (ctype.h) assume that its value is -1. The UNIX System V manual page for ctype(3C), for example, says explicitly that EOF equals -1. Thus the following usage rule:

Rule 1-3: If there are limitations on the modifiability of a defined constant, indicate the limitations with a comment:

```
#define EOF (-1)    /* DO NOT MODIFY: ctype.h expects -1 value */
```

Another application of this rule is the explicit indication of minimum and maximum values:

```
#define NBUFS 5    /* min 2, max 30 */
```

(to give a hypothetical example).

Rule 1-4: If one definition affects another, embody the relationship in the definition; do not give two independent definitions.

This pair of definitions

```
#define XX 5
#define XX2 (XX + 2)
```

follow the rule by showing the relationship, whereas

```
#define XX 5
#define XX2 7    misleading, no indication of relationship
```

does not. In the former case, we could reliably modify the program by changing the definition of XX; in the latter case, we would have to make a guess that XX2 should probably be changed to equal XX plus two.

Just giving the constant a name is not enough to ensure modifiability; you must be careful always to use the name, and remember that the value could change. One project had difficulties changing the value of BUFSIZ because some programmers had written

```
nblocks = nbytes >> 9;    hard to modify, uses "magic number"
```

in a number of places where

```
nblocks = nbytes / BUFSIZ;
```

was needed. The programmers figured that "everyone knows that BUFSIZ equals 512," and right-shifting nine bits is the same (for positive numbers) as dividing by 512. But when BUFSIZ changed to 1024 on some systems, modifications were difficult. Hence, this rule:

Rule 1-5: If a value is given for a #defined name, do not defeat its modifiability by assuming its value in expressions.

In most compilers, it is also possible to define a constant on the invocation of the compiler, rather than putting a #define in the code itself. Suppose, for example, that we wish to have the constant NBUFS specified at compilation time, rather than putting the value into the program. Using the UNIX compiler cc, we accomplish the definition like this:

```
cc -DNBUFS=10 pgm.c
```

This technique allows a program to be targeted to different environments without changing the source code for the program.

The UNIX function library has recently been standardized by /usr/group, the UNIX industry association. This standard specifies a new header named <limits.h>, wherein are defined environment-dependent limits. (ANSI C will probably standardize a similar capability.)

A sample version of <limits.h> for C on an IBM PC-type machine might contain definitions like these:

```
#define CHAR_BIT          8         /* number of bits in a char */
#define CHAR_MAX        255         /* largest char value */
#define CHAR_MIN          0         /* smallest char value */
#define INT_MAX       32767         /* largest int value */
#define INT_MIN      -32768         /* smallest int value */
#define LONG_MAX 2147483647         /* largest long value */
#define LONG_MIN -2147483648        /* smallest long value */
#define SHRT_MAX      32767         /* largest short value */
#define SHRT_MIN     -32768         /* smallest short value */
#define UCHAR_MAX       255         /* largest unsigned char value */
#define UINT_MAX      65535         /* largest unsigned int value */
#define ULONG_MAX 4294967295        /* largest unsigned long value */
#define USHRT_MAX     65535         /* largest unsigned short value */
```

Note that no extra definitions are needed for numbers like "number of bits in an int;" we can use sizeof(int) * CHAR_BIT, since every data type occupies an integral number of bytes.

Rule 1-6: Use limits.h for environment-dependent values.

1.2 Defined Types

Topics assumed from previous book: defined type [3.21], void [3.21], typedef [3.21].

It will be very important for purposes of reliability to make more precise definitions of data types than the basic types supplied by C. In this book, we will describe special semantic rules for various of these defined types. Here is a list of some useful defined types:

```
bits        /* an unsigned short integer used for bitwise operations */
ushort      /* an unsigned short integer used for arithmetic */
tbool       /* a char (one byte) to be tested for zero or non-zero */
metachar    /* a short integer holding a char value or EOF */
bool        /* an integer to be tested for zero or non-zero */
void        /* the "return type" for a function that returns no value */
```

These types can be defined using #define or typedef; here is a typedef version:

```
typedef unsigned short ushort, bits;
typedef char tbool;
typedef short metachar;
typedef int bool;
typedef int void;    /* delete if compiler supports void */
```

The important difference between #define and typedef is that #define replaces the name with its definition during preprocessing, whereas typedef is handled by the C syntax analysis. Thus, a defined type created via typedef cannot be "undefined" or re-defined, so its usage is more reliable. Also, if the name is mistakenly used as a variable name, the diagnostics are more intelligible.

This particular set of defined types are consistently used in the various Plum Hall books on C. In "publication" code, where one desires the fewest possible augmentations to standard C, an alternative approach is to use comments:

```
short status;      /* interface status: bits */
char is_open;      /* is device open?: bool */
int input_c;       /* most recent input character: metachar */
```

Even in publication code, however, the symbols ushort and void are important for portability reasons. Not all compilers currently accept the unsigned short type, but most that do not accept it are targeted for small machines where ushort can simply be translated into unsigned int.

Regarding void, any function that does not return a value should be indicated as being a void function. The following scr_beep function outputs the "bell" character, but does not return any value to the calling function, so we give it the void type:

```
void scr_beep()
    {
    putchar('\7');  /* "bell" - ASCII version */
    }
```

Recent C compilers implement void as a keyword. If your compiler supports void, you should not try to #define or typedef a definition for it; in this case, you should remove any such definitions from your headers. If your compiler does not support void, you should define it as int.

Rule 1-7: Use a consistent set of project-wide defined types.

1.3 Standard Headers

Topics assumed from previous book: #include [2.10], stdio.h [3,4]. math.h [3.17], ctype.h [3.5].

Headers are used for several purposes: creating defined constants, creating defined types, and declaring the type of various functions.

The modern treatment of libraries is to create a header for each related group of functions, along with any special symbols that are useful with those functions. Thus the math functions (and also the symbol HUGE_VAL) are declared in <math.h>:

acos	cos	fmod	modf	tan
asin	cosh	frexp	pow	tanh
atan	exp	ldexp	sin	
atan2	fabs	log	sinh	
ceil	floor	log10	sqrt	

The character-test functions are declared in <ctype.h>:

isalnum	isdigit	isprint	isupper	toupper
isalpha	isgraph	ispunct	isxdigit	
iscntrl	islower	isspace	tolower	

And the standard I/O functions (plus some useful symbols) are declared in `<stdio.h>`:

clearerr	fopen	fseek	printf	scanf	ungetc
fclose	fprintf	ftell	putc	setbuf	
feof	fputc	fwrite	putchar	setvbuf	
ferror	fputs	getc	puts	sprintf	
fflush	fread	getchar	remove	sscanf	
fgetc	freopen	gets	rename	tmpfile	
fgets	fscanf	perror	rewind	tmpnam	
BUFSIZ	EOF	FILE	NULL		
stdin	stdout	stderr			

Another standard header is `<assert.h>`, which provides an `assert` macro for debugging. This header will be covered in Section 1.6.

The logical extension of this approach is to partition each library entirely into related groups of functions, with each header declaring all functions in its group. ANSI C envisions two more headers, `<string.h>` and `<stdlib.h>`. (`<string.h>` is already found in UNIX libraries, beginning with System V. System V has another header named `<memory.h>`, which ANSI C will probably merge into `<string.h>`.)

In `<string.h>`, there should be declarations for these functions:

memchr	memset	strcoll	strncat	strrchr
memcmp	strcat	strcpy	strncmp	strspn
memcpy	strchr	strcspn	strncpy	strtok
memmove	strcmp	strlen	strpbrk	

In `<stdlib.h>` there should be declarations for several miscellaneous functions:

abort	atof	bsearch	exit	ldiv	rand	system
abs	atoi	calloc	free	malloc	realloc	
atexit	atol	div	getenv	qsort	srand	

Most of these names will be described in this book. Each header will be described when we need its functions; the names are given here just for completeness.

The variety of libraries available with existing compilers does create a portability problem for your code. Until the time that all your compilers conform to an ANSI standard, the following approach will help shelter your programs from library differences: The headers `<math.h>`, `<ctype.h>`, and `<stdio.h>` are well-nigh universal, and can simply be #included. For each of the other headers limits.h, string.h, and stdlib.h, create a header of your own which can be included without using the "angle-bracket" `<xxx.h>` form. In that header, provide declarations for all the functions that are supported on the environment that you are using. You might, of course, provide any missing functions yourself, and include their declarations in the header.

One other ANSI header needs to be mentioned. It is called <stddef.h> ("standard definitions") and it includes a few type definitions and named constants. The only one that we will need in this book is called size_t, and it is defined to be an integer that is big enough to hold the size of any object (unsigned int or unsigned long int).

The minimal versions of these "pre-ANSI" headers required for the programs in this book are as follows:

```
stddef.h:
    /* stddef.h - standard definitions (partial listing) */
    /* ENVIRONMENT-DEPENDENT - ADJUST TO LOCAL SYSTEM */
    #ifndef STDDEF_H
    #define STDDEF_H
    typedef unsigned size_t;      /* use unsigned long in large-object model */

    #ifndef NULL
    #define NULL 0                /* use OL if  int-size < long-size == ptr-size */
    #endif

    extern int errno;
    #endif

limits.h:
    /* limits.h - environment limits (partial listing) */
    #ifndef LIMITS_H
    #define LIMITS_H
    #define CHAR_BIT    8
    #endif
```

```
string.h:
    /* string.h - string functions (partial listing) */
    #ifndef STRING_H
    #define STRING_H
    #include "stddef.h"
    data_ptr memcpy();  /* PARMS(data_ptr s1, data_ptr s2, size_t n) */
    char *strcat();     /* PARMS(char *s1, char *s2) */
    char *strchr();     /* PARMS(char *s1, int c) */
    int strcmp();       /* PARMS(char *s1, char *s2) */
    char *strcpy();     /* PARMS(char *s1, char *s2) */
    size_t strlen();    /* PARMS(char *s1) */
    char *strncat();    /* PARMS(char *s1, char *s2, size_t n) */
    int strncmp();      /* PARMS(char *s1, char *s2, size_t n) */
    char *strncpy();    /* PARMS(char *s1, char *s2, size_t n) */
    #endif

stdlib.h:
    /* stdlib.h - miscellaneous library functions (partial listing) */
    #ifndef STDLIB_H
    #define STDLIB_H
    #include "stddef.h"
    double atof();      /* PARMS(char *s) */
    int atoi();         /* PARMS(char *s) */
    long atol();        /* PARMS(char *s) */
    data_ptr calloc();  /* PARMS(unsigned int n, size_t size) */
    void exit();        /* PARMS(int status) */
    void free();        /* PARMS(data_ptr ptr) */
    data_ptr malloc();  /* PARMS(size_t size) */
    int rand();         /* PARMS(void) */
    void srand();       /* PARMS(unsigned int seed) */
    #endif
```

Each header declares the returned type of various functions. The types of the function parameters are also specified in comments [1-2].

Assuming that you have all these headers, or have created your own versions, when and why should you use them? First of all, notice that several problems can arise from not declaring the returned type of a library function. For example, most of the functions in the math library return double values. If you use one of these functions, such as

```
x = sqrt(y);
```

without including the math.h header (and without declaring the function in your own program), the compiler assumes that sqrt returns an int value, which will give a garbage value to x in this example.

A more subtle problem arises in using the string functions. A number of these functions return a value of type char * ("pointer to character"), and can be embedded into expressions:

```
strcat(strcat(s, ".1"), ".a");
```

will end up catenating ".1.a" onto the end of s. In order for this to work reliably, the compiler must know that strcat returns a char * value. Otherwise, the compiler assumes that it returns int, and the program will not work in some environments where int and char * are different sizes. (The lint checker will complain in any case, if you have lint.)

For these reasons, it is important to declare the library functions. Should you use the headers, or declare each function yourself? In general, the headers are the more reliable way to be sure that you have all the correct declarations, but there is one (temporary) problem. Some compilers will link the object code for every library function that you declare, whether or not your program actually calls it. The ANSI C standard will probably say that functions should not be linked unless they are used, though it may be a while before all compilers behave this way. I recommend that you use the standard headers for the library, unless your compiler links everything.

If you are going to use the standard headers, I also recommend that you create your own local header file that brings in all the headers needed for your project. I have used the generic name local.h for this header; your own local version will presumably have its own name. The simplest course is to have your local.h include all the standard library headers, as the safest way to be sure that they are all included.

Rule 1-8: Be sure that all functions are declared before use; headers are the most reliable way.

Rule 1-9: Create a project-wide "local" header for standard definitions and inclusions.

One of the headers that we will use is called portdefs.h ("portability definitions header"). Into it are collected various defined types, defined constants, and macros which will be important in producing portable code. By including it in our local.h we ensure that all programs compile with these "portability definitions." The following listings of local.h and portdefs.h show the definitions that are needed for the Plum Hall books:

local.h:

```
    /* local.h - Definitions for use with Reliable Data Structures in C */
    #ifndef LOCAL_H
    #define LOCAL_H
    #include <stdio.h>
    #include <ctype.h>
    #include <math.h>
    #define FALSE           0           /* Boolean value */
    #define FOREVER         for(;;)      /* endless loop */
    #define NO              0           /* Boolean value */
    #define TRUE            1           /* Boolean value */
    #define YES             1           /* Boolean value */
    #define getln(s, n)     ((fgets(s, n, stdin)==NULL) ? EOF : strlen(s))
    #define ABS(x)          (((x) < 0) ? -(x) : (x))
    #define MAX(x, y)       (((x) < (y)) ? (y) : (x))
    #define MIN(x, y)       (((x) < (y)) ? (x) : (y))
    #define DIM(a)          (sizeof(a) / sizeof(a[0]))
    #define IN_RANGE(n, lo, hi) ((lo) <= (n) && (n) <= (hi))
    #ifndef NDEBUG
    #define asserts(cond, str) \
        {if (!(cond)) fprintf(stderr, "Assertion '%s' failed\n", str);}
    #else
    #define asserts(cond, str)
    #endif
    #define SWAP(a, b, t)   ((t) = (a), (a) = (b), (b) = (t))
    #define LOOPDN(r, n)    for ((r) = (n)+1; --(r) > 0; )
    #define STREQ(s, t)     (strcmp(s, t) == 0)
    #define STRLT(s, t)     (strcmp(s, t) < 0)
    #define STRGT(s, t)     (strcmp(s, t) > 0)
    #include "portdefs.h"   /* portability definitions */
    #include "stddef.h"     /* (ANSI) standard definitions */
    #include "limits.h"     /* (ANSI) machine parameters */
    #include "string.h"     /* (ANSI) string functions */
    #include "stdlib.h"     /* (ANSI) miscellaneous standard functions */
    #include "rdslib.h"     /* functions from Reliable Data Structures in C */
    #endif
```

portdefs.h:

```
/* portdefs.h - definitions for portability */
/* ENVIRONMENT-DEPENDENT - ADJUST TO LOCAL SYSTEM */
#ifndef PORTDEFS_H
#define PORTDEFS_H

/* adjust these names to local machine/compiler environment */
typedef unsigned short ushort;  /* or "unsigned" if short-size == int-size */
typedef unsigned char utiny;    /* to get unsigned byte */
typedef int void;               /* delete if compiler supports void */
typedef unsigned index_t;       /* may be chosen ad-lib locally */
typedef char *data_ptr;         /* use ANSI "generic ptr" if available */

/* next 5 names require no local changes, will work anywhere */
typedef char tbits;             /* one byte, for bitwise uses */
typedef char tbool;             /* one byte: {0:1} */
typedef ushort bits;            /* 16 bits (or more), for bitwise uses */
typedef int bool;               /* for function returns: {0:1} */
typedef short metachar;         /* return from getchar: {EOF,0:UCHAR_MAX} */

/* modulo function giving non-negative result */
#define IMOD(i, j) (((i) % (j)) < 0 ? ((i) % (j)) + (j) : ((i) % (j)))
/* if i % j is never negative, replace with the following line: */
/* #define IMOD(i, j) ((i) % (j)) */

/* portably convert unsigned number to signed */
#define UI_TO_I(ui) (int)(ui)   /* more complicated on ones complement */

/* structure offsets and bounds; adjust to local system */
#define STRICT_ALIGN int        /* adjust to local alignment requirement */
#define OFFSET(st, m) \
    ((char *)&((st *)&struct_addr)->m - (char *)&struct_addr)
#define BOUNDOF(t) \
    ((char *)(struct {char byte0; t byten; } *)&struct_addr)->byten - \
    (char *)&struct_addr)
static STRICT_ALIGN struct_addr = 0;
#define STRUCTASST(a, b) memcpy(&(a), &(b), sizeof(a))

/* defined constants */
#define FAIL      1             /* failure exit */
#define SUCCEED   0             /* normal exit */
#define STDIN     0             /* standard input */
#define STDOUT    1             /* standard output */
#define STDERR    2             /* standard error output */
#define SEEK_SET  0             /* seek relative to start of file */
#define SEEK_CUR  1             /* seek relative to current position */
#define SEEK_END  2             /* seek relative to end */
#endif
```

To be consistent with the approach of giving headers for all function declarations, we will also provide a header for all the utility functions that will be presented in this book. We will call it rdslib.h ("Reliable Data Structures library header") and it looks like this:

```
rdslib.h:
    #ifndef RDSLIB_H
    #define RDSLIB_H
    bool itoa();          /* PARMS(int n, char *str, int ndigits) */
    int fgetsnn();        /* PARMS(char *str, int size, FILE *fp) */
    int getsnn();         /* PARMS(char *str, int size) */
    int getreply();       /* PARMS(char *prompt, char *reply, int size) */
    bool getpstr();       /* PARMS(char *p, char *s, size_t n) */
    bool getplin();       /* PARMS(char *p, char *s, size_t n) */
    void plot_trk();      /* PARMS(int n, char c) */
    void reverse();       /* PARMS(char *s) */
    bool strfit();        /* PARMS(char *s1, char *s2, size_t n) */
    #endif
```

On any sizeable project that you work on, a significant part of the early work will be involved with choosing the project-wide set of headers to be used and putting them into the appropriate places in the system. Once the groundwork is done, however, the shared set of definitions makes everything else much easier.

1.4 Macro Functions

Topics assumed from previous book: macros with parameters [5.17].

A macro with parameters will be referred to as a *macro function,* for brevity. Of course, it is not *really* a function, but it is easier to talk about this way.

Our local.h specifies three macro functions:

```
#define ABS(x)       (((x) < 0) ? -(x) : (x))
#define MAX(x, y)    (((x) < (y)) ? (y) : (x))
#define MIN(x, y)    (((x) < (y)) ? (x) : (y))
```

Since each argument can contain operators, each parameter is parenthesized in the definition to avoid precedence conflicts. And since the entire result is an expression usable with other operators, the entire definition is also parenthesized. These are two reliability techniques totally under control of the programmer who writes the macro.

Unfortunately, one reliability problem is beyond the macro writer's control: side-effects on macro arguments. A typical example is

```
ABS(++n)     bug!
```

which increments n twice. To introduce some terminology, an *unsafe macro function* is one which evaluates a parameter more than once in the code expansion. Stated positively, a *safe* macro function evaluates each parameter only once in the code expansion. By this definition, all three macro functions (ABS, MAX, and MIN) are unsafe. As things stand now, the documentation for such macros must warn about putting side-effects on the invocation, and the responsibility is upon the programmer using the macro. (Some new compilers provide assistance in locating such bugs; see the appendix [1-3].)

Rule 1-10: Use UPPERCASE names for unsafe macro functions, to emphasize the restrictions on their usage.

For safe macros, there are some advantages to using lowercase names. Each safe macro could be replaced by an actual function call, and at different times during project development, one might want the macro version or the function version. For an example from the library, the character-type tests in ctype.h are usually implemented as safe macros; they could therefore be replaced with actual function versions.

Rule 1-11: Never invoke an unsafe macro with arguments containing assignment, increment/decrement, or function call.

Rule 1-12: Whenever possible, use safe macro functions.

To be more precise about our usage, all the macros described so far are what we will call *expression macros:* after replacement of arguments, they produce a valid C expression value. Thus, an expression macro (such as MAX(i, j)) can be used any place that C allows an expression.

An expression macro can be used purely for its side-effects, just like calling a void function. One such macro is useful for swapping two data objects using a third temporary:

```
#define SWAP(a, b, t) ((t) = (a), (a) = (b), (b) = (t))
```

Since the macro produces a single expression (three assignments connected with the comma operator), an invocation of the macro can be made into a statement just by adding a semicolon:

```
/* reverse the characters in a string */
for (i = 0, j = strlen(s) - 1; i < j; ++i, --j)
    SWAP(s[i], s[j], t);
```

Another form of macro is the *statement macro.* For example, the "swap" operation can also be written as a statement macro, like this:

```
#define SWAP_SHORT(a, b) {short _t; _t = (a); (a) = (b); (b) = _t;}
```

Because the definition constitutes a *block* (compound statement), it can have local variables, such as _t. This eliminates the need for an explicit parameter, but it limits the type of data to which the macro can be applied.

A statement macro like SWAP_SHORT, which contains code enclosed in braces, has one small syntactic restriction on its usage. We would like to put a semicolon onto each invocation of the macro, just because this looks more familiar:

```
if (a[i] < a[j])
    SWAP_SHORT(a[i], a[j]);
```

However, the macro replacement itself already *is* a statement, so the semicolon becomes an extra *null statement* tacked on. Usually, there is no harm, except for this one situation:

```
if (a[i] < a[j])
    SWAP_SHORT(a[i], a[j]);        syntax error
else
    /* ... */
```

Now we have a syntax error, because there are two statements between the if and the else. The unfortunate conclusion is that we need to be sure that the statement body following the if is enclosed in braces:

```
if (a[i] < a[j])
    {
    SWAP_SHORT(a[i], a[j]);
    }
else
    /* ... */
```

To keep things in perspective, statement macros comprise a small minority of the macros that you will typically use. The troublesome context is fairly uncommon, and the compiler will give a clear indication of any problem. Therefore, no special rules are necessary.

It would be nice to have a form for a statement macro which becomes a valid C statement when a semi-colon is appended. One interesting way to construct it is to terminate the macro with a trailing else:

```
#define SWAP_SHORT(a, b) if (1) {short _t; _t = a; a = b; b = _t} else
```

This does ensure that the macro will be syntactically valid when embedded into other C statements like this:

```
if (a[i] < a[j])
    SWAP_SHORT(a[i], a[j]);
else
    /* ... */
```

Unfortunately, the error of forgetting a semicolon is fairly common, and it will silently produce a very unreliable result in a common context like this:

```
SWAP_SHORT(i, j)          well-hidden bug
++n;
```

This generates

```
if (1) {short _t; _t = a; a = b; b = _t} else
++n;
```

Re-arranged for readability, it looks like this:

```
if (1)
    { short _t;   _t = a; a = b; b = _t }
else
    ++n;
```

The increment statement following the macro has become the body of the (never executed) else, producing a mysterious result with no chance of syntax diagnosis (unless the compiler complains about "unreachable code").

The "trailing else" form for statement macros is therefore not recommended.

A *control macro* is one which resembles a control structure. One simple example is the FOREVER macro:

```
#define FOREVER  for (;;)
```

which is sometimes used in implementing an "N+½-time loop":

```
FOREVER
    {
    perform some action
    if (time to quit)
        break;
    perform further actions
    }
```

A more involved example is useful in constructing highly optimized inner loops; our local.h header includes a macro named LOOPDN, which counts a variable downwards toward zero:

```
#define LOOPDN(r, n) for ((r) = (n)+1; --(r) > 0; )
```

In most environments, using LOOPDN (with a register variable r) is the most time-efficient way of specifying n iterations. (The expression is compared versus zero, and the decrement is part of an expression evaluation; see Plum and Brodie [1985].) Using the macro is preferable to writing the actual in-line code, because the code itself is rather obscure and ugly — the macro hides the messy details. If some environment allows a more efficient loop than this one, using the macro allows us to change the definition in just one place.

1.5 Undefining

Once a symbol has been #define'd, its definition can be deleted via #undef. For a dangerous example, consider

```
#define NBUFS 5
char b1[NBUFS][BUFSIZ];
/* ... one page of code here ... */
#undef NBUFS
/* ... another page of code here ... */
#define NBUFS 7
char b2[NBUFS][BUFSIZ];
```

This example is deliberately chosen to illustrate the reliability problems of #undef. The declarations for b1 and b2 appear to the reader to be of equal size, but the definition of NBUFS has changed underfoot. Thus, as a general rule, the re-definition of symbols is unreliable.

To put it in a positive way, we want each symbol to have an *invariant* meaning, so that each instance of the symbol denotes the same thing.

One usage of #undef may become more common, as a certain discipline of library construction becomes standard. Namely: each name in a library is declared in its associated header (as we saw in previous section). The header can #define a function name as a macro function (provided that it is a *safe* macro). Then, if the programmer wishes to be sure that a given name is a true function, it will be adequate to #undef that name.

ANSI C will probably specify that it is always allowable to #undef a name, even if it has not been #define'd. Some existing compilers, however, will complain about #undef'ing a non-existent name. For the time being, the safest course is to use this pattern:

```
#ifdef NAME
#undef NAME
#endif
```

1.6 Conditional Compilation

The preprocessor provides for *conditional compilation*, whereby some lines of code may be selectively excluded from compilation, depending upon the outcome of some test. This is the general pattern:

```
#if-line
    source lines
#else
    other source lines
#endif
```

The #else part can be omitted:

```
#if-line
    source lines
#endif
```

The #if-*line* can have any of these forms:

```
#if constant-expression
```
        True if *constant-expression* is non-zero.

```
#ifdef identifier
```
        True if *identifier* has been #define'd.

```
#ifndef identifier
```
        True if *identifier* has not been #define'd.

Recent C compilers provide two more capabilities:

```
#if defined(identifier)
```

or

```
#if defined identifier
```

means the same as

```
#ifdef identifier
```

And "else-if" logic is provided:

```
#if defined(A)
    n = A_LIMIT;
#elif defined(B)
    n = B_LIMIT;
#endif
```

means the same as

```
#ifdef A
    n = A_LIMIT;
#else
#ifdef B
    n = B_LIMIT;
#endif
#endif
```

Now we will look at some examples of the application of conditional compilation to practical programming situations.

Creating portable defined types

It is often useful to have a defined type to represent an unsigned short integer. Many compilers support this type directly, but some others (mostly 16-bit environments) do not. Suppose that our compile procedure ("shell script," "batch file," etc.) defines a constant named USHORT if the compiler supports the unsigned short data type. Then, we can specify the defined type ushort like this:

```
#ifdef USHORT
    typedef unsigned short ushort;
#else
    typedef unsigned ushort;     /* assumes 16-bit machine */
#endif
```

Using this definition in a local standard header, we can write our programs using ushort in declarations. Provided that our compilation procedure defines USHORT appropriately for the compilation environment, we will get the appropriate definition for each environment.

Tuning defined types for size

Suppose we need a defined type (to be called a TOKEN) which can represent any of a specified number of alternatives. (For simplicity, assume that the number of distinct "tokens" is never more than 64K.) We could define TOKEN like this:

```
#if MAXTOKEN <= 127
    typedef char TOKEN;
#else
    typedef ushort TOKEN;
#endif
```

Thus, for compilations in which the number of "tokens" is small, we can store each of them in a single char object (which can reliably hold a number between 0 and 127, in any environment).

Commenting-out sections of code

Sometimes one needs to "comment-out" several lines of code. Most compilers (and ANSI C) do not nest comments, so ordinary comments cannot be used. But the construct

```
#if 0
/* ... code to be commented-out ... */
#endif
```

will reliably delete the enclosed lines, even if they contain other #if constructs.

Rule 1-13: Use #if 0 if there is a need to comment-out sections of code.

Inclusion Sandwich

Until the early 1980's, large projects had a continual problem with the inclusion of headers. One group might have produced a graphics.h, for example, which started by including <stdio.h>. Another group might have produced keyboard.h, which also included <stdio.h>. And if <stdio.h> could not safely be included several times, arguments would break out about which header should include it. Sometimes an agreement was reached that each header should include *no* other headers, and therefore some application programs started with dozens of #include lines — and sometimes they got the ordering wrong, or forgot a header that was needed.

All these complications disappeared with the discovery of a simple technique: each header should #define a symbol which means "I have already been included." Then the entire header should be enclosed in a "sandwich":

```
#ifndef HEADER_H
#define HEADER_H
/* ... contents of the header ... */
#endif
```

Thus, the first time that header.h is #include'd, all of its contents will be included. If it should subsequently be #include'd again, its contents will be by-passed.

Rule 1-14: Enclose each header in an "inclusion sandwich."

Test drivers for library functions

When writing a library function — a general-purpose callable function, which has a source file to itself — it can be useful to provide a simple test harness within the same source file. The following pattern can be used:

```
code for the function
#ifdef TRYMAIN
main()
    {
    code for the test harness
    }
#endif
```

Now, when we want to compile the function with the test harness, we define the symbol TRYMAIN in the compilation procedure. When we want just the object code for the function, we do not define TRYMAIN, and compile for object-code only. Keeping the harness in the same source file as the function makes later modification easier to test, and provides useful documentation of how the function is supposed to be used.

Conditional debugging

One very important application of conditional compilation is the use of conditional debugging code. The macro name NDEBUG is conventionally used to turn *off* any conditional debugging code:

```
cc -DNDEBUG pgm.c
```

turns off debugging, while an ordinary compilation with

```
cc pgm.c
```

will enable debugging. For a specific example, the local.h header contains the following definition:

```
#ifndef NDEBUG
#define asserts(cond, str) \
    { if (!(cond)) fprintf(stderr, "Assertion '%s' failed\n", str); }
#else
#define asserts(cond, str)
#endif
```

If the program being compiled contains the line

```
asserts(x >= 0, "x is non-negative");
```

an ordinary compilation will generate a test for the non-negativity of x, while compilation with NDEBUG defined will turn off the checking.

Recent C compilers provide a more streamlined version of this facility, in the header <assert.h>. The assert macro takes only one argument, the condition being tested:

```
assert(x >= 0);
```

If the assertion fails during execution, a message of this form will be printed:

```
Assertion failed: "x >= 0", file pgm.c, line 17
```

Furthermore, the macro calls the function abort, which terminates program execution. (Under UNIX, a "core-image" file is produced, for further assistance in debugging.)

The assert macro is an excellent tool for putting executable assertions into a program, but its streamlined implementation requires several preprocessor features which are not yet universal. The preprocessor must provide the symbols _ _FILE_ _ and _ _LINE_ _ (which identify the source file name and current line number), the preprocessor must be able to make a string constant out of the macro argument, and the library must support the abort function. The asserts macro is intended to provide a more universally-portable substitute until these features are provided by all compilers. In the following chapters, there will be many uses for the asserts macro.

CHAPTER 2: SCALARS

A *data object* (or just *object*) is a sequence of bytes to be manipulated as a unit. For now, "object" is just a technical name for a variable. When we discuss pointers we will see that there are other objects besides variables.

We start our consideration of reliable data structures with the low-level objects, the individual scalars. In this book, a *scalar* object is one having floating, integer, or pointer type.

Throughout this chapter, we will address the reliable use of scalars. As always, our desire is that the program actually does what it appears to do. Our motto for reliable programming continues to be "No surprises!"

2.1 The Math Library, with <math.h>

Our search for non-surprising programs begins with the math library and the floating-point numbers that it supports. These are some of the more common math functions:

```
double ceil(x)      - smallest integer not less than x
double cos(x)       - cosine of x
double exp(x)       - exponential function of x
double floor(x)     - largest integer not greater than x
double log(x)       - natural log of x
double log10(x)     - base-10 log of x
double pow(x, y)    - raise x to the power y
double sin(x)       - sine of x
double sqrt(x)      - square root of x
double tan(x)       - tangent of x
```

All of these functions deal with floating-point numbers (of the size specified by double), which are only binary approximations of a "true" real number. Also, each library function that produces a fractional result may introduce some small error in the result. For example, in "real" numbers, multiplying the square root of x by itself should produce exactly the value of x. The actual results typically show a small error in the low-order bits, something like this [2-1]:

```
sqrtx.c:
    /* sqrttst - test accuracy of sqrt
     */
    #include "local.h"
    main()
        {
        double x, y;

        for (x = 1.; x <= 25.; x = x + 1.)
            {
            y = sqrt(x) * sqrt(x);
            if (y != x)
                printf("%5.1f %21.17f %10.2e\n", x, y, x-y);
            }
        }


sqrtx.out:
    2.0    2.00000000000000010    -5.55e-17
    3.0    3.00000000000000010    -5.55e-17
    7.0    6.99999999999999990     2.22e-16
    8.0    8.00000000000000020    -2.22e-16
   10.0   10.00000000000000000    -2.22e-16
   12.0   12.00000000000000000    -2.22e-16
   15.0   15.00000000000000000    -2.22e-16
   17.0   17.00000000000000100    -4.44e-16
   18.0   18.00000000000000000     4.44e-16
   21.0   21.00000000000000000     4.44e-16
   22.0   22.00000000000000000     4.44e-16
   23.0   22.99999999999999900     8.88e-16
```

Another aspect of floating representation concerns conversion from floating-point to integer. When a positive floating-point value is converted to an integer value, the fractional digits are lost, i.e., *truncated* [2-2]. When a negative floating-point value is converted, the truncation may be toward or away from zero, depending on implementation.

Rule 2-1: When exactness counts in converting floating-point to integer, be sure the value being converted is non-negative.

Another type of rounding behavior is needed when using floating-point numbers to represent decimal fractions such as currency. It is possible to use floating representations for small amounts of currency, such as six figures with two decimal places; errors in the low-order bits will not produce a noticeable error in addition or subtraction. However, when arbitrary fractions are computed, they must be rounded to the proper number of decimal places. For example, consider the computation of monthly payment on a mortgage [Plum, 1983, 3-45]:

```
pmt = bal * (intmo / (1. - pow(1. + intmo, (double)-npmts)));
```

With balance (bal) equal to $82,500.00, monthly interest (intmo) equal to 16.25% / 12, and number of payments (npmts) equal to 25 times 12 (i.e. 300), the C computation produces a result (pmt) equal to 1137.29654996 (showing just eight places). Since this result is about 35/100 different from an exact number of pennies, it will not take many additions or subtractions before the intermediate results start to differ noticeably from true figures.

Thus, we are able to use floating representations only if we make sure to round the intermediate fractional results (from multiplies, divides, and function calls) back to even pennies, with a function such as this one:

```
round:
    /* round - adjust floating dollars to even pennies */
    #include "local.h"
    double round(dollars)
        double dollars;
        {
        double pennies;

        pennies = floor(dollars * 100 + .5);
        return (pennies / 100.);
        }
```

which will give a "fair" or "symmetric" rounding. Thus, round(1137.2965) produces the result 1137.30, but round(1137.2925) would produce 1137.29.

The floor function produces a double result equal to the largest integer that is not larger than the argument; i.e., it "truncates" the argument's fraction. If we wanted a function that would round all fractional pennies upward (in favor of the bank), we could use the `ceil` function, which produces a `double` result equal to the smallest integer that is not smaller than the argument.

```
roundup:
    /* roundup - adjust floating dollars to even pennies
     * round all fractional pennies upward
     */
    #include "local.h"
    double roundup(dollars)
        double dollars;
        {
        double pennies;

        pennies = ceil(dollars * 100.);
        return (pennies / 100.);
        }
```

Using `roundup(1137.2925)` produces `1137.30`.

These observations on representation and rounding are a few of the simpler things that can be said about avoiding surprises with floating-point data. If you have uses for floating-point arithmetic that are more complex than these simple examples, consult a text on numerical analysis such as Hamming [1973].

We turn now from errors of representation to errors of computation. Most of the math functions can fail, if they are given arguments which do not produce a proper result. For example, the square root of a negative number, such as `sqrt(-1.0)`, has no meaning in "real" arithmetic. This is known as a *domain error*; the argument is outside the domain over which the function is defined. For another example, ten raised to the one-millionth power, `pow(10., 1e6)`, cannot be represented in any (current) floating representation. This is known as a *range error*; the result cannot be represented as a proper `double` number. In all such error cases, the function will return some value, but the value returned will not be the "correct" value [2-3]. The `sqrt` function returns zero, when given a negative argument. The `pow` function returns a very large number (appropriately positive or negative) on an "overflow" range error. This "very large number" is defined in `<math.h>` as `HUGE_VAL` (or in some versions, `HUGE`).

I would advise you against testing for errors by comparing the returned value against `HUGE_VAL` (or `-HUGE_VAL`, or zero), for several reasons. First of all, these are in general valid (albeit unlikely) data values. Secondly, making such tests requires detailed knowledge of the various error returns for each math function — knowledge which is otherwise useless. Also, there are three different possibilities — `-HUGE_VAL`, 0, and

HUGE_VAL — and you must know which are possible in each case. Finally, different versions of the library have differed in their error-return behavior.

A more reliable way to test for errors is by using the global variable errno. This variable is set to a non-zero value by any of the math functions that encounters an error. Thus, setting errno to zero prior to a computation, and testing it afterwards, will reveal whether any library errors were reported during the computation:

```
errno = 0;
perform computation
if (errno != 0)
    handle the error situation: report, compute differently, etc.
else
    computation was error-free
```

Rule 2-2: Test errno before using results from the math functions.

(See the appendix for a list of math functions in the library of recent C compilers [2-4].)

2.2 Error-handling

One important issue in "no surprises" programming is how to handle errors encountered during computation. To be general about it, we define "error" as any indication that the program cannot produce the expected result. Associated with each possible error is a "restart point," the place at which some action is taken so that the process can continue. The method of handling errors often depends upon whether the program is intended for use in a "stand-alone" environment, where execution must continue no matter what, or for use under an operating system, where a user is available to re-execute the command.

Throughout the rest of the book, we will refer to these categories of error-handling:

Diagnose and terminate: This is one of the simplest approaches, suitable to interactive use only. The restart point is re-execution of the entire program.

Diagnose and re-prompt: In this approach, computation does not begin until the program determines that input values will not cause errors in processing. If inputs are invalid, the program can prompt for replacement values. The restart point is the prompting for re-entry.

Re-try the operation: If the error is of a transient nature (e.g., a read error from disk), the program can re-try the operation, up to some pre-set maximum number of re-tries. The restart point is the re-try.

Terminate one transaction and proceed to the next: In this approach, the input is a series of independent transactions, such that one transaction can be diagnosed and terminated. This approach is common on batch systems in which the user is not assumed to be interactively monitoring the execution, but it may also be appropriate in some standalone systems. The restart point is the beginning of the next transaction.

Re-execute the computation with different algorithm: Sometimes one has a fast algorithm which sometimes fails, and a slower algorithm which always works. In this case, the restart point is the execution of the slower, more robust algorithm.

Ignore errors completely: This approach is only suitable when the error will be obvious to the user from the output of the program. Since no action is taken, there is no restart point. This is usually not suitable for reliable programming.

2.3 Character Tests, with <ctype.h>

Topics assumed from previous book: <ctype.h> [3.5].

In Chapter 1, a *safe* macro function is defined to be one which evaluates each argument exactly once, and observed that safe macro functions can reliably be used as replacements for function calls. This approach to macro-versus-function tradeoff is most simply illustrated by the "character-tests" in <ctype.h>. These have usually been implemented as safe macros. ANSI C requires that they also have true function versions in the library. As mentioned in Chapter 1, the true function version of, for example, isdigit can be obtained by using

```
#undef isdigit
```

(See the appendix for a list of the character-test functions from the library of recent C compilers [2-5].)

These functions are the most portable way of testing and converting characters, so their use is encouraged.

Rule 2-3: Use the <ctype.h> facilities for character tests and upper-lower conversions.

2.4 Boolean Data

Topics assumed from previous book: Semi-Boolean tests [3.2], bool [3.21], tbool [3.21].

As described in the introductory book, the logic of test conditions (if, while, for, do) is "semi-Boolean," in that zero means *false* and non-zero means *true*. In other words, any test expression is implicitly compared against zero, and many existing C programs employ this implicit comparison in shorthand uses. One often sees

```
if (c)   instead of   if (c != '\0')   and
if (p)   instead of   if (p != NULL)
```

There is no problem with portability here; nul character and NULL pointer are always guaranteed to be equal to zero in comparisons. However, the C syntax does have a potential for one common bug:

```
if (i = j)        either wrong or misleading
```

is syntactically valid; it means the same as

```
if ((i = j) != 0)
```

but the mistaken use of the "single-equal" assignment instead of the "double-equal" comparison is a common mistake. A new generation of C interpreters has the potential for eliminating this type of mistake, but the only simple way to achieve it is to require that *all* test conditions must clearly be "Boolean" expressions. Any expression whose top-level operators are relational and logical is obviously a "Boolean" expression, but what about Boolean variables? From the interpreter's point of view, any value other than zero or one might be assumed to be non-Boolean.

From the human reader's point of view, the program will be easier to understand if Boolean variables are clearly indicated as such. In the type scheme of *C Programming Guidelines* [Plum, 1984], two defined-types are provided for Boolean variables:

```
bool    designates an int-sized Boolean variable, and
tbool   designates a char-sized Boolean variable.
```

With an eye toward future automated assistance, we propose the following reliability rules:

Rule 2-4: Make sure that Boolean variables are assigned the values zero and one. This means that the type tbool is always adequate, and if this rule is part of local standards, the types bool and tbool could be made synonymous.

Rule 2-5: Make sure that each test condition is Boolean, involving only Boolean types or relational and logical operators.

In most modern compilers, there is no efficiency penalty for saying

```
while (*s1++ != '\0')
```

instead of

```
while (*s1++)        not strictly Boolean
```

2.5 Enumeration Types

Recent C compilers provide *enumeration types* , which allow declarations like this:

```
enum stoplight {red, yellow, green};
```

This establishes `enum stoplight` as a type which can be used in further declarations, such as

```
enum stoplight main_st, front_st;
```

And the enumeration constants (`red`, `yellow`, and `green`) become symbolic names for the integer constants `0`, `1`, and `2`. Each of the enumeration constants can be explicitly initialized, as in

```
enum stoplight {red = 'r', yellow = 'y', green = 'g'};
```

If an uninitialized enumeration constant follows one which is initialized, its value is one greater than the previous constant. To avoid surprises, we suggest this rule:

Rule 2-6: An enumeration's constants should all be initialized, or else none of them should be initialized.

There are some reliability problems with the semantics of `enum`. In a strict usage of `enum` data, the variables `main_st` and `front_st` would be assigned no values other than the named enumeration constants, `red`, `yellow`, and `green`, like this:

```
main_st = red;
```

That is not, however, what C requires. Instead, an enumeration variable is treated just like an `int` variable, except that its actual storage size might be optimized according to the range of the enumeration constants. The declaration of an enumeration type is therefore more or less equivalent to a listing of `#define`'d names, with a few minor advantages: The scope of the names is limited (just like ordinary identifiers), and it is marginally easier to add new constants to the list without having to manually change their values.

Future implementations could invoke stricter checking if programs were written according to stricter rules:

Rule 2-7: Write programs as if enumeration variables could receive no values other than the associated enumeration constants. Treat the enumeration types as if they were unique types, not for any arithmetic int usages. Convert between enumeration variables and integer values only by use of an explicit cast.

This allows, at least, easier inspection of the code by reviewers, and creates the possibility of stricter lint-like checking.

2.6 Range-Checking

Failure to attend to proper ranges of variables can lead to interesting reliability problems. One example from the field of computerized aircraft navigation: a heading variable was specified to be measured in degrees. But it was not discovered until airborne system test that one part of the system assumed that heading ranged from 0 to 360, while another part assumed that the range was -180 to 180.

For a concise representation of ranges in comments, we can use {low:high}. (Using a "two-dot" notation like "low..high" might seem more natural, but it becomes confusing when the range values are floating-point constants with decimal points.) The specification of a range comment could look like this:

```
double heading;     /* degrees: {0:360} */
```

If we follow the notational convention that the colon is taken to mean "must be," then the comment can be understood to mean "heading is measured in degrees, and must be between 0 and 360, inclusive."

Executable assertions can be useful for putting teeth into assumptions about ranges of data. In this case, an appropriate assertion on entry to a function using heading would look like this:

```
asserts(0 <= heading && heading <= 360, "heading range ok");
```

Tests of this form are common enough to deserve a macro:

```
#define IN_RANGE(n, lo, hi)  ((lo) <= (n) && (n) <= (hi))
```

which would allow the assertion to be given in this form:

```
asserts(IN_RANGE(heading, 0, 360), "heading range ok");
```

In C, it is often appropriate to consider the "one-too-far" value as part of the range of a variable. Consider, for example, a variable month_no which is a subscript into an array of monthly information. We might consider that its range would be from 0 through 11, but such variables are often used as loop indexes in contexts like this:

```
for (month_no = 0; month_no < 12; ++month_no)
    process array[month_no];
```

The `for` loop always involves a "one-too-far" value at the end of the loop; month_no must be incremented to 12 in order for the loop test (month_no < 12) to terminate the loop.

Rule 2-8: Include "one-too-far" values in the ranges for variables, if they are needed for loop terminations or other testing purposes.

The discussion of ranges would not be complete without considering the sizes of objects and the ranges of subscripts. C is moving toward the ability to handle objects whose size cannot be represented in an `unsigned int`; ANSI C envisions that some environments will need to use `unsigned long` to represent the `sizeof` anything. Several of the standard headers will define a type named `size_t`, which will be either `unsigned int` or `unsigned long`, according to the environment. Hence this rule:

Rule 2-9: Function parameters accepting the size of an arbitrarily large object should be declared with `size_t` type.

For an example of the use of `size_t`, consider the `reverse` function, which reverses the characters in a string. To be applicable to any string in any environment, the function needs to use a subscript of type `size_t`:

```
reverse:
    /* reverse - reverse the order of a string */
    #include "local.h"
    void reverse(s)
        char s[];
        {
        char t;
        size_t i, j;

        if ((j = strlen(s)) == 0)
            return;
        for (i = 0, j = j - 1; i < j; ++i, --j)
            SWAP(s[i], s[j], t);
        }
```

A related question concerns how a subscript variable should be declared. The lowest subscript of an array is always zero in C, but regarding the highest subscript there are new complications with recent versions of C. Some implementations allow declaration of arrays with more elements than the largest (signed) int value, whereas in K&R [Kernighan and Ritchie, 1978], subscripts were always representable as int values. Recent compilers for C allow for larger subscripts. For one example, the "large memory model" of the 8086 family of machines allows for objects larger than 32K elements, but the int is still 16 bits. Thus, in general, portable code (especially library functions callable in any context) must assume that a subscript could require an unsigned representation. Fortunately for portability, there is always a valid "one-too-far" value greater than the largest possible subscript, because in zero-origin indexing, the largest subscript is always one less than the largest dimension value for the array. However, a variable capable of holding the largest subscript must be an unsigned variety of integer, which eliminates the possibility of a "one-too-far" value at the low end.

One could always use size_t for subscripts, but this may be over-kill in many situations where the allowable range of subscripts does not need to span the memory space. We propose instead to use a type named index_t. What is the distinction between size_t and index_t? size_t is determined by the implementation, whereas index_t is chosen by the project. size_t is required for all general library functions, because there is no restriction upon the calling function. index_t could, by project-wide choice, be made smaller than size_t, if a maximum size for arrays is mutually agreed upon within the project. In the rest of this book, we will use index_t variables for subscripts. In our local.h header, index_t is defined as unsigned int. You can make the definition int, unsigned int, long, or unsigned long, according to the needs of your project. In stddef.h, size_t is also defined as unsigned int; you should change size_t to unsigned long if your implementation requires it.

2.7 Signed and Unsigned Arithmetic

Topics assumed from previous book: ones complement [2.1], twos complement [2.1], overflow [3.20].

In this section, all our examples will be easier to describe if we assume that int has 16 bits, but the principles are the same for any size of int. Most C machines use twos complement arithmetic, in which the smallest int has the value -32768, and the largest int has the value 32767. (These values are named INT_MIN and INT_MAX, respectively, in <limits.h>, as described in Section 1.1.) On a hypothetical 16-bit ones complement machine, INT_MIN would be -32767 and INT_MAX would be 32767. Notice that the very smallest twos-complement integer has no counterpart in ones complement, nor does it have a corresponding positive integer in either system.

While twos complement is the most popular usage in the C world, programmers aiming for the widest portability must consider various problems regarding ones complement, even if their current machine does not use it. More precisely, these are reliability problems for portable code, in that they can cause nasty surprises if not attended to. We shall see several such problems in this section.

Signed and unsigned arithmetic have significantly different properties in C. Ordinary signed integers correspond to positive and negative numbers along the number line, like a thermometer:

```
      +- ... +-+-+-+-+ ... -+
     INT_MIN        0 1 2   INT_MAX
```

Subtraction of two ordinary int values produces a (signed) int result, as in the subtraction of two temperatures:

```
int temp0, temp1, delta_temp;

delta_temp = temp1 - temp0;
```

This gives an algebraically correct result as long as the true difference lies between INT_MIN and INT_MAX, inclusive. But if temp1 and temp0 are too far apart, an overflow takes place in computing delta_temp, and the result is undefined.

Unsigned arithmetic is based on a "modulus" arithmetic, like an odometer or a timer counter. Consider two unsigned integers timer0 and timer1 which represent successive samples from a timer counter:

```
unsigned int delta_time, timer0, timer1;

delta_time = timer1 - timer0;
```

Assuming that our integers are 16-bit values, the largest unsigned int value (named UINT_MAX in <limits.h>) has the value 65535. If the value of timer0 is 12, say, and the value of timer1 (sampled some time later) is 10, then delta_time will have the value 65534; i.e., timer1 was sampled 65534 ticks later than timer0. By the definition of unsigned arithmetic, no overflow is possible in the computation. The "wrap-around" that can occur is not considered an error, whereas overflow is an error. From the formal point of view, any result of the subtraction is a well-defined result. From the practical point of view, the result corresponds to the actual delta_time only if the true value is less than or equal to UINT_MAX (65535, in this environment). This "timer" model corresponds closely to the underlying semantics of C, in that the difference between a later time and an earlier time is always a positive number.

Notice that it would be an error to assign the unsigned int value of delta_time to an int variable; all the values greater than INT_MAX would exceed the range of the int. Such an assignment is not a syntax error, however; the compiler would map a very large value into some negative integer value. The details of the mapping will be discussed shortly.

Programmers often use unsigned arithmetic as if it modeled the "positive number line," like the measurement of weight:

```
unsigned int weight0, weight1;
int delta_weight;

delta_weight = weight1 - weight0;
```

In this sort of usage, the difference between the two unsigned numbers is conceptually a signed number, according to whether one weight is greater or lesser than the other. In twos complement arithmetic, this computation is quite well-behaved and unobjectionable. The unsigned difference between weight1 and weight0 when converted into a signed number produces just the right result, as long as the "real" result is between INT_MIN and INT_MAX, inclusive.

In ones complement, however, there is an uncertainty about the conversion. Assigning the unsigned int value to the (signed) int variable can be done in any way that the compiler writer has chosen. The choice may have been to model the twos-complement behavior, in which case one possible result (-32768) is unrepresentable. (We will call this the "twos-complement mimic" treatment.)

Alternatively, the compiler writer may have chosen to simply assign the same bit representation, in which case all negative results will be "one greater" than expected. (We call this the "raw-bits" treatment.)

In either case, there are surprises, but the "twos-complement mimic" behavior is slightly less surprising than the "raw-bits" behavior. If a ones-complement environment uses the "raw-bits" treatment of conversion from unsigned to signed integers, we must do some work in order to reverse the "modulus" behavior of signed-to-unsigned conversion.

Here is an example. If the (signed) integer -1 is converted to an unsigned integer, the unsigned result consists of all 1-bits. When these "raw bits" are converted back to signed integer, the result is zero.

Here, then, is a 36-bit ones-complement version of an "unsigned int to int" conversion macro, called UI_TO_I, which can be found in the header portdefs.h:

```
#define UI_TO_I(n) (((n) & 0x800000000) == 0 ? (n) : -(n) -1)
```

Be aware that this is a non-unique mapping. Both 0 and 0x800000000 (2 to the 35-th power) are mapped into 0. Since 2 to the 35-th power could not occur in the typical 32-bit twos-complement environment, this is not likely to cause any portability problem.

In a twos-complement environment, all that UI_TO_I has to do is to cast the result to int:

```
#define UI_TO_I(n)  (int)(n)
```

The problems arising from subtraction of unsigned int values are not restricted to obscure portability problems regarding ones-complement systems. If they were, most programmers could safely ignore them. But as these examples show, the difference between unsigned values has a built-in duality of interpretation. The situation is as if C had a special type available for unsigned difference; let us call it "questionably signed," or qsigned, to invent a C-like notation. A qsigned number is a value on a number line with two different, coexisting value labelings:

```
UINT_MAX
          V 0 1 2   INT_MAX          [unsigned interpretation]
  +- ... +-+-+-+-+ ... -+
INT_MIN?  -1 0 1 2   INT_MAX         [signed (2s-comp) interpretation]
```

Any computations involving qsigned values are performed in the same (twos-complement) arithmetic that is used for unsigned values. (If the machine's signed arithmetic is ones-complement, the INT_MIN limit is actually equal to the smallest qsigned value plus one; this corresponds to the conversions that should take place when going from unsigned values to signed values in such environments.) When a qsigned int value is assigned to an unsigned int variable, the unsigned interpretation is followed. When a qsigned int value is converted to a (signed) int value (using the UI_TO_I macro), the signed (twos-complement) interpretation is followed.

So far, this is just an explanation of the underlying meaning of well-behaved computations. However, if a qsigned int value is assigned to a long int variable (in an environment where int is smaller than long), and no explicit conversion is used, there is an intrinsic confusion. In the examples above, one could be misled into thinking that

```
long delta_timer;

delta_timer = timer1 - timer0;
```

produces a non-negative value, and that

```
long delta_weight;

delta_weight = weight1 - weight0;
```

produces a signed value. Of course, both cannot be true; the difference between them is only in the mind of the programmer, not in the semantics of C. (The second example is the incorrect usage — the unsigned difference becomes a positive long integer.) Accordingly, we suggest that the conversion of a qsigned int result to a larger long int type should (for maximum reliability) be considered an *undefined* operation. In other words, before assigning or casting a qsigned value to a larger int type, one should convert the value explicitly either with UI_TO_I or with (unsigned). Thus, we should write

```
delta_timer = (unsigned)(timer1 - timer0);
```

and

```
delta_weight = UI_TO_I(weight1 - weight0);
```

This can all be summarized by a reliability rule:

Rule 2-10: When two unsigned int's are subtracted, convert the result using either (unsigned) or UI_TO_I.

One final observation about integer signs: the sign of the remainder (%) operator is implementation-defined, when the operands are of different sign. This sometimes constitutes a portability problem, when the programmer has assumed that i % j is always positive. To provide a true (never negative) modulo operation, we can use an IMOD ("integer modulo") macro from portdefs.h:

```
/* modulo macro giving non-negative result */
#define IMOD(i, j) (((i) % (j)) < 0 ? ((i) % (j)) + (j) : ((i) % (j)))
/* if i % j is never negative, replace with the following line: */
/* #define IMOD(i, j) ((i) % (j)) */
```

Rule 2-11: Use IMOD (or some similar mechanism) to ensure that a non-negative modulo result is produced.

2.8 Overflow

Strictly speaking, there are two different types of overflow. When an object is assigned a value that is too large for the object, we have a "range" overflow. And when an operation produces a result that is too large for the intermediate result, we have an "intermediate" overflow. The consequences are the same in both cases: the end result is incorrect. Range overflows have been discussed earlier; now we will attend to intermediate overflows.

Many C programmers have assumed that (on a twos-complement machine) overflows can be ignored in most cases. Consider the following (simplified) version of the `atoi` function:

```
atopi(#1):
    /* atopi - convert string to positive integer */
    int atopi(s)
        char s[];
        {
        int n = 0;
        int i;

        for (i = 0; isdigit(s[i]); ++i)
            n = 10 * n + s[i] - '0';
        return (n);
        }
```

We will refer to a "fussy" overflow as one which would not prevent the computation of the correct answer if overflow-checking were not performed. For example, during the computation of `atopi("32767")`, a "fussy" overflow takes place when the final `'7'` is added:

```
3276 * 10  =    32760
  + '7'          +    55
              -------
                32815    momentarily greater than INT_MAX
  - '0'          -    48
              -------
                32767    now within proper range
```

A "true" overflow takes place when the correct answer is not capable of being produced, as in `atopi("999999999999")`.

On a machine without overflow checking, "fussy" overflows are often ignored by the programmer. The overflow causes a "wraparound" in the temporary value, but the subsequent subtraction brings the result back into range. The programmer is often unaware of the overflow until the program is ported to a machine which checks for overflow in the machine hardware. One simple way to prevent fussy overflows is to perform the operation in unsigned arithmetic, since overflow checking is explicitly disabled for unsigned operations. A more precise way, in the case of atopi, would be to parenthesize the problematic expression like this:

```
n = 10 * n + (s[i] - '0');
```

If the operator inside the parentheses were a "plus," the technique would not work, because the compiler is free to re-arrange commutative-associative operators, even across parentheses. Since, however, it is a "minus," the subtraction is guaranteed to be performed before the addition (unless the compiler has a bug in this delicate area, that is).

Existing conversion functions in C libraries have tended to ignore overflows. In recent C libraries, there are conversion functions with a more constrained behavior. On overflow, they return a maximum value, and use errno to indicate that an error has taken place. In the case of atopi, we could more simply return a special value, such as -1, to indicate the overflow error. No overflows will take place during the computation, and an excessively-large argument value is diagnosed. Applying this philosophy to our atopi function would produce something like this:

```
atopi(#2):
    /* atopi - convert string to positive integer {0:INT_MAX} */
    #include <limits.h>
    int atopi(s)
        char s[];
        {
        unsigned n = 0; /* the converted number: {0:INT_MAX} */
        int i;

        for (i = 0; isdigit(s[i]) && n <= INT_MAX/10; ++i)
            {
            if (n > INT_MAX / 10)
                return (-1);
            n = 10 * n + (s[i] - '0');
            }
        if (n > INT_MAX || isdigit(s[i]))
            return (-1);
        else
            return (n);
        }
```

Rule 2-12: In (signed) integer arithmetic, assume that overflow is illegal, may be detected (hence should never be programmed), and cannot be trapped or ignored.

earlier, using unsigned can at least prevent "fussy" overflows.

2.9 Data Properties

Throughout the book, we will refer to three aspects of reliable use of data: type, properties, and allowable operations.

Type

By "type," we refer both to the way the data is represented in memory, and to the syntactic type on the declaration. Early C compilers were rather loose about the agreement of data types; code like this was allowable:

```
char *p;
int i;

i = p + 2;        loose and dangerous
```

Recent C compilers will flag this free interchange between pointers and integers as a syntax error. One reason for the tightening-up is that programmers have been found to make mistakes in mixing up pointers and integers, which leads to obscure bugs. Another reason is that, in some environments, an ordinary int is not large enough to hold a pointer. In the so-called "large model" of the Intel 8086 and 8088, a pointer takes 32 bits, while the int is only 16 bits.

C performs a number of conversions upon expression values, so there is an important distinction to make between the "declared" type and the "converted" type. For example, in

```
int i, j;
char c;

i = j + c;
```

the declared type of c is char, but when c appears in an expression like this, its converted type is int.

The main point is that C programmers must know the exact type of each variable and each expression in which the variable is used.

Properties

The most basic distinction when talking about data properties is the distinction between an *undefined* value (e.g., "garbage," or uninitialized), and a *defined* value. One common example of a "undefined" error comes from forgetting to initialize a counter:

```
long sum;
int i;

for (i = 0; i < N; ++i)
    sum += a[i];      error - sum not initialized
```

In C, automatic variables are undefined until they are initialized; static variables are initialized by default, so they are initially defined. A variable can acquire an undefined value as the result of an invalid operation;

```
n = m / 0;
```

causes n to become undefined, possibly terminating execution as well.

Similarly, when an overflow takes place in a computation, the result of the expression is undefined. And when a value is assigned to an object that is too small to hold the value, the object's value becomes undefined.

Besides this fundamental distinction between defined and undefined values, a variable may have other properties ascribed to it by the programmer. In Section 2.6, we discussed programmer-defined ranges for variables, documented like this:

```
double heading;      /* degrees: {0:360} */
```

By this comment, the programmer indicates that the property of being between 0 and 360 is an important property for this variable. If heading receives the value -1, the variable is "defined" from the point of view of C, but it is not properly defined according to the programmer's intention.

In previous sections, we saw other properties that the programmer can ascribe to a variable, by using an informative defined-type: metachar (a valid char-sized number or EOF), bool and tbool (zero or one), and bits (an unsigned number for bit manipulation).

We will use the term *well-defined* to refer to a value that conforms to the programmer's stated defining property. If, for example, a metachar variable were to receive the value 5000, the variable would not be "well-defined," because it exceeds the range of proper char-sized numbers.

Besides stating desired properties on the declaration of variables, the programmer can also document properties of function returned values. A function declared like this

```
bool is_empty();    /* is node empty? */
```

or like this

```
int is_empty();    /* is node empty?: bool */
```

is indicated to return only Boolean values. This documentation is important for determining that the function is producing a value that is appropriate for the context in which it is used.

We will be following a convention that a comment with a colon followed by a property name means "must have this property."

Rule 2-13: Document the defining properties of declared names in a comment on the declaration, using a convention such as "colon followed by property."

Allowable operations

The type and properties of a expression determine the operations that are allowable on that expression. For example, a bool variable should not be the operand of arithmetic operations like multiply or divide; the operations just do not make sense for the intended properties of the variable. Sometimes the type itself restricts the operations. For example, bitwise operations are not allowed upon any floating-point values.

In later chapters, we will see more complicated objects such as arrays, structures, stacks, and trees, each of which has its own repertoire of allowable operations.

CHAPTER 3: ARRAYS

An array is an *aggregate* object, which is composed of other objects, its *elements*. The *dimension* of an array is the number of objects that it contains. Its *size* is given by multiplying the dimension by the size of each element.

In C, arrays are used for storing character strings as well as for their more universal uses. As we shall see, this makes a reliable treatment of "properties of an array" somewhat more complex than in languages in which strings are objects in their own right. As always, our concern is for rules of programming which will ensure the reliable use of arrays.

3.1 Array Data

Topics assumed from previous book: arrays and subscripting [3.14], array arguments [5.4].

Just as we did for scalars, we will consider three aspects of array data: type, properties, and allowable operations.

Type

In C, the declaration of one variable, such as line in

```
static char line[10] = "msg";
```

consists of five components:

```
static        storage class (optional)
char          type specifier
line[10]      declarator
= "msg"       initialization (optional)
;             semicolon (of course)
```

Strictly speaking, the storage class and the type specifier can appear in any order, but declarations are clearer in a conventional order:

Rule 3-1: Storage class (if any) should precede the type specifier.

The examples will henceforth assume this rule.

For another variation, several variables can be declared in one declaration:

```
static char line_a[10], line_b[10];
```

declares two variables, line_a and line_b. This is in every way equivalent to two separate declarations:

```
static char line_a[10];
static char line_b[10];
```

It is a common error to assume that the following initialization applies to both line_a and line_b:

```
static char line_a[10], line_b[10] = "msg";  misleading
```

Rule 3-2: If a variable has an initialization, its declaration should have a source line to itself.

Setting aside the above complications, we will consider a declaration to consist of an optional storage class, a type specifier, a declarator, and an optional initialization. Now let us restrict our consideration to the non-optional parts, the type specifier and the declarator. For the rest of this section, when we refer to a "declaration," we will be referring only to the mandatory parts.

So declarations can be sliced into type specifier and declarator. But these syntactic categories are not of much practical importance to programmer; they are merely the syntactic terms. The important way to slice a declaration is into a *variable name* and a *type*. In a very simple declaration such as

```
short i;
```

the declarator consists only of the variable name (i), and the type specifier consists only of the type (short). But in a more complex declaration such as

```
short m[2];
```

the declarator m[2] contains the variable name m plus a part of the type. The type consists of what is left when the variable name is "scratched out" of the declaration, namely short [2]. In this sense, we can say that a declaration is a "sandwich" composed of a variable name and a type. The type is the "bread" wrapped around the variable name "meat" in the middle:

```
short m[2]  is the declaration
        m   is the name
short   [2] is the type
```

In C, the representation of an array consists of a sequence of contiguous objects (the *elements* of the array), running from low addresses to high addresses.

The meaning of an array declaration depends upon context. A parameter (typically declared with no stated dimension) is understood by C to be a pointer rather than an array (see Section 3.4). And a non-defining declaration of an external array, such as

```
extern short em[];
```

is an allowable form which declares an array of unknown size. (The size is determined by the defining instance, but a separately compiled function has no built-in way of determining that size.)

For an array whose size *is* known from the declaration (externally defined, or declared to be auto or static), we can define a useful macro for the dimension:

```
#define DIM(a) (sizeof(a)/sizeof(a[0]))
```

In other words, the dimension is the size of the array divided by the size of one element. Since both sizes are known at compile time, DIM(a) is effectively a constant, and can be used as such. One caution: the macro DIM should not be used with a *pointer* argument. The expression sizeof(p) always produces the size of one pointer, not the size of an array.

Properties

Reliability is often enhanced by maintaining a clear intuitive meaning for each data object. A data object, after all, reflects something about the world outside the program: a person's address, an amount of money, the pressure on an automobile brake pad, the temperature of a blast furnace, etc. Such interpretations are clearer if each object has a defining property which is maintained throughout a computation.

Rule 3-3: Document the defining property of a data object with a comment on its declaration. Ensure that this defining property remains invariant (unchanging) as much as possible throughout the computation, and document any exceptions.

This book's system of properties uses different names for aggregate properties than for scalar properties; this will allow us to say some simpler things about pointers later. An array is either *complete* (all scalar elements contained within the array are defined) or *incomplete* (one or more elements are not defined).

An array can become complete either by assignment to all its elements, or by an initializer on its declaration. (Any initializer causes the initialization of the entire array.)

Rule 3-4: A program is easier to write correctly and to understand if all arrays are made complete before the array is used.

Some arrays have other properties that are more important than "complete" or "incomplete." A "string," for example, requires defined characters only up to a nul (i.e., `'\0'`) terminator. The characters after the nul terminator can be total garbage, and the array still has its defining property satisfied, namely being a string.

Rule 3-5: If an array's defining property can be true even if not all elements are defined, indicate the property on the array's declaration. For example,

```
char s[10];     /* : string */
```

Lacking such mention, it is assumed that the array must be complete (all elements defined) before its value is used.

For any array, there are boundary values to be considered at the lowest and highest subscripts. These will always be important in determining valid access ("avoiding out-of-bounds reference"). Every array algorithm requires verification of the proper handling of the subscript boundaries.

A second issue concerns the "one-too-far" value required to terminate an ordinary for loop that walks over an array. As discussed in Section 2.7, if subscripts can be unsigned integers, there is always a valid "one-too-far" subscript value at the high end, but none at the low end.

In many cases, the defining property for an array is more restrictive than mere completeness. Let us now consider an array as an object to be *sorted*. In doing so, we will need a notation for a *subarray*, i.e. a contiguous sequence of elements of an array. The notation a[low:high]

will be used to mean the sequence of elements from a[low] to a[hi]. And the notation a[*] will mean "the entire array a." There are, of course, no such notations in C itself, but the notations will help us to speak more clearly about array algorithms.

To focus for now upon the general problem of sorting the elements of an array, the basic invariant property of such an array is that it contains individual-element values, the set of which remains unchanged from the start to the finish of the sorting process. In other words, the set of values remains invariant, although the positions of those values will be altered as the sort progresses. This is analogous to the sorting of a deck of cards; the values written on the cards do not change, but the ordering does change. To be precise, the array is a "multiset," which is like a set but individual values can occur more than one time. A deck of bridge cards is a proper set; each card appears only once (considering suits as distinct, as of course they are in bridge). A deck of Canasta cards is a multiset; each card appears several times in the deck.

We need to define one more property of an array. An array a is said to be *sorted in ascending order* if, for each i from 1 to DIM(a)-1, a[i] is greater than (or equal to) each element of a[0:i-1]. (An array containing only one element will be considered to be sorted, trivially.) More generally, a[low:high] is sorted (in ascending order) if, for each i from low+1 to high, a[i] is greater than (or equal to) each element of a[low:i-1].

The property of being sorted is not invariant during the operation of sorting an array. Being sorted is the *goal property*, not the invariant.

Allowable operations

C provides no built-in operators that act upon all elements of an array, but operations can be created from a succession of operations upon the individual elements. As we examine different data structures in this book, one common theme will be the creation of C functions and macros which perform specific operations upon a data structure. Designing the interface for a function is a subject in itself, and we will discuss the issue throughout the book. For now, our packaging criterion is minimal: we will employ the simplest C function that will encapsulate the data structure and algorithm that are our focus of attention.

The only allowable operations upon multiset arrays are those that perform a re-ordering without altering the actual values in the array. We have seen one such operation, in the form of the SWAP macro. Now we will examine the operation of *sorting an array*. For simplicity, we will restrict ourselves to an array of short integers. The "sorting" operation will take the form of a function with two arguments: an array parameter a designating the array to be sorted, and an integer n designating the number of elements in the array to be sorted. The function is supposed to arrange the n elements of a such that a[0:n-1] is sorted.

3.2 Sorting an Array

When we design the operations to be performed upon data, there are two more aspects of importance: *loop invariants* and *assertions*.

Loop invariants

In designing an algorithm to accomplish an operation such as sorting, the key design principle is to formulate a loop invariant which is true at each step of the computation, and which guarantees that the loop has attained its goal when the loop terminates.

The first sorting algorithm we will consider is called *insertion sort*. Using i as the loop subscript, the invariant of the insertion sort is "the subarray a[0:i-1] is sorted." The loop terminates when i reaches the "one-too-far" value, n. When it does, the invariant becomes "the subarray a[0:n-1] is sorted," which is the goal of the loop.

We will use the notation "*name* => *property*" to mean "*name* now has this *property*." Describing the loop invariants in program comments is often very useful documentation; we could, for example, write

```
for (i = 1; i < n; ++i)
    {
    /* a[0:i-1] => sorted */
    insert a[i] into its correct place
    }
/* a[0:n-1] => sorted */
```

To insert a[i] into the correct place, we copy it into a temporary (t), thus freeing up the location a[i]. Then, for each element of a[0:i-1] which is greater than t, we move it one position to the right, then insert t into its ordered position. (This is the insertion sort algorithm from Bentley [1984a].) Implemented as a function, this is what our algorithm looks like:

```
isort:
    /* isort - sort array a (dimension n) using insertion sort
     */
    #include "local.h"
    void isort(a, n)
        short a[];   /* array to be sorted; a[0:n-1]: multiset */
        index_t n;   /* dimension of a */
        {
        index_t i;
        index_t j;
        short t;

        for (i = 1; i < n; ++i)
            {
            /* a[0:i-1] => sorted */
            t = a[i];
            for (j = i; j > 0 && a[j-1] > t; --j)
                a[j] = a[j-1];       /* a[0:n-1] => !multiset */
            a[j] = t;                /* a[0:n-1] => multiset */
            }
        /* a[0:n-1] => sorted */
        }
```

During the inner loop, the array momentarily loses its "multiset" property, because the value a[i] has been removed into the temporary t. This is indicated by the comment in the inner loop. As soon as t is assigned into its proper place, the array once again becomes a multiset.

Assertions and run-time validation

We have placed comments in our code that indicate the intended invariant conditions, but unfortunately in real life, errors in creating and maintaining the program may cause such comments to be false and misleading. A more reliable way of stating such properties is to insert *executable assertions* in the code.

There are trade-offs to consider: The complexity of the assertion tests can exceed the complexity of the code being protected by the assertions, in which case the assertions can become a source of more, not fewer, errors. And the time to execute the assertions can swamp the execution time of the code itself. We do not mind if the assertions are more time-consuming than the program specification allows for the final production program; the assertions are all disabled by compilation with the NDEBUG flag.

Rule 3-6: Use executable assertions whenever they are simpler than the code being protected, and when the time to execute the assertions is not much greater than the time required to execute the code.

In the case of a sorting function, we could provide an executable method of asserting that a given array or subarray is sorted, something like this:

```
tst_sort:
    /* tst_sort - returns YES if array a is sorted
     * specialized "short" version
     */
    #include "local.h"
    bool tst_sort(a, n)
        short a[];
        index_t n;
        {
        index_t i;

        if (n <= 0)
            return (NO);
        for (i = 1; i < n; ++i)
            {
            /* a[0:i-1] => sorted */
            if (a[i] < a[i-1])       /* compare adjacent elements */
                return (NO);
            }
        /* a[0:n-1] => sorted */
        return (YES);
        }
```

According to our guidelines, we would not test this assertion inside the loop of isort. The time to test the assertions would become many times greater than the time to execute the code itself. But we could replace the final comment in isort.c

```
/* a[0:n-1] => sorted */
```

with this executable assertion:

```
asserts(tst_sort(a, n-1), "a is sorted");
```

The assertion is not required in the production version of the function; it checks the logic of the function itself, not any data provided from outside the function. Compiling with NDEBUG would turn off code generation for the assertion. We are using the executable assertions for documentation and for assistance during development, not for run-time checking in the final product.

Now we will consider the same underlying data structure, with a new algorithm, "quicksort."

For consistency, we will create a function with a calling sequence similar to that above:

```
void qksort(a, n)
    short a[];
    index_t n;
```

Loop invariants

Given an array or subarray, we pick the middle element and call it the *pivot*. Then the array is rearranged: those elements less than the pivot are moved to the left of the pivot, and those greater than the pivot are moved to its right. For convenience, we start by swapping the pivot with the initial element. The lowest subscript is lo, the highest subscript is hi, the subscript of the rightmost "less-than-pivot" element is lastlo, and the subscript of the element currently being tested is i. (This quicksort is somewhat simpler than most; it is adapted from Bentley [1984a].) During the loop of the sort, the invariant looks like this:

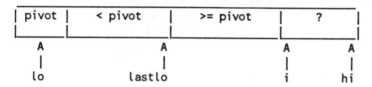

When the loop terminates, this is the picture:

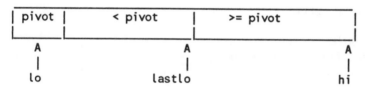

Swapping a[lo] with a[lastlo] gives

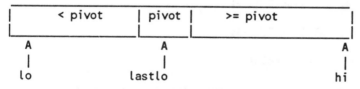

Thus we end up with two smaller subarrays, a[lo:lastlo-1] (all of whose elements are strictly less than a[lastlo]) and a[lastlo+1:hi] (all of whose elements are greater than or equal to a[lastlo]). If the array is trivial (only one element), then both subarrays are empty; there is no work to do, and the function returns immediately. If there is more than one element, at least one of the subarrays is non-empty. The function calls itself recursively for both subarrays. When it returns, the array a[lo:hi] is sorted.

Assertions and run-time validation

There is little to add here except to assert tst_sort after completion of the function. The function is so short that assertions during the algorithm would be needlessly complex in comparison.

Here is the qksort function:

```
qksort:
    /* qksort - sort array a (dimension n) using quicksort */
    #include "local.h"
    /* iqksort - internal function to partition a[lo:hi] */
    static void iqksort(a, lo, hi)
        short a[];  /* array to be sorted; a[lo:hi]: multiset */
        index_t lo; /* lowest subscript */
        index_t hi; /* highest subscript */
        {
        index_t mid = lo + (hi-lo)/2;   /* : {lo:hi} */
        index_t i;                       /* : {lo+1:hi+1} */
        index_t lastlo;                  /* : {lo:hi-1} */
        short tmp;

        SWAP(a[lo], a[mid], tmp);
        lastlo = lo;
        for (i = lo + 1; i <= hi; ++i)
            {
            if (a[lo] > a[i])
                {
                ++lastlo;
                SWAP(a[lastlo], a[i], tmp);
                }
            }
        SWAP(a[lo], a[lastlo], tmp);
        if (lastlo != 0 && lo < lastlo - 1)
            iqksort(a, lo, lastlo - 1);
        if (lastlo + 1 < hi)
            iqksort(a, lastlo + 1, hi);
        }
    /* qksort - external entry point */
    void qksort(a, n)
        short a[];  /* array to be sorted; a[0:n-1]: multiset */
        index_t n;  /* number of elements */
        {
        if (n > 1)
            iqksort(a, 0, n - 1);
        asserts(tst_sort(a, n), "a is sorted");
        }
```

The computation of mid is chosen to avoid a possible overflow. In the simpler expression

```
(lo + hi) / 2
```

the sum is susceptible to overflow for large values.

In Plum and Brodie [1985], optimization of this function is discussed at length. It is important to note that this recursive version of quicksort is vulnerable to some array values that cause the depth of the recursion stack to almost reach the number of elements in the array.

3.3 Strings

Topics assumed from previous book: string [2.4].

In C, a *string* is an array of char objects, containing a nul terminator '\0' that marks the end of the current string value. A *string constant* is written with double-quotes, like

```
"hello, world\n"
```

C does not require that every array of char's must be a string; indeed, the only built-in knowledge of "string" semantics is that string constants receive a nul terminator. Nonetheless, a char array is so frequently used to hold a string that we will identify a special property to signify a nul-terminated string: an array has the *string* property if all the characters up to the first nul terminator are defined.

If a char array has an initializer, the initializer will determine whether the array has the string property initially.

```
char a1[2] = {'a', 'b'};
```

is not a string, because there is no nul terminator within a1. On the other hand,

```
char a2[2] = "a";    and
char a3[2] = {'a'};
```

are both strings, according to the properties of string constants and of static array initializers.

It is often a useful style to declare an array of char's with an explicit +1 in its bound, to emphasize that space is reserved for the nul terminator. All other things being equal, algorithms involving char arrays are simpler if all the arrays involved remain proper nul-terminated strings during the execution.

3.4 Pointers as Array Parameters

Topics assumed from first book: pointers as function parameters [7.3], pointers and arrays [7.4].

In this book, we will follow the usage of declaring pointer parameters to scalars with the "asterisk" notation and declaring pointer parameters to arrays with the "empty brackets" notation. Thus the function definition

```
fn(a, b)
     char *a;
     char b[];
```

indicates that a points to a scalar char, and that b points to the initial element of an array of chars.

No strong semantics can be attached to the distinction, because the distinction is unavailable for non-parameter pointers. The distinction still seems worth keeping, because parameter pointers are so often used. This style leads to a more graceful notation for two-dimensional parameters:

```
fn(table)
     char table[] [20];
```

looks more natural than

```
fn(table)
     char (*table)[20];
```

Relying upon the foregoing context, we will henceforth refer to *array parameters* when talking about pointer parameters which point to the initial elements of arrays. Similarly, *string parameters* are pointer parameters which point to the initial char in a string.

Further generalizing, we will use the term *array pointer* for any pointer used to point to array elements. (The term "pointer into array" might be more precise, but the brevity of "array pointer" is worthwhile because the term will be used so often in discussing array algorithms.) Remember, it would be inaccurate to call such a pointer a "pointer to array" — an array pointer points to single elements, not to an entire array.

Array pointers (including array parameters) are different from array objects. The pointer itself can be undefined, or defined. It can be NULL, or it can point to valid storage. The array object being accessed through the pointer has its own properties: It could be complete or incomplete. It could be a multiset array (either sorted or unsorted). It could be a string. Or it could have any other property that we have defined for arrays.

In order to talk sensibly about the object being referenced we will need some new terminology. Because of the way C references arrays through pointers, the array being accessed is not simply the "indirect object" of the pointer (*p), because *p is just the individual array element pointed to by the pointer. We define the *target* of an array pointer to be the array object being accessed through the pointer. We will use the notation p[*] to mean "the entire array to which the pointer provides access."

In defining a meaning for p[*], we have reached the heart of an important reliability issue in the use of C: given an array pointer, exactly what object (i.e., what range of addresses) can we reliably access using that pointer? In the freest and least reliable usages, a pointer can be used to give access to the entire data space of the program:

```
int i;
int *p = &i;

printf("%d\n", p[12000]);    wild and dangerous usage
```

shows an access to whatever object is 12,000 elements further into the memory. But certainly this is not what we have in mind in using a pointer to access an array; the target of the pointer is meant to be only that array into which it is pointing.

In other words, *p ("indirect p") is only one array element; p[*] is the entire array accessed through p. In this example

```
short a[10];
short *pa = a;
```

the indirect object of p (*p) is the element a[0]. The target of p (p[*]) is the entire array a.

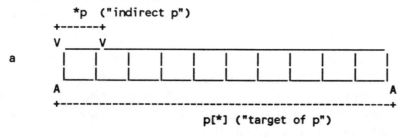

unsorted). It could be a string. Or it could have any other property that we have defined for arrays.

For single-dimension arrays, there is no ambiguity; in the example

```
short a[10];
short *pa = a;
```

it is clear that `a` is intended to be the target of `pa`. But what of this example:

```
short b[10][10];
short *pb2 = b[2];
```

Now we must make a choice and be consistent about it. Did we mean that `pb2` is meant only for providing access to `b[2]`, the second row of `b`, or that it is meant to provide access to the entire array `b`? Our choice is that when an array pointer is given a value, by assignment or passing an argument, the actual right-hand-side expression being assigned will be taken to indicate the target of the array. Thus, in the second example, the target of `pb2` is the array `b[2]` only.

One concession to common usage of C: The assignment

```
p = &a[n];
```

is taken to mean the same thing as

```
p = a + n;
```

which means that the entire array `a` is the target of the pointer.

One further notational convenience: The properties of the target can be attributed to the pointer itself. For example, "pointer `p` is a string" means that the target of `p` is an array with the "string" property. This allows more conventional and convenient documentation:

```
/* p: string */
```

means the same thing as

```
/* p[*]: string */
```

What are the *practical* implications of all these distinctions? There are two: determining the properties of the target of the pointer, and providing the possibility of range-checking the use of the pointer (i.e., avoiding "run-away pointers").

"Properties of the target" is the simpler of the two considerations. All that is meant here is that, for example, when an array of `char`'s is passed as the second argument to `strcpy`, that array should be a string. If we wish to state this constraint explicitly in documenting a function such as `strcpy`, we can use a notation like this:

```
char *strcpy(s1, s2)
    char s1[];       /* s1:!NULL, sizeof(s1[*]) > strlen(s2) */
    char s2[];       /* s2:string */
```

which means that the pointer s1 is not NULL, that the array to which s1 provides access is large enough to hold the result, and that the array to which s2 provides access is a string.

Regarding range-checking in reliable programming, we desire not to access any objects that are outside the extent of the pointer's target. (This is why the extent of the target must be unambiguous.) We will therefore adopt the convention that every pointer value has a range associated with it, which may actually be monitored by an interpreter or may just be a conceptualization guiding the programmer towards reliable code.

Section 2.6 discussed how scalar data objects could have a range associated with their declaration; the range lasts throughout the lifetime of the variable. For pointers, the situation is different; a pointer can be used to point into several different arrays as the computation progresses. Therefore, we will consider that the range of a pointer variable is dynamically set by each operation upon the pointer.

When a pointer is assigned an expression value involving an array target, the address range of the target determines the range of the pointer. When a pointer is assigned an expression value involving a pointer, the left-hand-side pointer acquires the range of the right-hand-side pointer. (By the rules of C, the right-hand-side can have only one array or pointer operand, so the source of range information is unambiguous.)

Before we say exactly what the range of the pointer is, we have to consider the possible "one-too-far" value of an array pointer. In a loop like

```
for (p = a; p < a + DIM(a); ++p)
    process *p;
```

we are counting upon p being eventually incremented to the address which is one byte greater than the last byte of the array a. The validity of the "one-too-far" value was agreed upon by the ANSI C committee in March 1985; it is vital to many existing C programs, which would be needlessly complicated otherwise. We will therefore always include the "one-too-far" value in the range of a pointer, with the understanding that this value is only good for arithmetic and comparisons, not for indirection.

If a pointer receives a value outside its range, we will consider that pointer to be *undefined*.

Now it is time for some examples. The comments will indicate the hypothetical addresses of the array elements:

```
static char m[10][10] = {0};    /* hypothetical address range: 2000:2099 */
char *p;

p = m[0];        /* p == 2000; range {2000:2010} */
                 /* p can access all of m[0], plus "one-too-far" */
p = (char *)m;   /* p == 2000; range {2000:2100} */
                 /* p can access all of m, plus "one-too-far" */
p = m[2];        /* p == 2020; range {2020:2030} */
                 /* p can access all of m[2], plus "one-too-far" */
p = p + 1;       /* p == 2021; range {2020:2030} */
                 /* value of p changes, but not its range */
++p;             /* p == 2022; range {2020:2030} */
                 /* again, value changes, but not range */
p += 8;          /* p == 2030; range {2020:2030} */
                 /* p is now "one-too-far"; valid value, */
                 /* but cannot be used for indirection */
++p;             /* p is now out-of-range; "undefined," strictly */
```

These rules for the range of pointers are, at the least, useful guidelines for the writing of reliable programs. They also can be enforced by compilers and interpreters which do dynamic bounds-checking [3-1]. They reflect the actual practice of working C programmers who write reliable programs that do not make out-of-bounds references in their use of pointers. The existence of precise rules such as these means that C is a language which can have both the expressive freedom of pointers plus the reliability of bounds-checking.

These concerns for the reliable uses of array parameters motivate the creation of a new general-purpose string-copying function. We will describe here a new function named strfit, which ensures that the target string is both bounds-checked and nul-terminated. If insufficient space was provided, the target is truncated but still nul-terminated. The function returns a bool value: a return of YES indicates that there was sufficient space for a complete copy.

```
strfit:
    /* strfit - copy s2 to s1, chopping to n chars
     * return YES if sufficient space, no if not
     */
    #include "local.h"

    bool strfit(s1, s2, n)
        char s1[];
        char s2[];
        size_t n;
        {
        size_t i;

        for (i = 0; i < n-1 && s2[i] != '\0'; ++i)
            s1[i] = s2[i];
        s1[i] = '\0';
        return (s2[i] == '\0');
        }
```

3.5 Arrays of Strings

An array of strings can be a handy format for the storage of simple tables. Consider

```
static char meas_codes[][6] =
    {"each", "box", "lb"};
```

This defines an array meas_codes with three rows of six char's each, which looks something like this:

```
meas_codes  [0] | e | a | c | h | \0| \0|
                |___|___|___|___|___|___|

            [1] | b | o | x | \0| \0| \0|
                |___|___|___|___|___|___|

            [2] | l | b | \0| \0| \0| \0|
                |___|___|___|___|___|___|
```

If we have a string to look up in this table, we can use a simple loop like this:

```
for (i = 0; i < DIM(meas_codes); ++i)
    if (strcmp(s, meas_codes[i]) == 0)
        found a match
```

We are passing the expression meas_code[i] to the strcmp function. According to the rules above, this means that we expect strcmp to be able to examine all the characters of the i-th row of meas_codes, but not to walk around in any other storage.

The strings are all self-contained in the array `meas_codes`; the table does not itself contain any pointers. For that variety of table, we must cover pointers in more detail. The details of pointers are the subject of the next chapter.

CHAPTER 4: POINTERS

Pointers are both powerful and dangerous in C. Programs can perform arbitrary manipulations of their data space in C. This is essential for many of the system-level uses of C. Because C has this expressive power, a style of programming oriented toward portability and reliability must place restrictions on the uses of pointers.

4.1 Declaration of Pointers

Topics assumed from first book: Pointers [7].

The first rule for reliable use of pointers requires that the programmer fully understand the declaration syntax of C:

Rule 4-1: In each pointer assignment, the right-hand-side value must have exactly the same ("converted") pointer type as the left-hand-side.

Recall from Section 2.9 that the "declared" type of the right-hand-side may differ from the "converted" type. In the assignment

```
char s[10], *p;

p = s;
```

the "declared" type of s is char [10] and the "converted" type is char *, so the assignment is proper. Here, by contrast, is an improper assignment:

```
char s[10];
int *pi;
```

pi = s; *improper mixed-type pointer assignment*

On some systems, pointers to char have a different representation than pointers to int. On many systems, the address of s could be an odd number which would cause a hardware trap if we attempted to reference an int at that location. These are some of the reasons why compilers enforce the agreement of pointer types.

We will, therefore, take some time now to attend to the exact form of pointer declarations in C.

As we saw in Section 3.1, a declaration in C is a "sandwich" of variable name and type; the declaration

```
short m[2];
```

says that the variable m has type short [2] (array of 2 short's).

Turning now to pointers, the asterisk (*) when used as a declarator-symbol means "pointer-to." Thus,

```
char *pc;
```

declares pc to be a pointer to objects of type char, or as it is more commonly said, a pointer to char. (The phrase "pointer to *type*" really means "pointer to an object of type *type*.") According to the "sandwich rule," the declaration is composed of the variable name (pc) and the type (char *). For another example,

```
char **ppc;
```

declares the name ppc to have the type char ** (pointer to pointer to char):

```
char **pc     declaration
       pc     name
char **        type
```

Another way of stating the "sandwich rule" is to list the possibilities:

```
if  x()  has the type  T,    then  x  has the type  "function returning T";
if  x[]  has the type  T,    then  x  has the type  "array of T";
if  *x   has the type  T,    then  x  has the type  "pointer to T";
```

One important aspect of the declaration rules of C is that each declarator-symbol (* [] ()) has a "precedence" that is strictly analogous to the precedence of the same symbol used as an operator. In other words, the parentheses and square brackets "bind tighter" in declarations than the asterisk does. As these examples get more complicated, we expand our interpretation of the "sandwich rule" to consider the type of expressions, not just names, like this:

```
char *a[N];  declaration
      a[i]   expression
char *        type
```

Since the square-brackets binds more tightly than the asterisk, the sandwich rule shows that a[i] is a char *. Or, in other words, a is an array of char *'s. Here is the contrasting case:

```
char (*pa)[N];  declaration
      (*pa)     expression
char      [N]   type
```

Here the parentheses cause the declarator *pa to be taken as a unit; the declaration says that *pa is an array of N char's. That is, pa is a pointer to an array of N char's.

Question [4-1] Just to be sure that you understand the "sandwich rule," jot down the variable name and type for the following declarations.

DECLARATION	VARIABLE NAME	TYPE ("DECLARED")
short **ap[5];	_____	_____
long (*pf)[2];	_____	_____
double **pps;	_____	_____

Having discussed the declaration of pointers, let us turn to some of the operators associated with them. Taking first the "address-of" operator (unary &), we note that it can be applied only to things that have an address, namely lvalues that are not declared with register storage class. (Bit-fields, which we have not yet discussed, are also not addressable.) If c is a char variable, then the expression &c evaluates to the address of c. The *type* of the expression &c is char * (pointer to char). To be more general, if an lvalue x has type T, then the expression &x has the type T *.

Thus, &c is a *pointer expression*, producing a value that is suitable for assignment to a pointer of type char *, such as pc.

Let us turn back to initializations for a moment. In any initialized declaration, the variable name designates the object that is being initialized. Thus in the declaration

```
char *pc = &c;
```

what gets initialized is the variable pc, not the declarator *pc. We could emphasize the point by writing the declaration as

```
char*   pc = &c;
```

which is fine as far as the compiler is concerned, but rather non-standard for human readers. The types are correct for the initialization; the name pc and the expression &c have the same type, char *. It would, however, be a type mismatch (and a serious bug) to write

```
char *pc = c;
```

The type of c is just char, and a char expression should not be assigned to a char * variable.

For a more complicated example, consider

```
char c = '1';    /* ASCII value is 49 decimal */
char *pc = &c;
char **ppc = &pc;
```

Here the pointer pc is being initialized to point to the character named c. And ppc is being initialized to point to the pointer named pc. A picture may help; hypothetical address values are being used for clarity:

```
ppc _____      pc _____        c _____
    | 112   |---->| 104   |---->| 49 |
120 |_____|  112|_____|  104|'1' |
```

What is the type of the expression &pc? The type is char ** (pointer to pointer to char), by the rules above. And this is an appropriate type to assign to ppc, because its type also is char **.

Now we will consider the *indirection* operator (unary *). This is, of course, the same character (asterisk) which means "pointer to" in a declaration. It has a different, but very compatible, meaning when used as "indirection" in an expression. Using the same example above, the expression *pc means "the thing that pc points to," or "indirect pc," for brevity. Assuming the initialization given above, *pc is an lvalue which could be used interchangeably with the variable c.

If an expression x has the type T *, then the expression *x has the type T. (Adding an asterisk to an expression removes an asterisk from its type.) Therefore, the type of *pc is simply char; *pc is a char lvalue. We can properly assign a char value to *pc, just as we could assign *pc to a char variable.

Similarly, *ppc has the type char *, and (with the initialization above) could be used interchangeably with the variable pc.

One reason why agreement of pointer types is so important is that in several implementations of C, pointers to different types have different internal representations, sometimes even different sizes. In these environments, it is especially important to be sure that all uses of pointer types follow the agreement rules strictly.

Sometimes we have a need to print the numeric **value** of a pointer itself, e.g. for debugging purposes. ANSI C envisions a new `printf` format for printing pointer values [4-2]. In the **meantime, we** suggest a macro `PR_PTR(p)` which will print pointer `p` in a fashion which will work in almost all current implementations.

```
#define PR_PTR(p) (printf("%10ld", (long)(p))
```

If we were to use this macro to print the two **pointers declared** above, we could do it like this:

```
PR_PTR(pc);
PR_PTR(ppc);
printf("\n");
```

And the output would look like this:

```
        104        112
```


4.2 Pointers to Scalars

Consider once again

```
char c = '1';
char *pc = &c;
char **ppc = &pc;
```

Assuming the same addresses as before, the memory looks like this after the initialization:

```
ppc _____    pc _____    c _____
   |   112  |---->|   104  |---->|   49  |
120|_____|  112|_____|  104|_'1'_|
```

We emphasized earlier that it is vital to be **clear about** the type of pointer variables and expressions. It is also important to be clear about their *values*.

In high-level languages like C, determination of the value of an expression depends upon whether the expression is an lvalue (something with storage). The value of an lvalue is found **by going to** the storage and loading the value that is found there. Thus in **the example above,** the value of `c` (assuming ASCII) is 49, the numeric **value of the constant** `'1'`. Similarly, the value of `pc` is the value that is **found in** the storage for `pc`, namely 104. And the value of `ppc` is currently 112.

On the other hand, an rvalue (an expression that is not an lvalue) simply *is* a value: the value of '1' is 49, assuming ASCII. This concept of *value* is regular and straightforward. It is the the concept that is followed in most high-level languages, including Basic, Fortran, and Cobol. It is, however, different from the behavior of assemblers, in which the value of a symbol is its address.

Consider the expression &x, where x is some lvalue expression. The expression &x is an rvalue: it has a value, but no storage for itself. Thus the value of &pc is (in this example) 112, the address of pc. The value of &c is 104.

If x is an expression of type "pointer to something," the expression *x is an lvalue, and its value is found in the storage that x is pointing to. Thus, *pc has the value 49 (assuming ASCII).

Question [4-3] Not all of the following "expressions" are valid. For each valid expression, write its value. Write "INVALID" otherwise.

&c _____   c _____   *c _____

&pc _____   pc _____   *pc _____

&ppc _____   ppc _____   *ppc _____

Question [4-4] The function call scanf("%c ", &c) will read one character into c. What is the value being passed as the second argument to scanf?

_____

Which of these expressions would accomplish the same result?

_____ scanf("%c", c)

_____ scanf("%c", pc)

_____ scanf("%c", &pc)

_____ scanf("%c", *pc)

_____ scanf("%c", *ppc)

In the Question above, the scanf function was told where to store something by being passed a pointer value (i.e. an expression of type "pointer to char"). We now look at short_order, a function which also expects pointer values for arguments:

```
short_order:
    /* short_order - put two short integers into order
     */
    #include "local.h"
    void short_order(pi, pj)
        short *pi, *pj;
        {
        short t;

        if (*pj < *pi)
            t = *pi, *pi = *pj, *pj = t;
        }
```

If the main program contained these declarations

```
short i1 = 1111;
short i2 = 22;
short *pi1 = &i1;
short *pi2 = &i2;
```

we could call short_order in several ways:

```
short_order(&i1, &i2);              short_order(pi1, &i2);

short_order(&i1, pi2);              short_order(pi1, pi2);
```

All of these would accomplish the same result.

But short_order(i1, i2) is incorrect, because the values passed to short_order must be pointer values (specifically addresses of short integers).

C is indeed a "call by value" language, but the arguments may be pointer values which tell the function where something is located.

Having discussed the types and values of simple pointers, we now turn to their semantic properties. A *NULL* pointer is one which contains the unique NULL value. A pointer becomes NULL when the integer zero is assigned to it. A NULL pointer always compares equal to integer zero. An *undefined* pointer is one that is not NULL, and yet is not pointing to an object of a compatible type (e.g., "garbage," uninitialized). Thus, a *defined* pointer is either pointing to valid storage, or else is NULL. And when we say that a pointer is non-NULL, we imply that it is defined. So a non-NULL pointer is one that points to valid storage. We can illustrate the importance of these concepts by considering various errors in calling short_order.

Undefined pointers: Suppose we invoked short_order like this:

```
short *ps1, *ps2;

short_order(ps1, ps2);
```

Then, without initializations or assignments, the values of ps1 and ps2 are undefined (uninitialized, "garbage"). We have, in effect, asked short_order to rearrange the contents of two random memory locations!

NULL pointers: Suppose instead that we invoked short_order like this:

```
short *ps1 = NULL;
short *ps2 = NULL;

short_order(ps1, ps2);
```

In the short_order function, the local variables pi and pj will receive the value NULL from the calling function. We then encounter a problem evaluating *pi and *pj. The problem is that NULL is not a proper value for indirection, because a NULL pointer does not point to any valid object. A strict checking environment could complain; most will attempt to access memory location zero, producing unpredictable results. So NULL pointers are also no good for the arguments to short_order.

The pointer parameters of short_order are used both to access already-existing values and also to modify the storage that is pointed to. We can refer to such pointer parameters as *in-out-pointer* parameters. (An *in-pointer* would be used only to access existing values, but not to modify anything. An *out-pointer* would be used only to modify something, but not to examine any existing value.) Let us define an *incomplete* pointer as a non-NULL pointer whose target contains one or more undefined scalars. In other words, an incomplete pointer is being used to access an object which is not totally defined. A *complete* pointer, then, is one whose target is totally defined. It is all right for an out-pointer to be incomplete, since the called function does not care what is already in the pointer's target. The safest default assumption regarding in-pointers and in-out-pointers is that they must be complete, since they must access the values that are in their target. In the short_order example, both pointers must be complete in order for the function call to be reliable.

It is an important part of the definition and documentation of a function to indicate what it expects of its pointer arguments.

Rule 4-2: The default requirement for pointer parameters is that they must point to storage that is entirely defined. Whenever a pointer parameter can accept something else, this should be explicitly stated on that parameter's declaration comment.

4.3 Dangling Pointers

There are further requirements for reliable programming with pointers. A pointer can become undefined if the object that it is pointing to should "disappear" during the lifetime of the pointer. Here is a simple example.

```
dangling.c:
    /* dangling - example of dangling pointer
     */
    #include "local.h"
    static short *pi = NULL;
    main()
        {
        void f1();

                        /* pi => NULL initially */
        f1();           /* pi => undefined suddenly! */
        }
    void f1()
        {
        short i;

        pi = &i;    /* pi => complete,  momentarily */
        }
```

The event which causes the pointer pi to become "undefined" is the *return from function* f1. The specific term for a pointer in this undefined state is a *dangling pointer;* the pointer points to storage no longer allocated. It is the programmer's responsibility to be sure that the program contains no instances of dangling pointers. (There are, however, techniques by which a strict-checking environment can detect dangling pointers [4-5].)

Rule 4-3: A function in which the address of an automatic variable is assigned to a non-automatic pointer must contain a comment to that effect. In any function with such a comment, each return from the function is an event requiring verification that no dangling pointers are left.

Further consideration of dangling pointers with respect to the free function will be found in Section 7.1.

4.4 Array Pointers and Strings

Remember that an "array pointer" (i.e., "pointer into array") is one used to access an array, not a "pointer to array." When declared as a parameter, an array pointer can be declared either with an asterisk or with empty brackets: `char *s` and `char s[]` are equivalent from the compiler's point of view. To make distinctions for the human reader, however, we can use `char s[]` to indicate an array pointer as opposed to a pointer to scalar. (However, a non-parameter pointer must be declared with the asterisk.)

Several languages provide string variables, and the compiler automatically keeps track of their current length. C does not. Loosely speaking, a *string* in C is a nul-terminated array of `char`s. More strictly, *string* is a particular *property* for a character array or character array pointer, namely the property of being nul-terminated. And a string constant, of course, always has the property *string*. Henceforth, when we use the noun "string," we are referring to a character array pointer, a character array, or a string constant, each with the property *string*.

There are advantages and disadvantages from this scheme in C. The main disadvantage is that more responsibility lies with the programmer for correct handling of strings. One advantage is that the compiler and the generated code are both simpler than in languages with built-in strings. Also, any appropriate region of memory can be treated as a string (which is useful in low-level programming).

Let us look at the string functions in the standard library, with an eye to the reliability requirements of each function.

```
size_t strlen(s)
char s[];                /* : string */
```

The parameter `s` must be a string. If it is not, most implementations of `strlen` will wander through the memory looking for a nul terminator. The "length" of a string, as always in C, is the number of characters prior to the nul terminator; thus,

```
strlen("hello")
```

returns the value 5.

```
int strcmp(s1, s2)
char s1[];              /* : string */
char s2[];              /* : string */
```

The parameters s1 and s2 must both be strings. The result is less than zero, zero, or greater than zero according to whether string s1 compares less than, equal to, or greater than string s2. Thus

```
strcmp("ab", "aa")
```

returns a positive number.

The result cannot be guaranteed to be portable if either string contains a character that is not in the machine's native character set, since the comparison may be a signed comparison on some machines. For example,

```
strcmp("\377", "a")
```

will yield a positive result if characters are signed, and a negative result if characters are not signed. Even for characters in the native character set, the collating sequence may be different on different machines.

```
char *strcpy(s1, s2)     /* at return, s1 => string */
char s1[];               /* : !NULL */
char s2[];               /* : string */
```

The s2 parameter must be a string. The s1 parameter must specify some storage into which the string can be copied, so it must be non-NULL. In general, strcpy should be used only when the program makes certain that the string length of s2 is less than the size of the array being referenced by s1. Otherwise, an out-of-bounds assignment will result.

The function strcpy returns the (original) value of s1, the address where the characters have been stored.

```
char *strcat(s1, s2)     /* at return, s1 => string */
char s1[];               /* : string */
char s2[];               /* : string */
```

The parameter s2 must be a string. The parameter s1 must be a string and its target (the storage that it accesses) must be larger than the sum of the string lengths of both parameters.

The parameter s1 is returned (the address of the new catenated string).

```
char *strchr(s, c)  /* returned value => string|NULL */
char s[];           /* : string */
int c;              /* : {CHAR_MIN:CHAR_MAX} */
```

Invoking

```
    strchr("abc", 'b')
```

will return a pointer to the second character in the string. If there
is no occurrence of character c in string s, strchr returns a NULL
pointer. Thus, the returned value is either a string (pointer) or a
NULL pointer.

```
char *strrchr(s, c) /* returned value => string|NULL */
char s[];           /* : string */
int c;              /* : {CHAR_MIN:CHAR_MAX} */
```

The behavior is the same as for strchr, except that the a pointer to
the *last* occurrence (or NULL) is returned. Thus,

```
    strrchr("aba", 'a')
```

will return a pointer to the third character of the string.

```
char *strpbrk(s1, s2)   /* returned value => string|NULL */
char s1[];              /* : string */
char s2[];              /* : string */
```

Parameters s1 and s2 must both be strings. The function returns a
pointer to the first occurrence in s1 of any character in s2. Thus

```
    strpbrk("abc123", "0123456789")
```

will return a pointer to the fourth character of the first string. If
no characters from s2 are in s1, strpbrk returns a NULL pointer.

```
size_t strspn(s1, s2)
char s1[];              /* : string */
char s2[];              /* : string */
```

Both parameters must be strings. The function returns the length
of the initial segment of string s1 which consists entirely of characters from string s2. Thus

```
    strspn("\t\tabc", " \t\n")
```

will return the number 2.

```
size_t strcspn(s1, s2)
char s1[];              /* : string */
char s2[];              /* : string */
```

Both parameters must be strings. The function returns the length of the initial segment of string s1 which consists entirely of characters *not* from s2. Thus

```
strcspn("abc\t", " \t\n")
```

will return the number 3.

```
char *strtok(s1, s2)    /* returned value => string|NULL */
char s1[];              /* : string */
char s2[];              /* : string */
```

This function splits string s1 into "tokens," more specifically, strings of characters delimited by occurrences of the characters in string s2. Calling strtok with a non-NULL argument will produce a pointer to the first token. Calling strtok with a NULL first argument will cause it to point to the next token from s1. Each token receives a nul terminator. Here is an example:

```
static char buf[] = "  abc  123\t\txyz\n";
static char seps[] = " \t\n";
char *p;

printf("first token=<%s>\n", strtok(buf, seps));
while ((p = strtok(NULL, seps)) != NULL)
    printf("next token=<%s>\n", p);
```

Three output lines will be printed:

```
first token=<abc>
next token=<123>
next token=<xyz>
```

The returned value is a string pointer, or else NULL.

One uses string comparisons so often in C that macros are sometimes useful. The local.h header defines three:

```
#define STREQ(s, t) (strcmp(s, t) == 0)
#define STRLT(s, t) (strcmp(s, t) < 0)
#define STRGT(s, t) (strcmp(s, t) > 0)
```

Besides being easier to type, the macros allow the possibility of various optimizations of the comparison. For example, in many classes of problems, strings usually differ in their first character. Each macro could be revised, to optimize speed at the expense of code space, something like this:

```
#define STREQ(s, t) ((*s) == (*t) && strcmp(s, t) == 0)
```

An array can be treated with semantics other than "string," if that is more convenient. For example, an alternative property for an array of char's is a property known as *nul-padded:* either the array is completely filled with (defined) non-nul characters, or else all characters after the first nul are also nul.

Similarly, one can maintain a *blank-padded* array: the array is completely filled with (defined) non-nul characters, of which the final sequence of blanks is considered "padding." Blank-padded arrays are often used in data-processing contexts where C is interfaced with other business-oriented software.

The string library contains the functions strncat, strncmp, and strncpy, which involve yet another array property. This one lacks a conventional name, but we can call it the *strn* property: An array with this property is either complete up to a nul-terminator, or complete up to the end of the array. In other words, if there is space for a nul-terminator, then one is present. Otherwise, the entire array is filled with (defined) non-nul characters. Here are the descriptions of the strn functions:

```
char *strncat(s1, s2, n)      /* at return, s1 => string */
char s1[];                    /* : string */
char s2[];                    /* s2[0:n-1] : strn */
size_t n;                     /* : {0:DIM(s2[*])} */
```

strncat copies at most n characters of the array s2 onto the end of string s1. Fewer than n characters are copied if a nul terminator is encountered first in s2. The resulting contents of s1 are always nul terminated, and the address of the resulting string is returned.

```
int strncmp(s1, s2, n)
char s1[];                    /* s1[0:n-1] : strn */
char s2[];                    /* s2[0:n-1] : strn */
size_t n;                     /* : {0:DIM(s2[*])} */
```

The arrays s1 and s2 are compared. The comparison stops when corresponding positions differ, or a nul terminator is reached, or all n characters of both arrays are equal. The returned value is less than zero, zero, or greater than zero according to the sense of the comparison.

```
char *strncpy(s1, s2, n)      /* at return, s1 => nul-padded */
char s1[];                    /* : !NULL, DIM(s1[*]) >= n */
char s2[];                    /* : strn */
size_t n;                     /* : {0:DIM(s2[*])} */
```

The contents of array s2 are copied into array s1. At most n bytes are copied. If the first n bytes of s2 include a nul terminator, the remainder of s1[0:n-1] is nul-padded. Otherwise, s1[0:n-1] is complete but not a string (no nul terminator).

Recent versions of C also include some new functions called the "memory" functions. These operate upon arrays of bytes with no regard for any special meaning of nul. In some environments this allows a more efficient implementation, since some machines have "block move" and "block compare" instructions.

These functions make use of a new concept in recent C, the *generic pointer*. This is a pointer which is much like a char * in that it can reference any particular byte, but its type allows it to be a "pointer to any data." Thus, you can assign any kind of data pointer to a generic pointer, or assign a generic pointer to any kind of data pointer. No pointer operations are allowed upon generic pointers, however. They are mostly useful for passing pointers to functions that can appropriately accept "pointer to any data." Inside the function, it is necessary to copy the generic pointer into some other pointer before doing pointer operations. In (draft) ANSI C, the generic pointer is a void *, but there are good reasons to use a defined type name instead. We will use the name data_ptr for the generic pointer.

One important reason to use a defined name such as data_ptr is that non-ANSI compilers will not know what a void * is. In these environments, we will need to define data_ptr as char *.

For maximum portability in non-ANSI environments, we should also cast each assignment (or argument passing) when going to or from generic pointers. This, of course, is unfortunate, since the original reason for generic pointers was to avoid so many nuisance casts. (If your compiler does not have lint-like checking of function arguments versus parameters, and it provides the same representation form for all varieties of pointers, you could safely eliminate the casts.) As long as we are still putting casts on function arguments, they might as well be (char *) casts, since this will work fine in both old and new environments.

Here, then, is the description of the memcpy function, using generic pointer notation. (In order to refer to the contents of the target of a generic pointer, we will refer to it as if it pointed to an array of char's.)

```
data_ptr memcpy(s1, s2, n)
data_ptr s1;                /* : !NULL */
data_ptr s2;                /* : !NULL */
size_t n;                   /* : {0:DIM(s1[*])-1 */
```

The array s2[0:n-1] is copied into s1[0:n-1]. The pointer s1 is returned.

All the "memory" functions are easy to implement in portable C, if your implementation does not already have them in the library. Here, for example, is a version of the memcpy function:

```
memcpy:
    /* memcpy - copy n bytes from b to a */
    #include "local.h"
    data_ptr memcpy(s1, s2, n)
        data_ptr s1;
        data_ptr s2;
        register size_t n;
        {
        register char *a = s1;
        register char *b = s2;

        for (; n > 0; --n, ++a, ++b)
            *a = *b;
        return (s1);
        }
```

For an example using memcpy, suppose that your compiler does not have structure assignments. You can efficiently copy one structure into another like this:

```
struct xxx a;
struct xxx b;

memcpy((char *)&a, (char *)&b, sizeof(a));
```

An even handier way to handle structure assignments is to define a macro:

```
#define STRUCTASST(a, b) memcpy((char *)&(a), (char *)&(b), sizeof(a))
```

This way, if your compiler does support structure assignments, you can change the definition like this:

```
#define STRUCTASST(a, b) ((a) = (b))
```

The macro STRUCTASST is defined in the local.h file described in Chapter 1.

Here are the definitions of the other "memory" functions:

```
data_ptr memchr(s, c, n)
data_ptr s;              /* : !NULL */
int c;                   /* : {CHAR_MIN:CHAR_MAX} */
size_t n;                /* : {0:DIM(s[*])-1} */
```

The array s[0:n-1] is searched for a match to the byte specified by
c. If one is found, a pointer to the matching byte is returned; otherwise, NULL is returned.

```
int memcmp(s1, s2, n)
data_ptr s1;             /* : !NULL */
data_ptr s2;             /* : !NULL */
size_t n;                /* : {0:DIM(s1[*])-1 */
```

The arrays s1[0:n-1] and s2[0:n-1] are compared byte-by-byte. If
they are identical, zero is returned. Otherwise, a number less than
zero or greater than zero is returned, according to the sense of the
comparison.

```
data_ptr memset(s, c, n)
data_ptr s;              /* : !NULL */
int c;                   /* : {CHAR_MIN:CHAR_MAX} */
size_t n;                /* : {0:DIM(s[*])-1 */
```

All the bytes of s[0:n-1] are filled with the byte value specified by
c. The pointer s is returned.

4.5 Changing Subscripts into Pointers

One often has the problem of converting an algorithm that uses
subscripts into one that uses pointers (usually for greater efficiency).
This works best when each subscript is used sequentially (with increments or decrements). Each subscripted reference like a[i] becomes a
pointer reference like *p_a. Each increment or decrement of a subscript
becomes an increment or decrement of a pointer instead. Instead of
comparing subscripts, we will compare pointers.

If, for example, we converted the qksort function of Section 3.2 to
use pointer references instead of subscript references, it would look
something like this:

```
qksortp:
    /* qksort - sort array a (dimension n) using quicksort */
    #include "local.h"
    /* iqksort - internal function to partition the array [*lo:*hi] */
    static void iqksort(p_lo, p_hi)
        short *p_lo, *p_hi;
        {
        short *p_mid = p_lo + (p_hi - p_lo) / 2;    /* : {p_lo:p_hi} */
        short *p_i;                                  /* : {p_lo+1:p_hi+1} */
        short *p_lastlo;                             /* : {p_lo:p_hi-1} */
        short tmp;

        SWAP(*p_lo, *p_mid, tmp);
        p_lastlo = p_lo;
        for (p_i = p_lo+1; p_i <= p_hi; ++p_i)
            {
            if (*p_lo > *p_i)
                {
                ++p_lastlo;
                SWAP(*p_lastlo, *p_i, tmp);
                }
            }
        SWAP(*p_lo, *p_lastlo, tmp);
        if (p_lo < p_lastlo && p_lo < p_lastlo - 1)
            iqksort(p_lo, p_lastlo - 1);
        if (p_lastlo + 1 < p_hi)
            iqksort(p_lastlo + 1, p_hi);
        }
    /* qksort - external entry point */
    void qksort(a, n)
        short a[];  /* array to be sorted; a[0:n-1]: multiset */
        size_t n;   /* number of elements */
        {
        if (n > 1)
            iqksort(a, &a[n-1]);
        }
```

Nothing has changed in the algorithm. All the invariants are the same as before. We have just replaced the subscripts with pointers.

4.6 Multi-dimensional Arrays

In C, a multi-dimensional array is really an array of arrays: if scores is declared via

```
static short scores[2][3] =        scores[0]
    {
    {2, 5, 3},                     scores[1]
    {2, 4, 4},
    };
```

scores consists of two elements, each of which is an array of three short integers. If, for instance, we were to typedef the name trio to stand for an array of three shorts, then scores could equivalently be declared to be an array of two trios.

```
typedef short trio[3];
trio scores[2];
```

As we saw earlier for pointers, there is a complementary relationship between array operations and array declarations. The "sandwich" rule tells us that the type of scores is short [2][3]. The same rule says that the type of the array scores[0] is short [3].

This becomes of particular importance when passing multidimensional arrays to functions, because what actually gets passed to the function is the address of the initial subarray. Consider a function weight which accepts n-by-three arrays of scores, and weights each column by one, two, and three.

```
long weight(a, n)
    short a[][3];
    int n;
    {
    index_t i, j;
    long sum = 0;

    for (i = 0; i < n; ++i)
        for (j = 0; j < DIM(a[0]); ++j)
            sum += (j + 1) * a[i][j];
    return (sum);
    }
```

The weight function should be passed the address of an array of three-element arrays. By C pointer parameter rules, the parameter declaration

```
short a[][3];
```

is understood as

```
short (*a)[3];
```

In other words, a is actually a pointer to three-element arrays. (The first form indicates the usage more clearly, but the second form reveals more clearly the nature of the parameter a.) Using the array scores above, we could call the function like this:

```
weight(scores, 2)
```

or like this:

```
weight(&scores[0], 2)
```

The two forms are equivalent, and the address of the array scores[0] is what gets passed. As discussed in Section 3.4, the range of pointer values that is associated with the argument is {&scores[0][0]:&scores[2][0]}, that is, all the elements of scores, plus the "one-too-far" address.

Note that in the called function, the compiler must be told the bounds of all dimensions except the major dimension. If the function needs to know the major dimension, it must be passed explicitly, as in weight above. Just as with single-dimensional arrays, there is no way to induce C to reveal the major dimension to the called function. It is certainly a mistake to use sizeof(a) to infer the dimension; sizeof(a) is only the number of bytes in a pointer, and has no relation to the size of the actual array.

4.7 Arrays of Pointers

An array of pointers is a compact way to store a table of strings. In Section 3.5 we saw a table that looked like this when stored in a two-dimensional array:

```
static char meas_codes[][6] =
    {"each", "box", "lb"};
```

```
meas_codes [0] | e | a | c | h | \0| \0|
               |___|___|___|___|___|___|
           [1] | b | o | x | \0| \0| \0|
               |___|___|___|___|___|___|
           [2] | l | b | \0| \0| \0| \0|
               |___|___|___|___|___|___|
```

We could store the same information using an array of string pointers:

```
static char *meas_codes[] =
    {"each", "box", "lb"};
```

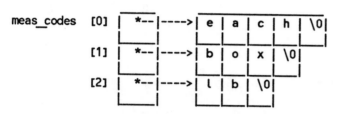

The ("declared") type of meas_codes[i] is char *, i.e., pointer to char. Each pointer meas_codes[i] is thus a proper argument to strcmp in the same loop that we used before:

```
for (i = 0; i < DIM(meas_codes); ++i)
    if (strcmp(s, meas_codes[i]) == 0)  or  if (STREQ(s, meas_codes[i]))
        found a match
```

A very simple lookup operation like this one sometimes has its practical uses. Recent C compilers provide a function called getenv ("get environment") which searches in a system-specific environment for a given name and returns a pointer to the definition associated with that name. One of the most common uses is as a way for a program to determine what type of terminal is being used:

```
char *termtype;
```

```
termtype = getenv("TERM");
```

will give us the answer, if the information is available. And if we were porting a program to a machine with no operating system, and hence no "environment," the getenv function would be one of the easiest ones to write, especially if all the "environment" definitions were constant:

```
getenv(dummy):
    /* getenv - get "environment" definition (dummy standalone version) */
    #include "local.h"
    char *getenv(s)
        char s[];
        {
        extern char *env_names[];    /* : array of string ptrs, last one NULL */
        extern char *env_defs[];     /* : array of string ptrs */
        int i;

        for (i = 0; env_names[i] != NULL; ++i)
            if (STREQ(s, env_names[i]))
                return (env_defs[i]);
        return (NULL);
        }
```

The function assumes that the array env_names will contain a NULL pointer as its last entry. This is a very common technique, since it eliminates the need for a separate variable to communicate the dimension of the array.

4.8 Command Line Arguments

Topics assumed from previous book: command line arguments [7.8].

The arguments to the main function are passed as an array of string pointers, along with a count which tells the number of non-NULL pointers in the array. Both the count and the array pointer are parameters of main, so their names can be whatever you like. The count is conventionally named argc or ac, and the array pointer is conventionally argv or av.

As with any array, the array accessed through av can be traversed either with a subscript or with a pointer. However, most programmers seem to make fewer mistakes when they use a subscript, as in the following function:

```
args.c:
    /* args - show command-line arguments, one line each
     */
    #include "local.h"
    main(ac, av)
        int ac;
        char *av[];
        {
        int i;

        for (i = 0; i < ac; ++i)
            printf("av[%d]=<%s>\n", i, av[i]);
        }
```

If we were to invoke args from the command line like this

```
    args  one  two  "quoted string for three"
```

most systems would pass the quoted string as one argument, giving this printout:

```
    av[0]=<args>
    av[1]=<one>
    av[2]=<two>
    av[3]=<quoted string for three>
```

4.9 Pointers to Functions

In most implementations, each function has an address, just as data objects do. Thus a pointer-to-function (or "function pointer") is typically an address-sized variable which can contain the address of a function. Declaring that pfn points to a function is equivalent to declaring that (*pfn) (the thing that pfn points to) *is* a function:

```
double (*pfn)();
```

says that (*pfn) is a function returning double, or that pfn is a pointer to a function returning double. The parentheses around *pfn are needed; the declaration

```
double *fnpd();
```

says that fnpd returns a pointer to double.

No operators are defined for function pointers, except for assignment, comparison, and (of course) indirection. And the only things that can be assigned to function pointers are the addresses of functions having the appropriate type:

```
extern int strcmp();
int (*cmpfn)() = &strcmp;
```

The address-of operator can be omitted; indeed, some current compilers prohibit it. We can write

```
int (*cmpfn)() = strcmp;
```

This is the more familiar style, once you understand that it is the *address* of strcmp that is being assigned to cmpfn.

The only useful thing to do with a function pointer is to call the function that it is pointing to. To call (*cmpfn) (the function that cmpfn is pointing to), with arguments s1 and s2, we write

```
(*cmpfn)(s1, s2)
```

Function pointers are useful for *dispatch tables*, i.e. tables of different functions to call. Instead of implementing a dispatch table like this

```
switch (code)   /* layout to highlight structure */
    {
case 0: initdb();    break;
case 1: opendb();    break;
case 2: readdb();    break;
    ...
case 7: closdb();    break;
    }
```

we could put the addresses of all the functions into an array:

```
typedef void (*pvoidfn)();  /* pvoidfn is ptr to fn ret void */
static pvoidfn dispatch[] = {initdb, opendb, readdb, ..., closdb};
    ...
if (0 <= code && code < DIM(dispatch))
    (*dispatch[code])();
else
    process invalid code
```

In other words, dispatch[code] is a function pointer (of the defined-type pvoidfn), so *dispatch[code] is the function that it points to.

The typedef for pvoidfn ("pointer to function returning void") makes the code more readable and less error-prone.

Another common use for function pointers is to provide a function as a parameter of another function. For example, the short-integer version of qksort could be made into a general-purpose sort function by passing a pointer to the comparison function, rather than programming the comparison operation into the function as we did in qksort. Thus, we will add a cmpfn parameter. The comparison function will be called with the addresses of two array elements, and it must return a value less than, equal to, or greater than zero, according to whether the first array element sorts before, equal to, or later than the second array element. (If the array elements are strings, the strcmp function would behave exactly in the right way.)

We will also need a new parameter to tell the size in bytes of the elements in the array, because the general-purpose version will not know the specific data type of the array elements. Accordingly, the interface will now look like this:

```
void qsort(a, n, size, cmpfn)
    data_ptr a;
    size_t n;
    size_t size;
    int (*cmpfn)();
```

Where earlier we had to re-compile a new sort function for each different array type, now one function will work for all array types. To sort an array of strings, call

```
qsort((char *)a, DIM(a), sizeof(a[0]), strcmp);
```

That is, we pass the starting address `a`, the number of array elements `DIM(a)`, the size of each element `sizeof(a[0])`, and the function to use for comparisons `strcmp`. Again, what gets passed to `qsort` is the *address* of the `strcmp` function.

Or to go back to the sorting of an array of `shorts`, we would need a little function to accomplish the `short` comparison.

```
short shortcmp(pi, pj)
    short *pi;
    short *pj;
    {
    if (*pi > *pj)
        return (1);
    else if (*pi == *pj)
        return (0);
    else
        return (-1);
    }
```

It is tempting to use a subtraction

```
return (*pi - *pj)
```

as a quick way to produce the three-way (positive, zero, negative) result, but this would be prone to overflow, as we discussed in Section 2.3. Then to sort an array of `shorts`, we would invoke

```
qsort((char *)a, DIM(a), sizeof(a[0]), shortcmp);
```

Because of this ability to parameterize the sort algorithm into a single function, it can become part of a general-purpose function library. (The specification, in fact, is taken directly from the UNIX library manuals.)

Thus, in almost all respects, we would consider the callable general-purpose library function (suitably parameterized) to be the more reliable implementation of the algorithm — there are fewer degrees of freedom for making mistakes.

Here is the C source for the `qsort` function:

```
qsort:
    /* qsort - sort array a (dimension n) using quicksort
     * based on Bentley, CACM April 84
     * Comments use notation A[i], a (fictitious) array of things
     * that are of size elt_size.
     */
    #include "local.h"
    /* swapfn - swap  elt_size bytes  a <--> b (internal routine)
     */
    static void swapfn(a, b, elt_size)
        register char *a;    /* pointer to one element of A */
        register char *b;    /* pointer to another element of A */
        size_t elt_size;     /* size of each element */
        {
        register size_t i;
        char tmp;

        for (i = 0; i < elt_size; ++i, ++a, ++b)
            SWAP(*a, *b, tmp);
        }

    /* iqsort - internal quicksort routine */
    static void iqsort(p_lo, p_hi, elt_size, cmpfn)
        char *p_lo;          /* ptr to low element of (sub)array */
        char *p_hi;          /* ptr to high element of (sub)array */
        size_t elt_size;     /* size of each element */
        int (*cmpfn)();      /* comparison function ptr */
        {
        char *p_mid = p_lo + ((((p_hi - p_lo) / elt_size) / 2) * elt_size);
        register char *p_i;          /* pointer to A[i] */
        register char *p_lastlo;     /* pointer to A[lastlo] */

        swapfn(p_lo, p_mid, elt_size);  /* pick the middle element as pivot */
        p_lastlo = p_lo;
        for (p_i = p_lo + elt_size;  p_i <= p_hi; p_i += elt_size)
            {
            if ((*cmpfn)(p_lo, p_i) > 0)
                {
                p_lastlo += elt_size;
                swapfn(p_lastlo, p_i, elt_size);
                }
            }
        swapfn(p_lo, p_lastlo, elt_size);
        if (p_lo < p_lastlo && p_lo < p_lastlo - elt_size)
            iqsort(p_lo, p_lastlo - elt_size, elt_size, cmpfn); /* lower */
        if (p_lastlo + elt_size < p_hi)
            iqsort(p_lastlo + elt_size, p_hi, elt_size, cmpfn); /* upper */
        }
```

```
/* qsort - the callable entry point */
void qsort(a, n, size, pf)
    data_ptr a;      /* address of array A to be sorted */
    size_t n;        /* number of elements in A */
    size_t size;     /* size of each element */
    int (*pf)();     /* comparison function ptr */
    {
    if (n > 1)
        iqsort((char *)a, (char *)a + (n-1) * size, size, pf);
    }
```

We started in Section 3.2 with the qksort function, which accepted an array of short integers and sorted it with subscripts. Then in Section 4.4 we transformed it into qksortp, which still worked upon short integers but used pointers. Finally, we transformed qksortp into qsort, shown just above. The next section will describe these transformations.

4.10 Pointer Transformations

The transformations that took qksort into qsort are typical of the messiest aspects of programming with pointers. It will be helpful to consider the transformations step-by-step.

First transformation: an ordinary array reference (such as a[lastlo]) is to be performed using a pointer. A pointer p_lastlo is created which will point to a[lastlo]. Then each reference to a[lastlo] becomes a reference to *p_lastlo. Finally, if any storage was dynamically allocated, it must be freed.

Second transformation: Pointers to known type are generalized into pointers to varying-size storage. Here, the rules are much trickier. The type (and therefore the size) that a pointer points to is fixed at compile time; there is no direct way to obtain a pointer to varying-size storage. The best we can do in C is to use a "byte" pointer (char *) and perform any scaling directly. (In the qsort example, the pointers are all scaled by elt_size, the size of each element in the argument array.) Thus the declaration (from qksortp)

        short *p_lastlo;

becomes (in qsort)

        char *p_lastlo;

And ++p_lastlo becomes p_lastlo += elt_size.

The difference between two pointers must be divided by the pointed-to size: (p_hi - p_lo) becomes (p_hi - p_lo) / elt_size. The difference between two pointers is an integer result, so multiplying and dividing both take place in transforming

```
short *p_mid;

p_mid = p_lo + (p_hi - p_lo) / 2;
```

into

```
char *p_mid;

p_mid = p_lo + ((p_hi - p_lo) / elt_size) / 2) * elt_size;
```

It is tempting to cut corners on the apparently redundant multiply-and-divide, but what gets added to p_lo must be an multiple of elt_size.

Third transformation: No operations can take place directly upon the pointed-to values; functions must be called for all operations. Thus

```
if (*p_lo > *p_i)
```

must be rewritten as

```
if ((*cmpfn)(p_lo, p_i) > 0)
```

Swapping two pointed-to values becomes too complicated for our simple SWAP macro; a new function (swapfn) is now used.

To summarize these transformation rules in a table:

Original	Transformed
(p_hi - p_lo)	(p_hi - p_lo) / elt_size
p_lo + expr	p_lo + expr * elt_size
++p_lastlo	p_lastlo += elt_size
SWAP(*p_lo, *p_mid, tmp)	swapfn(p_lo, p_mid, elt_size)

Such transformations must be done carefully, but it is testimony to the expressive power of C that they are possible at all. Certainly, in many languages it is difficult, if not impossible, to write a function which will accept an array of any dimension, composed of elements of any size, and then sort the elements according to an arbitrary ordering function. The C implementation of qsort does all this, in strictly portable code.

CHAPTER 5: STANDARD FILE AND TERMINAL I/O

In this chapter we examine the facilities for I/O on the "standard files": standard input, standard output, and the standard error file. Among these facilities are also the functions sprintf and sscanf for formatted operations to and from strings. Finally, we will look at methods for performing I/O with terminal screens and keyboards.

5.1 Formatted Output

Topics assumed from previous book: Basic printf formats [2.8], file redirection [3.22].

You are presumably familiar with the basic formats of printf: %c (character), %s (string), %d (decimal integer), %u (decimal unsigned integer), %o (octal integer), %x (hexadecimal integer), %f ("fixed-point" representation of floating-point number), and %e ("E-notation" floating-point number). The modifier l (for "long") can precede d, u, o, or x, to indicate a long int argument.

Format specifiers are actually somewhat more complicated than the simple examples above; the full syntax looks like this:

% *flag width . precision conversion*

In the simpler forms of printf (such as in K&R), the *flag* may consist of a minus sign, indicating left-adjustment of the output. The *width* is a string of digits indicating the minimum output width. (In K&R and in UNIX Version 7, a *width* beginning with a zero digit indicated that extra output places were to be filled with zeros, not blanks. This feature disappeared in later UNIX manuals, but not always from the library code itself!) The *precision* (for floating-point formats) is the number of decimal places; for strings, it is the maximum number of characters to print. And the *conversion* characters were covered in the previous paragraph.

One other format completes the capabilities of basic printf: the g format. When g is specified, printf tries the output both in e and f formats and prints whichever takes less space. This can be useful for outputs of widely differing magnitude.

Over the years, other features have been found useful and incorporated in newer libraries. New *flags* are provided: A plus sign (+) produces either a plus (+) or a minus (-) sign on the printed output. A *blank* produces either a blank or a minus sign. And a # flag produces an "alternate form." For example, %#o causes the (octal) printed result to have a high-order zero, and %#x causes the (hex) printed result to begin with 0x.

One innovation most useful for reliability is that the *width* and/or *precision* can be replaced by an asterisk, in which case the appropriate number will be taken from the argument list. For example,

```
printf("%*.*f\n", fld_width, dec_places, x);
```

will print the (floating) number x with dec_places number of decimal places and fld_width total field width. Previously, the hard-coded numbers appearing in format strings were likely to be missed when modifying programs with new output parameters.

Some cosmetic changes were also provided: the *conversion* characters X, E, and G cause the appropriate alphabetic characters to appear in upper case, to the delight of former FORTRAN programmers who never adapted to 1.86272E5 being printed as 1.86272e5. (For a detailed comparison of the K&R, /usr/group, and ANSI C libraries, see the appendix [5-1].)

All of the printf formatting is available for formatted output into a string, using the sprintf function. For example, the invocation

```
sprintf(s, "%3s %3s %2d %2d:%02d:%02d %4d",
    weekday, mo, day, hh, mm, ss, yr);
```

could leave s looking like this:

```
"Fri Nov 11 15:47:04 1982"
```

Exercise 5-1. Write a function

```
char *fround(x, s, nsignif, width, precis)
    double x;
    char s[];
    int nsignif;
    int width;
    int precis;
```

which will round x to nsignif significant digits and then "print" the result into the string s in %f format with width and precision specified by width and precis. The function should return the (address) value of s. For example,

```
printf("%s\n", fround(x, buf, 3, 8, 3));
```

would produce, when given successive x values of 12.345, .6666, and 4853.4836, the output

```
  12.3
   .667
4850.
```

There are some reliability limitations to the printf family of functions. Since numeric output will occupy as many characters as are needed, it is dangerous to use sprintf to write into strings which are not large enough for the largest possible output, nor should we use printf to write into files whose contents are strictly formatted in size. The only way to be certain of the size of numeric output is to bounds-check each number before printing or to allow the absolute maximum output size for each number.

Oftentimes it is more convenient to use a more specialized, but more reliable, function for converting numbers into strings. The itoa function below is one example. This is much less powerful than the printf functions, but it is suitable for converting integers into small strings. It assumes that the stated string size is inviolate, so a string of 9's is the best response to an out-of-bounds argument, with a Boolean return of NO if the full result would not fit. Here is the itoa function:

```
itoa:
    /* itoa - convert integer n to string (ndigits max) */
    #include "local.h"
    bool itoa(n, str, ndigits)
        int n;
        char str[];
        int ndigits;
        {
        int sign;
        short i;
        bool success;
        unsigned un = n;      /* need room for most-negative n */

        success = YES;
        if (ndigits < 1 || n < 0 && ndigits < 2)
            return (NO);          /* can't even get started */
        else if (n == 0)
            {
            strcpy(str, "0");   /* dispose of a special case */
            return (YES);
            }
        else if (n < 0)
            {
            sign = -1;
            un = -n;
            --ndigits;             /* sign consumes one print digit */
            }
        else
            sign = 1;
        for (i = 0; i < ndigits && un != 0; ++i)
            {
            str[i] = '0' + un % 10;
            un /= 10;
            }
        if (un != 0)          /* still more digits to print, and no room */
            {
            for (i = 0; i < ndigits; ++i)
                str[i] = '9';
            success = NO;
            }
        if (sign < 0)
            str[i++] = '-';
        str[i] = '\0';
        reverse(str);
        return (success);
        }
```

5.2 Standard Files

Before the main function is invoked, three *standard files* are opened, known as the *standard input*, the *standard output*, and the *standard error* files. The standard input is used by getchar and scanf; the standard output is used by printf and putchar. All the information needed to keep track of each file is kept in a struct declared in <stdio.h> with the defined-type FILE [5-2]. Also in <stdio.h> are definitions of three symbols — stdin, stdout, and stderr — each of which is defined to be the address of a FILE structure. Thus, stdin has the type FILE *, or "pointer to FILE," as do stdout and stderr.

Most hosted environments for C provide a method for *redirecting* the standard input and the standard output on the command line:

```
pgm <file1 >file2
```

will associate stdin with file1, and stdout with file2. This redirection is accomplished by the command language interpreter (e.g., "shell" or COMMAND.COM)   on UNIX systems, MS-DOS (since Version 2.0), and many other systems. Other environments provide special startup code in the program itself. In either event, the redirection is accomplished before the main function is called.

Files that are accessed through the FILE mechanism provided by <stdio.h> are known as *stream files*, or (less officially) as *buffered files* — "buffered," because most implementations provide a char array (whose size is named BUFSIZ in <stdio.h>) to provide in-memory temporary storage of characters being read or written.

The main advantage of buffering is execution speed. On many systems, input and output are vastly more efficient if done in large chunks; disk transfers in particular are often more efficient in blocks of 256, 512, or 1024 characters. Taking putchar as an example, its usual implementation involves storing the output character into the buffer, updating a pointer to the next buffer location, and decrementing a count of the space left in the buffer. When the buffer is full, a physical I/O transfer then takes place to write out all the characters in the buffer. This scheme is known as "fully buffered" I/O.

Each of the default-file I/O functions has an equivalent version that accepts a FILE * argument :

getchar()	is equivalent to	getc(stdin)
putchar()	is equivalent to	putc(stdout)
scanf(fmt, ...)	is equivalent to	fscanf(stdin, fmt, ...)
printf(fmt, ...)	is equivalent to	fprintf(stdout, fmt, ...)

Until we discuss how to open files by name, the most useful of these functions is fprintf for the printing of error messages onto stderr:

```
if (x < x_low_lim)
    fprintf(stderr, "x=%.6e is below x_low_lim=%.6e\n", x, x_low_lim);
```

It is often advantageous not to buffer the standard error file, since the last error message printed by a program in deep trouble might get lost in the buffer if the program's demise is untidy. Many environments provide an unbuffered stderr by default, but the safe course is to use the setbuf function:

```
setbuf(stderr, NULL);
```

will, if called before the first I/O operations upon stderr, put stderr into the "unbuffered" mode. Some environments will also put stdin and/or stdout into unbuffered mode if they are associated with an interactive terminal.

One final advantage of the "buffered" scheme of stream input is that "pushing-back" a character is easily provided for. If c contains a character read from stdin, calling ungetc(c, stdin) will cause the next input operation to read that character again. This is often useful in scanning an input file in which some punctuation character marks the end of each word or item. The punctuator can be "pushed back" onto the stream for another part of the program to handle.

5.3   Reading Lines of Input

For reading lines of input, two functions are provided in the standard library: gets and fgets. The gets function has the simpler calling sequence:

```
gets(buf)
```

reads one line from stdin, stores it in buf (with a nul-terminator but *without* a newline), and returns NULL at end-of-file. Since it provides no means of specifying the size of the receiving string, it can seldom be used in reliable programs. Furthermore, it gives no convenient way to tell whether a newline was present in the input. The fgets function is more reliable, but oftentimes awkward to use. Calling

```
fgets(buf, n, stdin)
```

will store at most n bytes into buf, reading from the file specified by the FILE * third argument (stdin, in this example). Of these bytes, the last byte stored is always a nul-terminator. If a newline is encountered in the input, it will precede the nul-terminator. Like gets, fgets returns NULL at end-of-file.

In many applications, the newline in the string is a nuisance, and the more useful returned value would be the length of the stored string. I have many times found more use for a slightly different function, named getsnn ("get string with no newline"). This function deletes the newline, and returns the length of the stored string, or EOF at end-of-file. If the length is less than its maximum (i.e., the specified size minus one), a newline was present in the input; if the length reaches the maximum, no newline was present. The function looks like this:

```
getsnn:
    /* getsnn - get one line, omitting the newline (if any)
     * Returns the number of characters stored,
     * which equals size-1 only if no newline was found to that point.
     * Returns EOF at end of file.
     */
#include "local.h"
    int getsnn(s, size)
        char s[];
        int size;
        {
        int i;
        metachar c;

        for (i = 0; i < size-1 && (c = getchar()) != EOF && c != '\n'; ++i)
            s[i] = c;
        s[i] = '\0';
        if (c == EOF)
            return (EOF);
        return (i);
        }
```

Question [5-3] Modify getsnn into fgetsnn, a function with identical specification except for a third (FILE *) argument:

```
    int fgetsnn(s, size, fp)
        char s[];
        int size;
        FILE *fp;
```

As an example of the use of getsnn, consider the function getreply, designed for the common task of printing a prompting message and receiving a reply. If the user types more characters than are wanted, we are not interested in them. (In the next chapter we will see more sophisticated means of receiving replies in which the user sees immediately that no more characters are allowed on input. The getreply function will adequately handle the simple cases such as getting a 'y' or 'n' reply.) The function prints the prompt, gets a reply using getsnn, consumes the rest of the line if getsnn did not consume the newline, and returns the length of the reply string, or EOF if end-of-file.

```
getreply:
    /* getreply - print a prompt and get one-line reply
     * Returns length of reply string, or EOF if end-of-file
     * Consumes an entire input line, even if over-long.
     */
    #include "local.h"
    int getreply(prompt, reply, size)
        char prompt[];
        char reply[];
        int size;
        {
        metachar last_char;              /* the last char read */
        int get_ret;                     /* getsnn return: length of reply or EOF */

        printf("%s", prompt);
        get_ret = getsnn(reply, size);
        if (get_ret == EOF)
            return (EOF);
        else if (get_ret == size-1) /* no newline was read */
            while ((last_char = getchar()) != EOF && last_char != '\n')
                ;
        if (last_char == EOF)
            return (EOF);
        return (get_ret);
        }
```

5.4 Formatted Input

Topics assumed from first book: Basic scanf formats [3.12].

The combinations of basic conversion characters for scanf can be illustrated by the following table:

```
data size
short    int   long        conversion

  %hd    %d    %ld         decimal integer
  %ho    %o    %lo         octal integer
  %hx    %x    %lx         hexadecimal integer
  %hu    %u    %lu         unsigned integer


float         double

%e or %f    %le or %lf    floating-point number
```

A "one-word" string (delimited by whitespace) can be read with the %s format:

```
char next_word[LARGE_ENOUGH];

if (scanf("%s", next_word) != 1)
    /* must be EOF if scanf failed */
```

The value of LARGE_ENOUGH must be adequate for the largest possible input word.

For all the input formats discussed so far, scanf will skip over any input whitespace (including newline!) to find the next input item. If a *width* specification precedes the conversion character, leading whitespace is still skipped, and then only the specified number of input characters are considered in the conversion. Thus,

```
char next_char[2];

scanf("%1s", next_char)
```

will read into next_char the next non-whitespace input character, followed by a nul-terminator. If the percent-sign is followed by an asterisk (the "assignment-suppression flag"), the corresponding input item will be matched but not assigned. This means that

```
scanf("%*1s%1s", next_char)
```

will read into next_char the *second* non-whitespace character from the input.

The %c input format behaves somewhat differently: it produces the next input character, whitespace or not. For example, an input file consisting of 80-character "card-images" could be read by

```
scanf("%80c", card_image)
```

Note that no nul-terminator will be placed after the characters.

For discussion of recent additions to scanf, as well as a comparison of different versions, see the appendix [5-4].

Now we will consider some of the reliability problems of the scanf functions. Numeric input is not checked for overflow. This means that numerical input using scanf can be trusted only if the inputs are somehow known to be in-bounds (perhaps previously produced by a reliable program). As alluded to earlier, strings read by the %s format have no guaranteed upper bound on their length. And character input, such as %80c, works reliably only when the input file is known to have the proper number of characters available. A format like this would be a disaster if applied to input lines of varying length; the newlines would just be swallowed up into the 80-character inputs.

Another problem with scanf is that its returned value is a very crude indicator of the success of the scan. The format argument can specify literal text characters that are supposed to be matched in the input, but scanf tells only how many arguments were successfully assigned. In particular, if a format string ended with literal text instead of a format specifier ("percent-sign something"), there would be no way to tell whether the text was successfully matched or not. For example, if a format string ends with a whitespace character, this requests scanf to skip over any trailing whitespace after the last input item — but there is no way to tell if there was any such trailing whitespace after scanf returns.

Finally, there is scanf's "push-back" behavior: unless the final format stopped because of a specified width bound, there is one input character which scanf pushed back onto the input stream, using ungetc, or its equivalent. This makes for problems when scanf input conversion is combined with other input functions. For example, unless the format ends with whitespace, scanf will not consume the newline at the end of a line that it has read, so calling a line-oriented function must be done with full awareness that the input is still on the same line that scanf partially consumed.

Somewhat finer control is available by reading an entire input line with a line-oriented function such as getsm, and then splitting it up with sscanf. This works for reasonably error-free inputs where "diagnose-and-terminate" (or "diagnose and re-prompt") is adequate for errors.

The scanf functions provide no control over the size of strings read via %s formats. When the input can be expected not to exceed some generous maximum line length, an intermediate buffer can solve the problem. For example, we can make a getpstr function which looks for a specified "prompt" sequence in the input and passes back the whitespace-delimited "word" which follows:

```
getpstr:
    /* getpstr - get a string from input
     * string must be preceded by specified "prompt" text
     * return YES if text matched, NO otherwise
     */
    #include "local.h"
    #define FMTSIZE 84   /* arbitrary limit on size of "prompt" */

    bool getpstr(p, s, n)
        char p[];               /* : !NULL */
        char s[];               /* : string */
        size_t n;               /* : {1:sizeof(p[*])} */
        {
        char buf[BUFSIZ];       /* : string */
        char fmt[FMTSIZE];      /* : string */
        metachar c;

        if (!strfit(fmt, p, FMTSIZE - 4))   /* copy "prompt" into fmt */
            return (NO);        /* prompt text is too long */
        strcat(fmt, "%s");      /* make fmt into a scanf format */
        while (isspace(c = getchar()))
            ;                   /* skip leading whitespace */
        ungetc(c, stdin);       /* put the non-whitespace back */
        if (scanf(fmt, buf) != 1)
            return (NO);        /* scanf match failed */
        if (!strfit(s, buf, n))
            fprintf(stderr, "<%s> chopped to <%s>\n", buf, s);
        return (YES);
        }
```

Here is a typical usage: the input is expected to contain the characters `"Name: "` (preceded and followed by any amount of whitespace) and then one "word" (whitespace-delimited string) which is to be read into a string (name_str, say). The corresponding call to getpstr would look like this:

```
    if (!getpstr("Name:", name_str, sizeof(name_str)))
        error("Expected   Name: ...", "");
```

The getpstr function consumes only one word after the expected "prompt" prefix. If we want a similar function which will consume the entire remainder of the line, it is simpler to read the rest of the line with a line-oriented function such as getsnn. Here is the function getplin ("get prompted line") which does so:

```
getplin:
    /* getplin - get a line from input
     * line must start with specified "prompt" text
     * return YES if text matched, NO otherwise
     */
    #include "local.h"
    #define FMTSIZE 84
    bool getplin(p, s, n)
        char p[];
        char s[];
        size_t n;
        {
        char buf[BUFSIZ];
        char fmt[FMTSIZE];
        metachar c;

        if (!strfit(fmt, p, FMTSIZE - 4))
            return (NO);      /* prompt text is too long */
        strcat(fmt, "%c");
        while (isspace(c = getchar()))
            ;
        ungetc(c, stdin);
        if (scanf(fmt, buf) != 1)
            return (NO);
        if (getsnn(buf, BUFSIZ) == EOF)
            return (NO);
        if (!strfit(s, buf, n))
            fprintf(stderr, "<%s> chopped to \n<%s>\n", buf, s);
        return (YES);
        }
```

5.5 Direct Terminal I/O

Most of the reliability problems discussed above are eliminated by using direct terminal I/O. In this mode, the program reads the user's inputs character-by-character, accepting only good data as it is typed. If the user types too many characters, or the wrong kind of characters (e.g., non-numeric in a numeric field), the program can "beep" and refuse to echo the character. This mode also has the advantage of controlling the physical appearance of the screen directly.

To accomplish this, we need control over the cursor position and control over the echoing of characters. There is, unfortunately, no portable means to enter this mode in standard C; the best that we can do is to define a minimal set of functions and write an implementation for them in each different environment. (The libraries known as curses, termcap, and terminfo in the UNIX world provide all of this and more, but these libraries are not available on most non-UNIX C implementations.)

Our functions will address the screen by line and column numbers. Line zero, column zero is the "home" position, in the upper left corner. Global variables scr_lins and scr_cols give the number of lines and columns on the terminal:

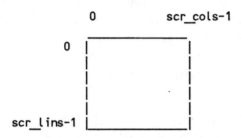

These are the functions that we will need:

scr_open() will do whatever is necessary in order that each key be received by the program as it is typed.

scr_close() will restore the ordinary terminal state.

scr_clear() erases the screen and moves the cursor to the home position.

scr_cel() clears to the end of the current line.

scr_curs(line, col) causes the cursor to move to the specified location.

scr_putc(c) prints the character c at the current screen position and moves the cursor accordingly.

scr_print(fmt, ...) performs a printf at the current screen position.

scr_refresh() forces any buffered screen changes to be written to the physical screen.

To achieve the needed control over the terminal screen, some environments have to turn off the usual mapping of newline ('\n') into carriage-return+linefeed. (The newline character when unmapped produces a linefeed only, dropping down one line without return to the margin.) If we need to accomplish a carriage-return+newline, we will have to transmit "\r\n" explicitly. If newline mapping is still turned on, nothing has been lost in doing so.

The scr_refresh macro forces the flushing of the standard-output buffer by calling the library function fflush.

Regarding the input, there is a function scr_getkey which performs some useful mappings. Many terminals now have cursor-control keys (typically left-arrow, right-arrow, up-arrow, down-arrow, and home) but the actual code sequences which they generate are not standard. The scr_getkey function interprets these special sequences and returns a single scalar value, which is either an ordinary character or a special code for each of the mapped keys.

The screen functions work together to ensure that the terminal screen has an invariant property that we might call the screen-sync property: The program knows what the screen looks like. There are no characters on the screen that were not known to the program.

To be very strict about the screen-sync property, we should take steps to ensure that no other programs or other users can write to the screen during execution of the program. The details will vary, of course, from system to system.

The code examples below are simple implementations of the above operations. One implementation (screenU.c) works on a UNIX system with an ANSI terminal (DEC VT-100, Zenith Z-19 and Z-29, etc.), the other one works on an IBM PC-compatible system with the "ANSI.SYS" driver.

screen.h:

```
/* screen.h - header for terminal package
 * Assumes ANSI terminal
 */
#ifndef SCREEN_H
#define SCREEN_H

typedef short SCR_CMDCHAR;
#define SCR_RETURN '\r'
#define SCR_EXIT    0x101
#define SCR_UP      0x102
#define SCR_DOWN    0x103
#define SCR_LEFT    0x104
#define SCR_RIGHT   0x105
#define SCR_HOME    0x106
#define SCR_CLEAR   "\33[2J"     /* clear entire screen, go HOME */
#define SCR_CEL     "\33[K"      /* clear to end of line */
#define SCR_TTY 1   /* screen is in ordinary (non-direct) mode */
#define SCR_RAW 2   /* screen is in "total-control" mode */

#define SCR_CMD(c) \
    (c == SCR_RETURN || c >= 0x101 && c <= 0x106)

extern short scr_mode;      /* {SCR_TTY, SCR_RAW} */
extern short scr_lins;      /* number of lines on screen */
extern short scr_cols;      /* number of columns on screen */

void scr_close();           /* PARMS(void) */
SCR_CMDCHAR scr_getkey();   /* PARMS(void) */
void scr_open();            /* PARMS(void) */

#define scr_beep()      putchar('\7')
#define scr_clear()     printf(SCR_CLEAR)
#define scr_cel()       printf(SCR_CEL)
#define scr_curs(r, c)  printf("\33[%d;%dH", (r)+1, (c)+1)
#define scr_print       printf
#define scr_putc(c)     putchar(c)
#define scr_refresh()   fflush(stdout)
#endif
```

```
screenU.c:
    /* screen - environment-specific terminal functions
     * UNIX version for ANSI terminal
     */
    #include "local.h"
    #include "screen.h"
    #define get_7bit_char() (getchar() & 0177)  /* "raw" getchar never EOF */
    short scr_mode = SCR_TTY;    /* screen mode - TTY or RAW */
    short scr_lins = 24;     /* screen lines (default) */
    short scr_cols = 80;      /* screen columns (default) */
    /* scr_getkey - get a (coded) keyboard char */
    SCR_CMDCHAR scr_getkey()
        {
        char c1, c2;

        scr_refresh();
        if ((c1 = get_7bit_char()) != '\33')
            return (c1);
        else if ((c2 = get_7bit_char()) == 'O')
            {
            if (get_7bit_char() == 'S')     /* F1 function key */
                return (SCR_EXIT);
            scr_beep();
            return (scr_getkey());
            }
        else if (c2 == '[')
            {
            switch (get_7bit_char())
                {
            case 'A':   return (SCR_UP);     /* no "break" needed - all returns */
            case 'B':   return (SCR_DOWN);
            case 'C':   return (SCR_RIGHT);
            case 'D':   return (SCR_LEFT);
            case 'H':   return (SCR_HOME);
            default:    scr_beep();
                        return (scr_getkey());
                }
            }
        else
            {
            scr_beep();
            return (scr_getkey());
            }
        }
```

```
/* remark - print error message, appropriate for scr_mode */
void remark(s1, s2)
    char s1[], s2[];    /* strings to be printed */
    {
    if (scr_mode == SCR_TTY)
        fprintf(stderr, "%s %s\n", s1, s2);
    else
        {
        scr_curs(scr_lins-1, 0);
        scr_print("%s %s; hit any key to continue", s1, s2);
        scr_getkey();
        scr_curs(scr_lins-1, 0);
        scr_cel();
        }
    }
/* scr_open - initialize the terminal */
void scr_open()
    {
    system("stty raw -echo");    /* slow but universal */
    printf("\33[>6h");           /* keypad-shifted; not universal ANSI */
    scr_mode = SCR_RAW;
    }
/* scr_close - re-establish normal terminal environment */
void scr_close()
    {
    printf("\33[>6l");           /* exit keypad-shifted mode */
    system("stty -raw echo");    /* slow but universal */
    scr_mode = SCR_TTY;
    }
```

screen86.c:

```c
/* screen - environment-specific terminal functions
 * PC Version - uses  bdos  function
 */
#include "local.h"
#include "screen.h"
short scr_mode = SCR_TTY;   /* screen mode - TTY or RAW */
short scr_lins = 24;     /* screen lines (default) */
short scr_cols = 80;     /* screen columns (default) */
/* scr_getkey - get a (coded) keyboard char */
SCR_CMDCHAR scr_getkey()
    {
    char c1;

    scr_refresh();
    if ((c1 = bdos(8)) != '\0')
        return (c1 & 0x7F);
    switch (c1 = bdos(8))
        {
    /* no "break" needed - all returns */
    case 'H':   return (SCR_UP);
    case 'P':   return (SCR_DOWN);
    case 'M':   return (SCR_RIGHT);
    case 'K':   return (SCR_LEFT);
    case 'G':   return (SCR_HOME);
    case ';':   return (SCR_EXIT);   /* F1 function key */
    default:    scr_beep();
                return (scr_getkey());
        }
    }
/* remark - print error message, appropriate for scr_mode */
void remark(s1, s2)
    char s1[], s2[];     /* strings to be printed */
    {
    if (scr_mode == SCR_TTY)
        fprintf(stderr, "%s %s\n", s1, s2);
    else
        {
        scr_curs(scr_lins-1, 0);
        scr_print("%s %s; hit any key to continue", s1, s2);
        scr_getkey();
        scr_curs(scr_lins-1, 0);
        scr_cel();
        }
    }
/* scr_open - enter "raw" screen mode */
void scr_open()
    {
    scr_mode = SCR_RAW; /* otherwise no work; bdos(8) is unbuffered */
    }
```

```
/* scr_close - restore normal tty state */
void scr_close()
    {
    scr_mode = SCR_TTY;
    }
```

This simple implementation of scr_putc outputs each character with putchar, which may be totally unbuffered in some environments. A significantly more efficient implementation would store up characters internally until the "screen-refresh" function (scr_refresh) was called. Even more sophisticated is the scheme of the curses library. Output to the screen is saved in a screen-image buffer until a refresh function is called. Then, the desired new screen image is compared with the existing image, and only those screen positions which have changed are output, with appropriate cursor motions, character-inserts, character-deletes, etc. Both approaches to screen refreshing are easy to add onto the basic scheme, if you want to.

As a simple demonstration of cursor addressing, the function plot_trk (listed below) simulates a pseudo-oval track around the screen. (There are 100 points on the track, chosen so that the physical distance between points is roughly equal.)

```
plot_trk:
    /* plot_trk - plot position around a pseudo-oval track */
    #include "local.h"
    #include "screen.h"
    #define LIN_ORIGIN 11
    #define COL_ORIGIN 40
    #define NPOINTS 26
    #define IMAX (NPOINTS - 1)
    #define POS(n, signlin, signcol) \
        scr_curs(LIN_ORIGIN + (signlin) * coords[n].lin, \
            COL_ORIGIN + (signcol) * coords[n].col)
    static struct coords
        {
        short lin, col;
        } coords[NPOINTS] =
        {       /* points for one quadrant (quarter-screen) */
        {11,  0}, {11,  2}, {11,  4}, {11,  6}, {11,  8},
        {11, 10}, {11, 12}, {11, 14}, {11, 16}, {11, 18},
        {11, 20}, {11, 22}, {11, 24}, {11, 26}, {11, 28},
        {10, 29}, { 9, 30}, { 8, 31}, { 7, 32}, { 6, 33},
        { 5, 34}, { 4, 35}, { 3, 36}, { 2, 36}, { 1, 36},
        { 0, 36},
        };
```

```
/* plot_trk - plot a point */
void plot_trk(n, c)
    int n;
    char c;
    {
    asserts(n >= 0, "plot_trk: n is non-negative");
    n %= 4 * IMAX;
    if (n < IMAX)
        POS(n, 1, 1);                    /* 1st quadrant - lower right */
    else if (n < 2 * IMAX)
        POS(2 * IMAX - n, -1, 1);    /* 2nd quadrant - upper right */
    else if (n < 3 * IMAX)
        POS(n - 2 * IMAX, -1, -1);   /* 3rd quadrant - upper left */
    else
        POS(4 * IMAX - n, 1, -1);    /* 4th quadrant - lower left */
    scr_putc(c);
    }
```

A simple "test-drive" function runs four times around the track, then stops.

```
plot_m.c:
    /* plot_m - demonstrate plot_trk function */
    #include "local.h"
    #include "screen.h"
    main()
        {
        short i;

        scr_open();
        scr_clear();
        for (i = 0; i < 400; ++i)    /* four times around the track */
            plot_trk(i, 'X');
        scr_curs(scr_lins-1, 0);
        scr_close();
        }
```

Those of you programming race-track simulations will immediately see the applicability. In the next chapter, we will have more substantive uses for all these new functions.

CHAPTER 6: STRUCTURES

Structures are useful for grouping a collection of objects into a single aggregate object. Structures can even be subdivided down to the level of machine bits, using bit-fields. Unions are syntactically very similar to structures, allowing the same memory to be used in different ways.

In this chapter, we will examine various uses for structures and unions, as well as relevant reliability rules. The chapter concludes with a complex data structure known as a "menu," which provides a convenient generalized user interface.

6.1 Records

Topics assumed from previous book: structures [8.1], members [8.2].

One of the oldest uses of structures is the *record*, a collection of information about a single entity. For example, a structure can be used to collect information about a specific part in an assembly:

```
struct part
    {
    char part_no[14];    /* part number: string */
    short lead_time;     /* lead time (in weeks): {0:99} */
    char unit_meas[6];   /* unit of measure: string {"each", "lb", "box"} */
    float unit_cost;     /* cost for one unit_meas: {0.00:9999.99} */
    short cost_qty;      /* quantity required for price: {0:9999} */
    };
```

In a typical environment where short takes two bytes and float takes
four bytes, the memory layout of a struct part might look like this:

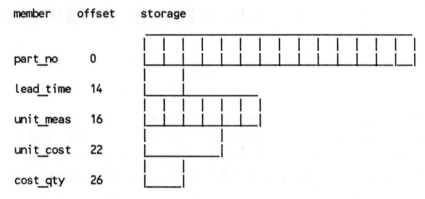

Each data type has its own *alignment requirement*, a requirement
(imposed by the CPU hardware and/or the compiler) that the address of
this type of data must be evenly divisible by some number. In the
example above, we have assumed that each alignment requirement is no
more restrictive than "even address" (divisible by two). In such implementations, a struct part occupies 28 bytes.

   Suppose, however, that we are compiling for a machine on which
float data is required to have an divisible-by-four address. Such an
alignment requirement would force the compiler to leave a *hole* in the
structure, an unused portion of the storage which exists solely to
preserve alignment. Furthermore, a structure has its own alignment
requirement, which is the most restrictive of its members' alignment
requirements. Thus, in this implementation, a struct part would be
required to have a divisible-by-four address. Another hole would be
required at the end, to cause the size of a struct part to be evenly divisible by four. (If a structure's size were not an even multiple of its alignment requirement, an array of structures would come out mis-aligned.)
In this more restrictive implementation, the memory layout would look
like this:

part_no	0	
lead_time	14	
unit_meas	16	
unit_cost	24	
cost_qty	28	

And the size of a struct part would be 32 bytes, in this more restrictive implementation.

Rule 6-1: In portable programming, do not hard-code the numeric values of structure offsets. The values may be different in each environment. Refer to members by their symbolic member names only.

The advantage of a structure over an array is that the members can have different data types. In this example, the information recorded for each part consists of two char arrays for strings, two short integers, and one float.

The declaration given above does not reserve any storage for any variable; it merely describes a "shape" or *template* for a part record. The template is identified by a *tag* name (part, in this example). We can declare one or more variables to have this template by using the type struct part in a declaration:

```
struct part part1;
```

This creates storage for the variable part1. Thus, the entire structure part1 and also its individual *members* (part1.part_no, part1.lead_time, part1.unit_meas, ...) are all *lvalues*.

6.2 Structures for Information-Hiding

One of the important uses for C structures is to encapsulate interface information. Consider, for example, the FILE structure provided by the standard I/O library. On many systems, the header stdio.h defines the name FILE something like this:

```
#define FILE      struct _file
struct _file
    {
    char    *_cur_ptr;    /* where to get/put the next character: !NULL */
    int     _size;        /* how big is the buffer: {0:INT_MAX} */
    char    *_buffer;     /* where is the buffer: char[_size] | NULL */
    int     _rcount;      /* how many more gets left: {0:_size} */
    int     _wcount;      /* how many more puts left: {0:_size} */
    char    _status;      /* file state: bits */
    char    _fd;          /* file descriptor: {0:_NFILES-1} */
    };
```

Thus the name FILE becomes a synonym for the type struct _file. The tag name (_file) and each of the member names (_cur_ptr, _size, etc.) are given names that start with a leading underscore. There is an associated reliability rule:

Rule 6-2: Names with leading underscore should only appear in code that is privy to the internal details of the associated data structure, not in "user-level" portable code.

In particular, you can see that if a supposedly portable program were to use one of these "private names," the program would probably not even compile correctly on another system, since the actual names themselves will very likely be different. If the user uses only the name FILE, the program will portably conform to each target environment.

In C, the "information-hiding" of private names is purely advisory, enforced by style conventions rather than compilers. The advantage for simplicity in programming is that the header provided with a functional package (such as the stdio functions) can easily define macros that allow efficient use of the data structure, just by using the private member names needed.

The main advantage of this defined-type approach is that the internal details of the representation are somewhat more "hidden" from the functions that use the type. This allows the internal details to be tailored to each particular target system, or to be changed to incorporate more efficient algorithms when needed. Furthermore, those functions that do not examine the internal representation of the object need no source-code changes if the object is changed from a structure to a scalar (or to a union — see Section 6.4).

Creating defined-types for structures can also be done with typedef. For example, the FILE type could be declared like this:

```
typedef struct _file
    {
    char    *_cur_ptr;  /* where to get/put the next character */
    int     _size;      /* how big is the buffer: {0:INT_MAX} */
    char    *_buffer;   /* where is the buffer: char[_size] | NULL */
    int     _rcount;    /* how many more gets left: {0:_size} */
    int     _wcount;    /* how many more puts left: {0:_size} */
    char    _status;    /* file state: bits */
    char    _fd;        /* file descriptor: {0:_NFILES-1} */
    } FILE;
```

The typedef approach has the minor advantage of preventing any subsequent re-definition of the name, but either approach will serve adequately.

Using either approach, we will assume that for each generally-useable structure, both the defined (upper-case) name and the tag (lower-case) name will be available. Here is another useful convention: Structures used in several different source files should be declared in a header to be included wherever needed. The "part-record" structure might, for example, be declared like this:

```
part.h(#1):
    /* part.h - header for PART structure */
    #ifndef PART_H
    #define PART_H
    typedef struct part
        {
        char part_no[14];   /* part number: string */
        short lead_time;    /* lead time (in weeks): {0:99} */
        char unit_meas[6];  /* unit of measure: string {"each", "lb", "box"} */
        float unit_cost;    /* cost for one unit_meas: {0.00:9999.99} */
        short cost_qty;     /* quantity required for price: {0:9999} */
        } PART;
    #endif
```

Rule 6-3: Use the "leading underscore" name format for tag and member names if the internal details of the structure are not to be inspected by functions outside of the package. Conversely, avoid leading underscores if the details of the structure are available for inspection by functions that use the structure.

6.3 Properties of Structures

Recall from Section 2.9 that an object is well-defined if it conforms to the programmer's stated defining property. Since structures are an aggregate of individual members, it will be useful to provide a default meaning for "well-defined" as applied to structures. In the absence of a specific defining property, a structure will be said to be well-defined if all its scalar constituents are well-defined. Referring back to the definition of the PART structure, in order for a PART to be well-defined, all of the following must be true:

```
part_no     must be a (nul-terminated) string
lead_time   must be within the range {0:99}
unit_meas   must contain the string "each", "lb", or "box"
unit_cost   must be within the range {0.00:9999.99}
cost_qty    must be within the range {0:9999}
```

Why is it important to be clear about whether a structure is well-defined? We desire that we be able to talk about the behavior of a program in simple terms without a lot of qualifying phrases. For example, in talking about a particular program, we want to be able to say "part1 is a well-defined PART structure" rather than having to verbalize a whole list of qualifications such as "the part_no member is a nul-terminated string, lead_time is within its allowable range, ..."

One of the common abbreviations allowed by C is the initialization of a structure to "all zeros":

```
PART part1 = {0};
```

This convention of zero-initialization is sufficiently common that it deserves a reliability rule:

Rule 6-4: If a structure is not well-defined when initialized to zero, document this fact in a comment. (The program will in general be simpler if the members are defined such that the zero-initialized structure is well-defined.)

Examine for a moment the declaration of a PART structure. Most of its members conform to their defining property when initialized to zero, all except for unit_meas, which is required to be one of three specific strings. Since the result of initializing a string to all zeros is a null string, the rule above suggests that we consider re-defining the properties of the unit_meas member like this:

```
char unit_meas[6];   /* unit of measure; string {"", "each", "lb", "box"} */
```

Alternatively, we would have to add a comment to the declaration of PART to the effect that it is not well-defined upon zero-initialization.

Oftentimes a structure has other properties that go beyond "well-definedness" as described above. Regarding the FILE structure, for example, we might wish to document two properties of a FILE structure called "is-open" and "is-closed." Hypothetically, let us say that the cur_ptr member is NULL if the file is closed and non-NULL if the file is open. We might then add these lines to the declaration:

```
/* cur_ptr != NULL ==> FILE is open */
/* cur_ptr == NULL ==> FILE is closed */
```

Consideration of the "zero-initialization" rule would suggest one more comment:

```
/* A zero-initialized FILE is closed */
```

6.4 Unions

A union is basically a struct in which all the offsets are zero. That is, all the members of a union start at byte zero of the object's storage, and hence occupy the same space.

The most portable use for a union is to *overlay* two or more data objects in the same space. For example,

```
struct rec
    {
    char name[20];
    char type;
    union
        {
        TYPE_A_INFO a;
        TYPE_B_INFO b;
        } info;
    };
```

contains a member named info which contains *either* "type-a" information *or* "type-b" information. Presumably, the type member tells which of the alternatives is used in each particular instance. In C, there is no automatic way for the compiler to tell which member of the union is being used; it is entirely the programmer's responsibility to keep track of the state of the union. For portable programming, the state of a union object includes (at least in concept) the name of the member last assigned into. Any use of the value of a union member should be used through the last member assigned into.

Another use for union is alignment-forcing:

```
union buffer
    {
    int align;
    char buf[BUFSIZ];
    };
union buffer dsk_block;
```

will provide an array of characters (named dsk_block) which is aligned on
an int boundary. The program will probably never refer to the align
member except in the declaration; the only purpose of the member is to
force alignment. The actual array of characters is accessed by the
expression dsk_block.buf (the buf member of dsk_block). One of the more
common reasons for alignment-forcing is interfacing with specific
hardware or operating system interfaces.

6.5 Bit Fields

C provides a storage-compaction capability for structure members,
in which each member occupies only a specified number of bits. Such a
member is known as a *bit-field*. Bit-fields can be useful for reducing
the storage needed for a large array of structures. They are also useful
for defining various hardware interfaces which specify the individual
bits within a machine word.

Consider the representation of time-of-day in hours, minutes,
seconds and milliseconds. Bit-fields provide one way to represent such
times:

```
time_day.h(#1):
    /* time_day.h - bit-field structure for  hh:mm:ss.fff */
    #ifndef TIME_DAY_H
    #define TIME_DAY_H
    typedef struct time_day
        {
        unsigned h1 : 2;     /* tens digit of hours     {0:2} */
        unsigned h2 : 4;     /* units digit of hours    {0:9} */
        unsigned m1 : 3;     /* tens digit of minutes   {0:5} */
        unsigned m2 : 4;     /* units digit of minutes  {0:9} */
        unsigned s1 : 3;     /* tens digit of seconds   {0:5} */
        unsigned s2 : 4;     /* units digit of seconds  {0:9} */
        unsigned f1 : 4;     /* first digit of fraction {0:9} */
        unsigned f2 : 4;     /* second digit of fraction {0:9} */
        unsigned f3 : 4;     /* third digit of fraction {0:9} */
        } TIME_DAY;     /* 32 bits total */
    #endif
```

The last millisecond of the day is

```
23:59:59.999    (hh:mm:ss.fff)
```

Each member (bit-field) is declared to be unsigned (int); this is the only bit-field type that is guaranteed to be portable to all current compilers. Each member is declared to have only as many bits as are necessary to represent the possible digits at its position in the time representation. Representing h1 (first digit of hours) takes only two bits to represent the possible values (0, 1, and 2). And the largest members need only four bits to represent ten digits, 0 through 9. The total number of bits is 32.

Consecutive bit-field members are allocated by the compiler to the same int-sized word, as long as they fit completely. Thus, on a 32-bit machine, a TIME_DAY object will occupy exactly one int-sized word. On a 16-bit machine, the first five members (totalling 16 bits) will fit into one int-sized word, and the last four members will fit into an immediately following word. Such an exact fit is rare, however. Add another member such as "day-of-year" to the structure, and the nice size-fitting property disappears. Thus, bit-fields are useful for storage-saving only if they occupy most or all of the space of an int, and if the storage-saving property is to be reasonably portable, they must occupy most of the space in a 32-bit integer [6-1].

The order of allocation within a word is different in different implementations. Some implementations are "right-to-left": the first member occupies the low-order position of the word. Most PDP-11 and VAX compilers allocate right-to-left. Following the convention that the low-order bit of a word is on the right, the right-to-left allocation would look like this:

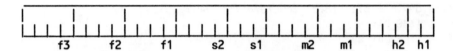

Most other implementations are "left-to-right":

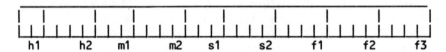

This variability of allocation order leads to a portability rule:

Rule 6-5: In portable code, do not depend upon the allocation order of bit-fields within a word.

Of course, in machine-specific non-portable code one knows exactly how the bit-fields are laid out, and the internal details can be inspected with bitwise operations. A union provides a convenient way to say what is going on:

```
typedef union time_overlay        /* MACHINE DEPENDENT */
    {
    struct time_day time_as_fields;
    long time_as_long;
    } TIME_OVERLAY;

TIME_OVERLAY time_port;
```

This allows bitwise operations like `time_port.time_as_long & 0xF00` as well as providing access via bit-field names like `time_port.time_as_fields.h1`.

Specifying a field size of zero causes any subsequent allocations to begin on a new word boundary. Un-named bit-fields are allowed; they occupy space but are inaccessible, which is useful for "padding" within a structure.

Since most C machines do not support bit-addressing, the "address-of" (&) operator is not allowed upon bit-field members.

Aside from these complications, bit-fields can be treated just like any other structure member. The following declaration

```
#include "time_day.h"

struct time_day last_msec = {2, 3, 5, 9, 5, 9, 9, 9, 9};
```

initializes `last_msec` to the last millisecond of the day.

```
struct time_day now;

/* ... */
if (now.h1 == 0 || (now.h1 == 1 && now.h2 < 2))
```

tests whether now is less than "noon."

If we wish to use the TIME_DAY structure for an "information-hiding" purpose, so that it could be changed without affecting the programs that use it, we should employ the "leading-underscore" convention mentioned earlier in Section 6.2 :

```
time_day.h(#2):
    /* time_day.h - bit-field structure for  hh:mm:ss.fff */
    #ifndef TIME_DAY_H
    #define TIME_DAY_H
    typedef struct _time_day
        {
        unsigned _h1 : 2;    /* tens digit of hours     {0:2} */
        unsigned _h2 : 4;    /* units digit of hours    {0:9} */
        unsigned _m1 : 3;    /* tens digit of minutes   {0:5} */
        unsigned _m2 : 4;    /* units digit of minutes  {0:9} */
        unsigned _s1 : 3;    /* tens digit of seconds   {0:5} */
        unsigned _s2 : 4;    /* units digit of seconds  {0:9} */
        unsigned _f1 : 4;    /* first digit of fraction {0:9} */
        unsigned _f2 : 4;    /* second digit of fraction {0:9} */
        unsigned _f3 : 4;    /* third digit of fraction {0:9} */
        } TIME_DAY;      /* 32 bits total */
    #endif
```

We chose the TIME_DAY example because it illustrates the use of bit-fields nicely, but there are numerous other ways to represent time-of-day. One obvious method is simply to count milliseconds since midnight. Adding and subtracting times is easier this way, but printing or displaying times is easier with the bit-field structure. The choice of representation ultimately depends upon the intended uses for the data.

6.6 Structures of Strings

One of the simplest and most useful structures is one containing nothing but (nul-terminated) strings. For ordinary string data (such as names and addresses), this approach requires only that the programmer be careful to allow space for each nul-terminator.

Numeric data, if present, is stored in readable string form. This may necessitate conversion from numeric representation to string representation, which takes a significant amount of CPU time.

Coded data (a choice among a small number of alternatives) can usually be represented by a single char. But in order to preserve the consistent "string" property of all the structure members, an array of two char's is needed, to allow space for the nul terminator.

The advantage is that data stored in this fashion can be processed in a uniform manner; each member of the structure is a nul-terminated string. We will shortly describe a "menu" program which deals with data stored uniformly in strings. Its version of the part structure will look like this:

```
part.h(#2):
    /* part.h - header for parts structure
     */
    #ifndef PART_H
    #define PART_H
    typedef struct part
        {
        char part_no[14];     /* part number: string */
        char lead_time[3];    /* lead time (in weeks): num string {0:99} */
        char unit_meas[2];    /* unit of measure: coded string */
                              /* {"0"=each, "1"=lb, "2"=box, other=each} */
        char unit_cost[8];    /* cost: num string {0.00 : 9999.99} */
        char cost_qty[5];     /* qty required for price: num string {0:9999} */
        } PART;
    extern PART part1;
    #endif
```

6.7 Pointers to Structures

Structures and unions may be used as operands for address-of (&), member (.), and sizeof operators. If part1 has the type struct part, then the expression &part1 has the type struct part * (pointer to struct part), and produces the address of part1. The member operator, as in part1.part_no, we have seen before. And sizeof(part1) gives the size (in bytes) of part1.

Recent versions of C also allow assignment, argument passing, and function return for structures and unions. One could, for example, write a function which would accept a structure argument, update the structure, and return it to the calling function, where the returned value could be assigned to a structure variable:

```
#include "part.h"
main()
    {
    struct part part1;
    struct part chg_part();

    /* ... */
    part1 = chg_part(part1);
    /* ... */
    }
struct part chg_part(arg_part)
    struct part arg_part;

    /* get new values for arg_part.lead_time, ... */
    return (arg_part);
    }
```

However, passing and returning structures can cost considerable CPU time; the entire structure is copied each time. Often it is more efficient to pass a pointer to a structure. The declaration

```
struct part *part_ptr;
```

declares that part_ptr points to struct part's. To access the members of the structure that part_ptr points to, we use the "arrow" (->) operator, as in

```
part_ptr->lead_time
```

Changing the definition of the function chg_part for use with a pointer to struct part's would produce something like this:

```
#include "part.h"
main()
    {
    struct part part1;
    void chg_part();

    /* ... */
    chg_part(&part1);
    /* ... */
    }
void chg_part(ppart)
    struct part *ppart;
    {
    /* Get new values for ppart->lead_time, ... */
    /* The changes take place directly in the pointed-to structure. */
    }
```

The "dot" and "arrow" member operators can be written in terms of each other:

part_ptr->lead_time   *is equivalent to*   (*part_ptr).lead_time

part1.lead_time   *is equivalent to*   (&part1)->lead_time

The rules for when to use each form are simple: If ps is a pointer to a structure, the members of the pointed-to structure are accessed via the "arrow"; if s *is* a structure, its members are accessed via the "dot."

Now let us consider the properties of pointers to structures. As discussed in Section 4.2, a pointer value can be either undefined (not valid in any pointer contexts), or defined (either NULL or pointing to a valid object of the proper type). In order to speak simply about programs, if a pointer points to a structure, we will say that the pointer is well-defined if the structure that it points to is well-defined.

Since one of the common uses of pointers to structures is as function parameters, we should consider some rules for their reliable usage. Taking the simplest case first, an "out" pointer (used only to modify the pointed-to object) does not care what properties the object has when its address is passed to the function. It is usually an error to pass NULL to an "out" parameter, since it does not point to any object. (A NULL parameter could be used to mean "do not store anything this time," but an explicit comment should be given.) An "in" pointer (used only to read values from the pointed-to object) should, for reliability, be passed the address of a "well-defined" structure. If, however, the structure is supposed to have some other defined property, the parameter declaration should so indicate in a comment. The same conditions apply to an "in-out" pointer (used both to read values from, and change values in, the pointed-to structure).

Rule 6-6: Regarding parameters which are pointers to structures, an "out" pointer parameter is assumed to be non-NULL, pointing to the storage for a structure of the specified type. "In" and "in-out" pointer parameters are assumed to point to a well-defined structure of the specified type. Any exceptions should be noted in a comment on the parameter declaration.

6.8 Example: Menu Processor

Topics assumed from previous book: array of structures [8.5].

We can now apply these observations about structures to a practical problem, the execution of screen-oriented *menus*.

In screen-oriented programming, the keyboard is handled in a "raw no-echo" fashion. The typed key does not automatically echo on the screen. The program determines whether a character will be echoed to the screen, or whether it will instead cause some action.

As described in Section 5.5, we can make use of scr_getkey, which returns the user's latest input character with no intermediate buffering and no echoing of the input. The scr_getkey function returns each ordinary character entered, but also returns special coded values for the keys EXIT, UP, DOWN, RIGHT, LEFT, and HOME.

The particular menu processor that we will present is somewhat generalized. We will call each component of a menu a *field*. In the most conventional usage, the fields of the screen are actions to be performed:

```
|--------------------------------------|
|                                      |
|       MAIN PART MENU                  |
|                                      |
|   Add a part record                  |
|                                      |
|   Change a part record               |
|                                      |
|   Delete a part record               |
|                                      |
|                                      |
|--------------------------------------|
```

In this example, there are three fields, each one a possible action.

The location of the screen cursor indicates the "current field." (On our diagrams, the cursor is indicated by an underscore.) The cursor is moved among the fields by cursor-movement keys. The DOWN key moves to the next field downward; the UP key moves upward; the HOME key moves to the first field. The UP and DOWN movements "wrap around" from first to last, or vice-versa. When the current field is an action field, hitting RETURN causes that action to be invoked, and typing the first letter of a field description (A, C, or D, here) moves the cursor to that field.

Thus, in our sample MAIN PART MENU, if the user were to type C then RETURN, the action field entitled "Change a part record" would be invoked. An action can lead to the presentation of another menu, and a menu can contain *data fields* as well as, or instead of, action fields:

```
|---------------------------------------|
|                                       |
|         CHANGE A PART RECORD          |
|                                       |
|                                       |
|   Part number: 39849-02_              |
|                                       |
|   Lead time (weeks): 12               |
|                                       |
|   Unit of measure: each               |
|                                       |
|   Unit cost: 17.25                    |
|                                       |
|   Cost qty: 100                       |
|                                       |
|---------------------------------------|
```

All fields of the CHANGE A PART RECORD menu are data fields. Cursor keys UP, DOWN, and HOME work as before. Hitting RETURN moves the cursor to the next field. The cursor always appears at the righthand end of the data value. Hitting BACKSPACE moves the cursor leftward, erasing the rightmost character of the data value. Hitting the EXIT key returns control to the place where the current menu was invoked, back to the main menu, in this example. Typing an ordinary text character appends that character to the current field, until the maximum field length is reached. (Special handling of a "coded choice" field will be described later in this section.)

Before we turn to the overall design of the menu processor, it will be helpful to show the details involved in updating one data field's value. A string data value is described by a STRING_VAL structure:

```
typedef struct string_val
    {
    char edit_type; /* 'n' = numeric, 'a' = anything */
    char *string;   /* ptr to the string value */
    short maxsize;  /* maximum size of string; {2:SHORT_MAX} */
    short *pnum;    /* ptr to short; NULL=store as string */
    } STRING_VAL;
```

The function which updates string values is mu_sval ("menu string value"). It is called when the cursor is sitting just to the right of the displayed contents of the current field's value, like this:

```
+---------------------------------------+
|                                       |
|   Part number: 39849-02_              |
|                                       |
|              ...                      |
|                                       |
+---------------------------------------+
```

The associated STRING_VAL structure would look something like this, when mu_sval is called:

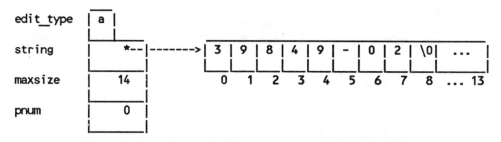

```
edit_type  | a |
           +---+
string     |  *--|------->| 3 | 9 | 8 | 4 | 9 | - | 0 | 2 |\0|  ...  |
           +---+          +---+---+---+---+---+---+---+---+---+------+
maxsize    | 14|            0   1   2   3   4   5   6   7   8  ... 13
           +---+
pnum       |  0|
           +---+
```

mu_sval reads the next input character. If it is a command character, work on this string is complete for now, and mu_sval returns. If it is a backspace, the prior character is erased (if there is one). If the character is invalid for entry in a numeric field, mu_sval calls the scr_beep function to indicate the problem. If there is space to store the new character, it is added to the string and echoed. Otherwise, a scr_beep indicates the out-of-bounds situation.

Before showing the mu_sval function, one refinement needs discussion. The STRING_VAL structure allows for the possibility that the field is actually stored as a short int instead of as a string. All of the editing and user interaction are the same as is provided for numeric strings, using an auxiliary string of the appropriate size. Upon leaving the field, this numeric string is converted into an integer value in *pnum. During the modification of the string, the function preserves a property that we can call "string-sync": the displayed image on the screen agrees with the memory contents of the string. Furthermore, the string contents are valid, according to the specification of the field: the length is within the stated bound, and numeric strings consist only of digits with a possible leading minus sign.

Here, then, is the code for the mu_sval function.

```
mu_sval:
    /* mu_sval - get the string contents for a STRING_VAL field
     * Assumes cursor is just to right of string
     */
    #include "menu.h"
    SCR_CMDCHAR mu_sval(psv)
        STRING_VAL *psv;        /* ptr to the STRING_VAL structure : str_sync */
                                /* str_sync = screen agrees with contents of  */
                                /*               psv->string                  */
        {
        char *s;                /* ptr to start of string */
        short i;                /* index of current nul-terminator */
        SCR_CMDCHAR c;          /* latest SCR_CMDCHAR returned from scr_getkey */

        s = psv->string;
        i = strlen(s);
        FOREVER
            {
            c = scr_getkey();
            if (SCR_CMD(c))              /* if c is a command character, */
                return (c);              /* return it */
            else if (c == '\b')
                {
                if (i > 0)
                    {
                    scr_print("\b \b"); /* erase previous character */
                    s[--i] = '\0';      /* shorten the string */
                    }
                }
            else if (psv->edit_type == 'n' && !isdigit(c) &&
                !(i == 0 && c == '-'))
                {
                scr_beep();             /* non-digit invalid */
                }
            else if (i < psv->maxsize - 1)
                {
                scr_putc(s[i++] = c);   /* append the char, and echo it */
                s[i] = '\0';
                }
            else
                scr_beep();             /* no room left in string */
            }
        }
```

Notice that the parameter, psv, is a pointer to STRING_VALS. The edit_type member of the object pointed to by psv is accessed by writing psv->edit_type. Similarly, we see psv->string and psv->maxsize.

A data field may be a "choice field" instead of a string field. A choice field has a fixed set of possible values. In the "part record" example, the "unit-of-measure" field (unit_meas) might allow the values "each", "lb", and "box", which are coded into the strings "0", "1", and "2".

The user cycles among the possible values by typing LEFT or RIGHT; like the other special keys, these are interpreted by scr_getkey. The structure which controls a choice field is called a CHOICE_VAL:

```
typedef struct choice_val
    {
    short nchoices;      /* number of possible choices: {2:10} */
    char **choices;      /* ptr to start of array of choice strings */
    char *pc;            /* ptr to the one-char coded choice value */
    } CHOICE_VAL;
```

A CHOICE_VAL structure for the unit_meas component of the part record might look like this:

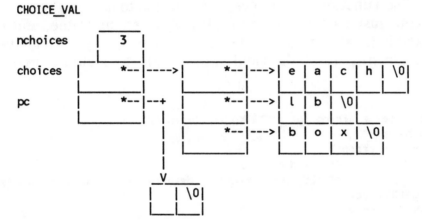

This diagram corresponds to the following initialized declarations:

```
PART part1 = {0};
char *Tunit_meas[] = {"each", "lb", "box"}; /* table of code meanings */
CHOICE_VAL Cunit_meas =
    {DIM(Tunit_meas), Tunit_meas, part1.unit_meas};
```

Having seen how structures like STRING_VAL and CHOICE_VAL are used to control the access to an individual data value, let us look now at the overall design. Each field is specified by a C structure, FIELD:

```
typedef struct field
    {
    short line, col;       /* co-ordinates of screen display position */
    char *desc;            /* description (title) of this field: string */
    char val_type;         /* what type of field is this? */
    STRING_VAL *psv;       /* non-NULL iff val_type == 's' or 'S' */
    CHOICE_VAL *pcv;       /* non-NULL iff val_type == 'c' */
    struct menu *pmenu;    /* non-NULL iff val_type == 'm' */
    bool (*pfn)();         /* function to do after string or choice field */
    } FIELD;
```

A more sophisticated way of declaring val_type would have involved defining an enumeration,

enum val_types {STRING_TYPE, CHOICE_TYPE, MENU_TYPE, FN_TYPE};

and declaring val_type as

enum val_types val_type;

We chose the more primitive method, a simple char, mainly because enum is still not universally supported in existing compilers, and because the enumeration does not add any noticeable clarity.

If a FIELD structure's val_type equals 's' or 'S', then this field is a string field. The function mu_str accepts a pointer to a string FIELD, positions the cursor just past its currently-displayed string value, and calls mu_sval to update the string value. The relevant property ("field-sync") is that the screen display of the field agrees with the field's stored contents.

```
mu_str:
    /* mu_str - get a string for a STRING_VAL field */
    #include "menu.h"
    SCR_CMDCHAR mu_str(pf)
        FIELD *pf;        /* : fld_sync */
        {                 /* fld_sync = field in data rec agrees with screen */
        SCR_CMDCHAR ret;
        STRING_VAL *psv;

        psv = pf->psv;  /* get the string-value pointer for this field */

        /* position scr_curs just to right of string value */
        scr_curs(pf->line, pf->col + strlen(pf->desc) + 2 + strlen(psv->string));

        ret = mu_sval(psv);                    /* get string value */
        if (psv->pnum != NULL)                 /* pf => !fld_sync */
            *psv->pnum = atoi(psv->string);    /* pf => fld_sync */
        return (ret);
        }
```

If a FIELD structure's val_type equals 'c', then this field is a choice field. The function mu_chv ("get choice value") allows the user to change the current value of a choice field:

```
mu_chv:
    /* mu_chv - get a value for a CHOICE_VAL field
     * Return the SCR_CMDCHAR that terminated the input of this field.
     * fld_sync = field in data rec agrees with screen
     */
    #include "menu.h"
    SCR_CMDCHAR mu_chv(pf)
        FIELD *pf;                  /* ptr to current FIELD : fld_sync */
        {
        short nchoice;             /* current choice value: {0:9} */
        CHOICE_VAL *pcv;           /* ptr to this field's CHOICE_VAL */
        SCR_CMDCHAR c;             /* most recent user input char */
        short prevlen;             /* length of previous choice display string */
        short curlen;              /* length of current choice display string */
        short i;

        prevlen = 0;
        pcv = pf->pcv;
        if ('0' <= *pcv->pc && *pcv->pc <= '9')
            nchoice = *pcv->pc - '0';
        else
            nchoice = 0;
        FOREVER
            {
            /* scr_curs to start of choice display, display current choice */
            scr_curs(pf->line, pf->col + strlen(pf->desc) + 2);
            scr_print("%s", pcv->choices[nchoice]);       /* pf => fld_sync */

            /* erase any leftover from previous choice */
            curlen = strlen(pcv->choices[nchoice]);
            for (i = 0; i < prevlen - curlen; ++i)
                scr_putc(' ');
            for (i = 0; i < prevlen - curlen; ++i)
                scr_putc('\b');
            prevlen = curlen;

            /* get user input and process it */
            c = scr_getkey();
            if (c != SCR_LEFT && c != SCR_RIGHT)
                return (c);
            else if (c == SCR_RIGHT)
                nchoice = IMOD(nchoice + 1, pcv->nchoices);
            else /* c == SCR_LEFT */
                nchoice = IMOD(nchoice - 1, pcv->nchoices);
            *pcv->pc = '0' + nchoice;                      /* pf => !fld_sync */
            }
        }
```

Each time the keys LEFT or RIGHT are hit, nchoice is decremented or incremented, modulo pcv->nchoices, the number of choices for this field. (The IMOD macro from Section 2.7 is used to ensure that the new nchoice is positive.)

For both string and choice fields, the user can terminate the entry of the current field by typing the cursor keys UP, DOWN, or HOME. Additionally, the user can leave a choice field by typing a letter which matches the initial letter of a field description. In either case, if a non-NULL pointer to function (the "post-function") is provided for this field, that function is called (with a pointer to the current menu). If the post-function returns NO, the cursor returns to the current field. Thus the post-function could perform arbitrarily complicated validation of the current field.

A menu is specified by a structure, MENU:

```
typedef struct menu
    {
    char *title;            /* alphabetic title for menu: string */
    FIELD *fields;          /* ptr to beginning of array of FIELDs */
    short nfields;          /* how many fields in this menu */
    short cur_field;        /* index of the current field */
    } MENU;
```

In English translation, these structures are saying that a menu has a title, a specified number of fields, a current field, and an array of individual fields. Each field has screen co-ordinates for its display, a description, a value-type (string, choice, menu, or function),and four pointers: a pointer to a STRING_VAL structure, to a CHOICE_VAL structure, to another menu, and to a C function. (If the field is a function field, the menu processor simply calls the function that is pointed to. For simplicity of design, the processor ignores any return value from the function.) Here is a schematic picture of the data structures:

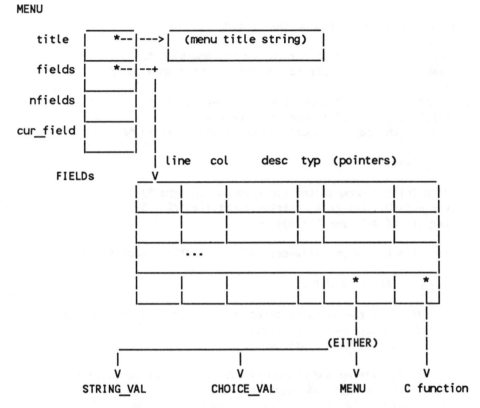

There is a function mu_pr for the displaying of menus. It makes use of two environment-dependent functions: scr_clear (to erase the screen) and scr_curs (to move the cursor to a specified (line, col) location). Its job is to create a certain property for the menu, namely that the screen display agrees with the contents of all the field descriptions and field contents ("menu-sync"). It accomplishes this by clearing the screen and then looping over all the fields, moving the cursor to the proper place on the screen for each field, and then displaying the field description and field contents.

```
mu_pr:
    /* mu_pr - display a menu on the screen */
    #include "menu.h"
    void mu_pr(pm)          /* at return, pm => menu-sync */
        MENU *pm;           /* ptr to the MENU to be displayed */
        {
        short i;            /* index for loop over fields */
        FIELD *pf;          /* pointer to each FIELD */
        short i_choice;     /* numeric value of choice field */

        scr_clear();

        /* print the menu title, centered on top line */
        scr_curs(0, (scr_cols - strlen(pm->title))/2 - 3);
        scr_print("%s", pm->title);

        for (i = 0; i < pm->nfields; ++i)        /* for each field */
            {
            pf = &pm->fields[i];

            /* print the field description at proper x,y location */
            scr_curs(pf->line, pf->col);
            scr_print("%s  ", pf->desc);

            /* for string and choice fields, print current value */
            if (tolower(pf->val_type) == 's')
                {
                if (pf->psv->pnum != NULL)        /* field has numeric form */
                    itoa(*pf->psv->pnum, pf->psv->string, pf->psv->maxsize -1);
                scr_print("%s", pf->psv->string);
                }
            else if (pf->val_type == 'c')
                {
                if ('0' <= *pf->pcv->pc && *pf->pcv->pc <= '9')
                    i_choice = *pf->pcv->pc - '0';
                else
                    i_choice = 0;
                scr_print("%s", pf->pcv->choices[i_choice]);
                }
            }
        scr_refresh();
        }
```

Now we are ready for the function which processes the user responses to a menu. The mu_ask function allows the user to move around among the fields of a menu, entering or altering the values of data fields, until the user selects a MENU field, selects a function field, or hits EXIT. It is the job of mu_ask to call any associated post-function for each field. If the post-function returns failure (NO), mu_ask prevents the user from moving to another field. (EXIT is allowed, to prevent locking the user into a "no-exit" situation.) mu_ask embodies one special case: a string field with capitalized value-type 'S' is "mandatory": mu_ask will

not allow movement to another field until a non-null string has been
entered in this field.

```
mu_ask:
    /* mu_ask - get responses to menu items
     * Keeps looping over string and choice fields;
     * terminates when user selects an action field, or hits SCR_EXIT.
     */
    #include "menu.h"
    FIELD *mu_ask(pm)
        MENU *pm;        /* ptr to current MENU */
        {
        FIELD *pf;       /* ptr to current FIELD */
        FIELD *pfj;      /* ptr to j-th FIELD of this MENU */
        SCR_CMDCHAR c;   /* most recent user key input */
        char vtype;      /* value type of current FIELD */
        bool legal;      /* is  c  valid input in this state? */
        short j;         /* index over FIELDs of this MENU */

        pm->cur_field = 0;      /* start with first field */
        FOREVER
            {
            pf = &pm->fields[pm->cur_field];
            legal = YES;
            vtype = pf->val_type;

            /* accept user input, get user's SCR_CMDCHAR */
            if (vtype == 'c' || tolower(vtype) == 's')
                {
                if (vtype == 'c')
                    c = mu_chv(pf);
                else            /* vtype == 's' OR 'S' */
                    c = mu_str(pf);
                if (pf->pfn != NULL)
                    legal = (*pf->pfn)(pm);
                if (c == SCR_EXIT)
                    return (NULL);
                }
            else
                {
                scr_curs(pf->line, pf->col);
                c = scr_getkey();
                }
            /* at this point, c is the user's response, and */
            /* legal records validity of 'c' or 's' field */
            /* (more) */
```

```
/* determine next action, based on c */
if (c == SCR_RETURN && (vtype == 'm' || vtype == 'f'))
    return (pf);
else if (c == SCR_EXIT)
    return (NULL);
else if (!legal)
    ;           /* no actions allowed if validation failed */
else if (vtype == 'S' && pf->psv->string[0] == '\0')
    legal = NO;
else if (!SCR_CMD(c) && tolower(vtype) != 's')
    {
    legal = NO; /* tentatively */
    for (j = 0; j < pm->nfields; ++j)
        {
        pfj = &pm->fields[j];
        if (toupper(pfj->desc[0]) == toupper(c))
            {
            pm->cur_field = j;
            legal = YES;
            break;
            }
        }
    }
else if (SCR_CMD(c))
    {
    switch (c)
        {
    case SCR_UP:
        pm->cur_field = IMOD(pm->cur_field - 1, pm->nfields);
        break;
    case SCR_DOWN:
    case SCR_RETURN:
        pm->cur_field = IMOD(pm->cur_field + 1, pm->nfields);
        break;
    case SCR_HOME:
        pm->cur_field = 0;
        break;
    default:
        legal = NO;
        break;
        }
    }
if (!legal)
    scr_beep();
} /* end FOREVER */
}
```

The top-level function of the package is mu_do. In a FOREVER loop, mu_do prints a menu and calls mu_ask. As long as the user remains within string fields and choice fields, mu_ask handles the dialog. If mu_ask returns NULL, the user requested to exit, and mu_do returns. Otherwise, the return specifies either a menu field or a function field. If a menu

field, mu_do is called recursively to process the sub-menu; if a function
field, the function is called.

```
mu_do:
    #include "menu.h"
    /* mu_do - present a menu, process actions until user SCR_EXIT
     */
    void mu_do(pm)
        MENU *pm;
        {
        FIELD *pf;
        static short level = 0;

        if (level == 0)
            scr_open(); /* initialize the terminal state */
        ++level;
        FOREVER
            {
            mu_pr(pm);                           /* print the menu */
            pf = mu_ask(pm);                     /* get a new field ptr */
            if (pf == NULL)
                break;
            else if (pf->val_type == 'm')   /* new field is a menu */
                mu_do(pf->pmenu);
            else /* pf->val_type == 'f' -- new field is a C fn */
                {
                asserts(pf->val_type == 'f', "val_type is 'f'");
                (void)(*pf->pfn)(pm);
                }
            }
        --level;
        if (level == 0)
            {
            scr_curs(scr_lins-1, 0);
            scr_close();    /* restore terminal state */
            }
        }
```

One utility function is provided for use by the user program. It is
called mu_reply, and it behaves just like the getreply function shown in
Section 5.3, except that in SCR_RAW mode the dialog takes place at the bottom of the screen.

```
mu_reply:
    /*  mu_reply -- get a reply in response to a prompt
     *               on the last screen line
     */
    #include "local.h"
    #include "menu.h"

    mu_reply(prompt, reply, size)
        char prompt[];       /* : string */
        char reply[];        /* : !NULL */
        int size;            /* max number of chars allowed in reply */
        {
        STRING_VAL rsv;      /* reply string value structure */

        if (scr_mode == SCR_TTY)
            return (getreply(prompt, reply, size));
        else
            {
            scr_curs(scr_lins - 1, 0);
            scr_print("%s", prompt);
            reply[0] = '\0';         /* reply string initially empty */
            rsv.edit_type = 'a';     /* initialize the STRING_VAL rsv */
            rsv.string = reply;
            rsv.maxsize = size;
            rsv.pnum = NULL;         /* rsv => well-defined */
            mu_sval(&rsv);           /* let mu_sval handle the dialog */
            return (strlen(reply));
            }
        }
```

Finally, here is the header menu.h:

```
menu.h:
    /* menu.h - header for menu pgm */
    #ifndef MENU_H
    #define MENU_H
    #include "local.h"
    #include "screen.h"
    typedef struct string_val
        {
        char edit_type;      /* 'n' = numeric, 'd' = short int, 'a' = anything */
        char *string;        /* ptr to the string value */
        short maxsize;       /* maximum size of string: {2:SHORT_MAX} */
        short *pnum;         /* if non-NULL, ptr to numeric storage */
        } STRING_VAL;
    typedef struct choice_val
        {
        short nchoices;      /* number of possible choices: {2:10} */
        char **choices;      /* ptr to start of array of choice strings */
        char *pc;            /* ptr to the one-char coded choice value */
        } CHOICE_VAL;
    /* (more)
```

```
    */
    typedef struct field
        {
        short line, col;        /* co-ordinates of screen display position */
        char *desc;             /* description (title) of this field: string */
        char val_type;          /* what type of field is this?  */
        STRING_VAL *psv;        /* non-NULL iff val_type == 's' or 'S' */
        CHOICE_VAL *pcv;        /* non-NULL iff val_type == 'c' */
        struct menu *pmenu;     /* non-NULL iff val_type == 'm' */
        bool (*pfn)();          /* function to do after str or choice field */
        } FIELD;
    typedef struct menu
        {
        char *title;            /* alphabetic title for menu: string */
        FIELD *fields;          /* ptr to beginning of array of FIELDs */
        short nfields;          /* how many fields in this menu */
        short cur_field;        /* index of the current field */
        } MENU;
    FIELD *mu_ask();            /* PARMS(MENU *pm) */
    SCR_CMDCHAR mu_chv();       /* PARMS(FIELD *pf) */
    void mu_do();               /* PARMS(MENU *pm) */
    void mu_pr();               /* PARMS(MENU *pm) */
    int mu_reply();             /* PARMS(char *prompt, char *reply, int size) */
    SCR_CMDCHAR mu_str();       /* PARMS(FIELD *pf) */
    SCR_CMDCHAR mu_sval();      /* PARMS(STRING_VAL *psv) */
    #endif
```

This completes the source listing for the menu processor. It is a rather concise program, considering the capabilities that it provides. This is largely due to the encoding of so much information into the structures that drive it.

Much more flexibility and many more features are available in commercially available menu and screen-generator software. Here are a few simple extensions that could be added to this menu processor, left as exercises:

Exercise 6-1. An extra member (e.g., horizontal_ok) could be added to the MENU structure; if its value is YES, this menu allows the LEFT key as synonym for UP and RIGHT for DOWN. (This is an intuitive behavior for horizontal menus.)

Exercise 6-2. The cursor can be turned off except when entering strings. The current field can instead be highlighted (underscore, reverse video, etc.).

Exercise 6-3. The distinction between string fields and other types of field can be emphasized by emboldening the first character of other-field names.

Exercise 6-4. All data fields are currently stored as nul-terminated strings. Revise the program so that fields are blank-padded to their full size. (This creates a more traditional data processing record.)

For a concrete example of the use of the menu processor, let us consider the "change part record" menu. The first field ("part number") is mandatory, as indicated by the capitalized 'S' in its field entry. Its description string "Part number " is to be displayed at row 2 and column 0. The field specifies the address of a STRING_VAL structure named Spart_no. This field has a C function, is_part, associated with it; when the user attempts to leave this field, the is_part function will be called. Movement to another field succeeds only if a YES return is received. (More about is_part shortly.) The "unit of measure" field is a choice field, and all the others are string fields. Here is the C source file that defines the "change part record" menu:

```
chg_menu.c:
    /* chg_menu - CHANGE A PART RECORD */
    #include "local.h"
    #include "menu.h"
    #include "part.h"
    extern bool is_part();
    static STRING_VAL Spart_no =
        {'a', (part1).part_no, sizeof((part1).part_no), NULL};
    static STRING_VAL Slead_time =
        {'n', (part1).lead_time, sizeof((part1).lead_time), NULL};
    static char *Tunit_meas[]=
        {
        "each", "lb", "box",
        };
    static CHOICE_VAL Cunit_meas =
        {DIM(Tunit_meas), Tunit_meas, (part1).unit_meas};
    static STRING_VAL Sunit_cost =
        {'a', (part1).unit_cost, sizeof((part1).unit_cost), NULL};
    static STRING_VAL Scost_qty =
        {'n', (part1).cost_qty, sizeof((part1).cost_qty), NULL};
    static FIELD Fchg_menu[] =
        {
        {2, 0, "Part number", 'S', &Spart_no, NULL, NULL, is_part},
        {4, 0, "Lead time (in weeks)", 's', &Slead_time, NULL, NULL, 0},
        {6, 0, "Unit of measure", 'c', NULL, &Cunit_meas, NULL, 0},
        {8, 0, "Cost per unit", 's', &Sunit_cost, NULL, NULL, 0},
        {10, 0, "Qty required for price", 's', &Scost_qty, NULL, NULL, 0},
        };
    MENU chg_menu = {"CHANGE A PART RECORD", Fchg_menu, DIM(Fchg_menu), 0};
```

The other submenus (add_menu, acd_menu, and del_menu) are similar. The source file for the main program, part_menu, also contains, for convenience, the functions called by each of the menus.

```
part_menu.c:
    #include "menu.h"
    #include "part.h"
    /* main menu */
    /* menu-sync = screen agrees with menu contents */
    PART part1 = {0};
    PART null_part = {0};
    extern MENU add_menu, chg_menu, del_menu, acd_menu;
    /* isn_part - verify that no record exists for this key */
    bool isn_part(pm)
        MENU *pm;          /* : menu-sync */
        {
        if (db_find_part(&part1))
            {
            /* pm => !menu-sync, new part contents */
            remark("This part is entered already", "");
            STRUCTASST(part1, null_part);   /* clear the part struct */
            mu_pr(pm);                       /* pm => menu-sync */
            return (NO);
            }
        return (YES);
        }

    /* is_part - verify that record exists and read it into part1 */
    bool is_part(pm)
        MENU *pm;
        {
        if (!db_find_part(&part1))
            {
            remark("Unknown part number", "");
            STRUCTASST(part1, null_part);        /* clear the part struct */
            mu_pr(pm);        /* display the cleared record, pm => menu-sync */
            return (NO);
            }
        /* pm => !menu-sync, new part contents */
        mu_pr(pm);              /* display the found record, pm => menu-sync */
        return (YES);
        }
```

```c
/* addpart - add a part record */
bool addpart(pm)
    MENU *pm;
    {
    char reply[2];

    STRUCTASST(part1, null_part);
    mu_do(&add_menu);
    /* if no valid transaction occured, exit without change to db */
    if (part1.part_no[0] == '\0')
        return (NO);
    mu_reply("Add this part [y/n]? ", reply, 2);
    if (reply[0] == 'y')
        {
        return (db_add_part(&part1));
        }
    else
        return (NO);
    }

/* chgpart - change a part record */
bool chgpart(pm)
    MENU *pm;
    {
    char reply[2];

    STRUCTASST(part1, null_part);
    mu_do(&chg_menu);
    /* if no valid transaction occured, exit without change to db */
    if (part1.part_no[0] == '\0')
        return (NO);
    mu_reply("Change this part [y/n]? ", reply, 2);
    if (reply[0] == 'y')
        return (db_chg_part(&part1));
    else
        return (NO);
    }
```

```
/* delpart - delete a part record */
bool delpart(pm)
    MENU *pm;
    {
    char reply[2];

    STRUCTASST(part1, null_part);
    mu_do(&del_menu);
    /* if no valid transaction occured, exit without change to db */
    if (part1.part_no[0] == '\0')
        return (NO);
    mu_reply("Delete this part [y/n]? ", reply, 2);
    if (reply[0] == 'y')
        return (db_del_part(&part1));
    else
        return (NO);
    }

/* part_menu (main) - execute the parts menu */
main()
    {
    db_open_part();
    mu_do(&acd_menu);
    db_close_part();
    }
```

The simulated database of parts records is provided by part_db.c, containing several functions which manipulate a small array of PART records.

```
part_db.c:
    /* part_db.c - simulated database access to parts */
    #include "local.h"
    #include "part.h"
    static PART parts[3] = {0};
    static short n_part = 0;

    /* db_locate_part -- see if a part is in the database */
    static int db_locate_part(partp)
        PART *partp;
        {
        short i;

        for (i = 0; i < n_part; ++i)
            if (STREQ(partp->part_no, parts[i].part_no))
                return (i);      /* this is the part, return its index */
        return (-1); /* no part from 0 to n_part matches this part_no */
        }
```

```
/* db_add_part - add a part record to database */
bool db_add_part(partp)
    PART *partp;
    {
    if (n_part >= DIM(parts))
        {
        remark("Part storage is full", "");
        return (NO);
        }
    STRUCTASST(parts[n_part], *partp);
    ++n_part;
    return (YES);
    }

/* db_find_part - find a part record in database */
bool db_find_part(partp)
    PART *partp;
    {
    short i;

    i = db_locate_part(partp);
    if (i == -1)
        return(NO);
    STRUCTASST(*partp, parts[i]);
    return(YES);
    }

/* db_del_part - delete a part record in database */
bool db_del_part(partp)
    PART *partp;
    {
    short i;

    for (i = 0; i < n_part; ++i)
        {
        if (STREQ(partp->part_no, parts[i].part_no))
            {
            --n_part;
            STRUCTASST(parts[i], parts[n_part]);
            return (YES);
            }
        }
    return (NO);
    }
```

```
/* db_chg_part - change a part record in database */
bool db_chg_part(partp)
    PART *partp;
    {
    short i;

    for (i = 0; i < n_part; ++i)
        {
        if (STREQ(partp->part_no, parts[i].part_no))
            {
            STRUCTASST(parts[i], *partp);
            return (YES);
            }
        }
    return (NO);
    }

/* db_open_part - open the parts database
 * Dummy - no action needed
 */
void db_open_part()
    {
    }
/* db_close_part - close the parts database
 * Dummy - no action needed
 */
void db_close_part()
    {
    }
```

Thus, the entire program consists of the main program file (part_menu), the part_db package, and the three source files for the submenus (add_menu, chg_menu, and del_menu.)

Lest you think that I am teaching you the wrong lessons, let me add a few words about the overall functionality. This example is chosen primarily for its recognizability and its simplicity. In a real application, the separation of "add," "change," and "delete" would be considered rather awkward; the three operations could be combined into one somewhat more complicated menu. Also, the user must EXIT from each menu in order to affect a change to the database, which is distracting.

All these shortcomings could be overcome with a different approach to the problem, which is left as an exercise to the reader:

Exercise 6-5. Program part_menu with all operations combined into one menu that would look something like this:

```
 _____
|                                   |
|     UPDATE PART RECORDS           |
|                                   |
|                                   |
|  Part number:                     |
|                                   |
|  Action [a, c, d, p]:             |
|                                   |
|                                   |
|  Lead time (weeks):               |
|                                   |
|  Unit of measure:                 |
|                                   |
|  Unit cost:                       |
|                                   |
|  Cost qty:                        |
|                                   |
|_____|
```

In your design, you may find it useful to add a new function (or macro) to the menu package: mu_set_fld(n) will set the current field number to n.

6.9 A Translator for Menus

Preparing the C source code for a menu is highly repetitive work with the potential for introduction of errors. We will look at a simple program which will allow menus to be written in a more human-readable form. The user is assumed to be a C programmer who is familiar with the conventions of the menu package; the translator will just make the programmer's job a bit easier.

The human-readable form for a menu looks something like this:

```
chg_menu.mu:
     Menu name: chg_menu    Menu title: CHANGE A PART RECORD
         Header: part.h        C-struct: part1

     Field name: part_no    Desc: Part number
        Line: 2 Col: 0   Type: S      Edit: a      Post-fn: is_part

     Field name: lead_time    Desc: Lead time (in weeks)
        Line: 4 Col: 0   Type: s      Edit: n      Post-fn: 0

     Field name: unit_meas    Desc: Unit of measure
        Line: 6 Col: 0   Type: c               Post-fn: 0
        {
        "each", "lb", "box",
        };

     Field name: unit_cost    Desc: Cost per unit
        Line: 8 Col: 0   Type: s      Edit: a      Post-fn: 0

     Field name: cost_qty    Desc: Qty required for price
        Line: 10 Col: 0   Type: s      Edit: n      Post-fn: 0
```

Compare this with the corresponding C source given at the end of the previous section.

The menu generator itself is a straightforward application of the functions getpstr and getplin shown in the previous chapter. Whenever the data required is a single "word," getpstr will read it for us. Whenever an input string may contain more than one word, we use getplin. Thus, the input format is extremely free-form, and the menu inputs may be formatted ad-lib. The only inputs that are not read with either of these functions are the list of alternatives for a choice field. Here we simply accept a comma-separated list of C strings. The end of the list is marked by a line consisting only of initial whitespace followed by }; .

Purely for purposes of simplification, the Edit: input is coded like this:

```
a        String of any characters
n        String of digits only (with possible leading '-')
n1       short integer, 1 digit
n2       short integer, 2 digits (with possible leading '-')
              ... etc. ...
n6       short integer, 6 digits (with possible leading '-')
```

The full program is quite large but unsophisticated. The only deviation from a straight translation of input to output is the buffering of FIELD lines so that they can be printed at the end to initialize the array of FIELDS.

gen_menu.c:

```
/* gen_menu - generate C source for menu from description file */
#include "local.h"
#define MAXBFLDS 8000
#define C_ID_LEN 31
#define FILE_NM_LEN 64        /* max length of file name */
#define C_EXPR_LEN 80         /* arbitrarly limit on length of struct ref */
#define TITLE_LEN 80          /* max length of displayed title */
#define SCR_POS_LEN 3         /* max digits in screen position */
#define FTYPE_LEN 1           /* field type is only one char */
#define EDIT_LEN 2            /* edit type is 1 char plus 1 optional digit */
#define MAXFLINE (TITLE_LEN+FTYPE_LEN+EDIT_LEN+SCR_POS_LEN+SCR_POS_LEN+50)
#define GETPSTR(p, s)  \
    { if (!getpstr(p, s, sizeof(s)))  error("Cannot match" , p);  }
#define OPTPSTR(p, s)  \
    getpstr(p, s, sizeof(s))
#define GETPLIN(p, s)  \
    { if (!getplin(p, s, sizeof(s)))  error("Cannot match" , p);  }

/* internal variables */
static char buf[BUFSIZ] = {""};
static char buf_flds[MAXBFLDS] = {""};
static short i_flds = 0;
static char mname[C_ID_LEN+1] = {""};
static char mstruct[C_EXPR_LEN+1] = {""};
static char mtitle[TITLE_LEN+1] = {""};
static char mheader[FILE_NM_LEN+1] = {""};
static char fname[C_ID_LEN+1] = {""};
static char fline[SCR_POS_LEN+1] = {""};
static char fcol[SCR_POS_LEN+1] = {""};
static char ffn[C_ID_LEN+1] = {""};
static char ftype[FTYPE_LEN+1] = {""};
static char fedit[EDIT_LEN+1] = {""};
static char fdesc[TITLE_LEN+1] = {""};
void do_1_menu(), do_1_fld(), pr_s_fld(), pr_c_fld(), pr_m_fld(), pr_f_fld();
```

```
/* gen_menu (main) */
void main()
    {
    do_1_menu();
    while (OPTPSTR("Field name:", fname))
        do_1_fld();      /* process one field */
    printf("static FIELD F%s[] =\n", mname);
    printf("\t{\n");
    for (i_flds = 0; buf_flds[i_flds] != '\0'; ++i_flds)
        putchar(buf_flds[i_flds]);
    printf("\t};\n");
    printf("MENU %s = {\"%s\", F%s, DIM(F%s), 0};\n",
        mname, mtitle, mname, mname);
    }

/* do_1_menu - process the menu information */
void do_1_menu()
    {
    GETPSTR("Menu name:", mname);
    GETPLIN("Menu title:", mtitle);
    GETPSTR("Header:", mheader);
    GETPSTR("C-struct:", mstruct);
    printf("/* %s - %s */\n", mname, mtitle);
    printf("#include \"local.h\"\n");
    printf("#include \"menu.h\"\n");
    printf("#include \"%s\"\n", mheader);
    }
```

```
/* do_1_fld - process the info for one field */
void do_1_fld()
    {
    asserts(IN_RANGE(i_flds, 0, MAXBFLDS - MAXFLINE), "buffer space ok");
    GETPLIN("Desc:", fdesc);
    GETPSTR("Line:", fline);
    GETPSTR("Col:", fcol);
    GETPSTR("Type:", ftype);
    if (tolower(ftype[0]) == 's')
        GETPSTR("Edit:", fedit);
    if (ftype[0] != 'm')
        GETPSTR("Post-fn:", ffn);
    if (!STREQ(ffn, "0") && !STREQ(ffn, "NULL"))
        printf("extern bool %s();\n", ffn);
    switch (ftype[0])
        {
    case 's':
    case 'S':
        pr_s_fld();
        break;
    case 'c':
        pr_c_fld();
        break;
    case 'm':
        pr_m_fld();
        break;
    case 'f':
        pr_f_fld();
        break;
    default:
        error("Unknown field type", ftype);
        }
    i_flds += strlen(&buf_flds[i_flds]);
    if (i_flds > MAXBFLDS - MAXFLINE)
        error("out of buffer space", "");
    }
```

```
/* pr_s_fld - print the info for a string field */
void pr_s_fld()
    {
    sprintf(&buf_flds[i_flds],
        "\t{%s, %s, \"%s\", '%c', &S%s, NULL, NULL, %s},\n",
        fline, fcol, fdesc, ftype[0], fname, ffn);
    if (fedit[1] == '\0')
        {
        printf("static STRING_VAL S%s =\n", fname);
        printf("\t{'%c', (%s).%s, sizeof((%s).%s), NULL};\n",
            fedit[0], mstruct, fname, mstruct, fname);
        }
    else
        {
        printf("static char N%s[%c+1] = {0};\n",
            fname, fedit[1]);
        printf("static STRING_VAL S%s =\n", fname);
        printf("\t{'%c', N%s, sizeof(N%s), &(%s).%s};\n",
            fedit[0], fname, fname, mstruct, fname);
        }
    }

/* pr_c_fld - print the info for a choice field */
void pr_c_fld()
    {
    int ret;

    sprintf(&buf_flds[i_flds],
        "\t{%s, %s, \"%s\", '%c', NULL, &C%s, NULL, %s},\n",
        fline, fcol, fdesc, ftype[0], fname, ffn);
    printf("static char *T%s[]=\n", fname);
    do {
        ret = getsnn(buf, BUFSIZ);
        if (ret != EOF && ret > 0)  /* skip blank lines */
            printf("%s\n", buf);
        } while (ret != EOF && strchr(buf, ';') == NULL);
    printf("static CHOICE_VAL C%s =\n", fname);
    printf("\t{DIM(T%s), T%s, (%s).%s};\n",
        fname, fname, mstruct, fname);
    }
```

```
/* pr_m_fld - print the info for a menu field */
void pr_m_fld()
    {
    printf("extern MENU %s;\n", fname);
    sprintf(&buf_flds[i_flds],
        "\t{%s, %s, \"%s\", '%c', NULL, NULL, &%s, %s},\n",
        fline, fcol, fdesc, ftype[0], fname, ffn);
    }
/* pr_f_fld - print the info for a function field */
void pr_f_fld()
    {
    sprintf(&buf_flds[i_flds],
        "\t{%s, %s, \"%s\", '%c', NULL, NULL, NULL, %s},\n",
        fline, fcol, fdesc, ftype[0], ffn);
    }
```

Exercise 6-6. Write a program (using menus) which will write ".mu" menu files.

CHAPTER 7: DYNAMIC DATA STRUCTURES

In this chapter, we will look at data structures which dynamically grow and shrink as the computation progresses. By contrast, the structures that we saw in the previous chapter were totally determined at program-initialization time.

7.1 Dynamic Storage Allocation

The function `malloc` provides dynamically-allocated storage;

```
char *p;
```

```
p = malloc(N);
```

will set aside a contiguous "chunk" of N bytes of data storage and return the address of this chunk to be stored in the pointer p. This memory is guaranteed not to overlap the storage of any declared variable or any other memory obtained by the allocation functions.

Besides the `malloc` function, there is also a `calloc` function, which behaves like `malloc` with two extra features: the allocated memory is filled with 0-bits, and the number of bytes requested is given by the product of the two arguments.

```
p = calloc(N, M);
```

will cause p to point to a new chunk of N * M bytes filled with zeroes.

The conventional term for the location of allocated storage is *the heap*. In many environments, the heap starts at the low addresses of the dynamic data segment and grows upwards to high addresses, while the stack starts at high addresses and grows downwards. If a function call needs more stack space than the dynamic segment has available for it ("stack-heap collision"), this is a fatal error. Nothing reliable can happen afterwards. Most environments will terminate the program with a severe error.

If a request for allocated memory asks for more bytes than are available in the heap, the malloc (or calloc) function returns a NULL pointer. Thus, the returned pointer should always be tested to be sure that it is non-NULL. Moreover, early in the program design, if the program uses dynamic memory allocation, an error-handling strategy must be determined for the "out-of-heap" condition. (On many non-UNIX systems, it is necessary to specify a maximum size for the program's dynamic memory; the details depend upon the environment [7-1].)

When allocation is successful, the memory provided will have the most restrictive alignment of any data type on the target machine. In other words, it is safe to store any kind of data in the allocated memory, because the alignment will always be adequate.

One of the most common uses of dynamic allocation is storing a structure. In this case, the pointer by which we will access the memory will be a pointer to some type of structure, and the returned pointer from malloc (or calloc) should be cast to the type of the pointer:

```
struct x *px;

px = (struct x *)malloc(sizeof(struct x));
```

When allocated storage has been used and is no longer needed, it can be returned to the heap by the free function:

```
free(px);
```

will give back to the heap the storage which px is pointing to. Note carefully that each time storage is allocated, the allocation functions record internally the size that was given to this allocation. When free is called, this internally-recorded size is used to determine the amount of storage that is being given back. It is very important that the pointer value passed to the free function *must* be one which was originally delivered by malloc (or calloc).

One of the important reliability aspects of dynamic allocation is the avoidance of dangling pointers. After calling free(px), the pointer px should be considered to have an *undefined* value. To be sure, the pointer does still contain a valid machine address, but the storage that it points to may subsequently be allocated to some other use. One useful style convention is to immediately assign NULL to a pointer after passing it to the free function:

```
free(px);
px = NULL;
```

In some environments, this will ensure that any further access using px will generate an execution error [7-2]. And in any environment, it will warn the reader that px should not be used to access data.

This convention is not a complete preventative measure by itself, because more than one pointer may be pointing to the freed storage. Here is a more general rule:

Rule 7-1: When a pointer p is passed to the free function, the programmer must determine how many pointers are pointing into the freed storage. (This number is known as the "reference count" of the storage.) Steps must be taken (such as assigning NULL) to ensure that none of these pointers are subsequently used to access the freed storage.

We have seen that a "dangling pointer" results from continued use of a pointer to freed storage. There is a complementary problem known as *dead storage* which results from failure to free a chunk of storage when it is no longer needed. Here is an unusually blatant case of dead storage:

```
p = malloc(N);
p = NULL;
```

Access to the allocated storage is immediately lost, and there is no way to let the allocation functions know that the storage is available for other uses. A few isolated cases of dead storage are unlikely to be noticed; the storage available is simply decreased. But as the dead storage begins to accumulate, the odds increase that the program will run out of allocatable storage. The preventive measures are fairly simple:

Rule 7-2: For every instance in which a program allocates storage, there should be an easily identifiable instance in which that storage is later freed.

7.2 Singly-linked Lists

A structure can contain a pointer to the same type of structure, which is useful for building data structures which can grow and shrink during execution. The simplest such data structure is a *singly-linked list,* or *chain*.

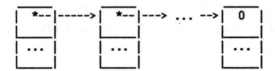

Each box represents a *node* on the stack. Each node contains a pointer to another node; we will conventionally name this member of the node structure the next pointer. The bottom node is distinguished by having a null next pointer. In the other nodes, the next pointer points one node further down the chain.

One common use of a chain (singly-linked list) is to implement a *stack*, a data structure where insertions and deletions take place at one end, called the "top" of the stack. Thus, one pointer (pointing to the top node) is all that is needed to access the stack.

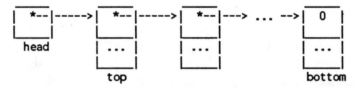

Note that we have here a situation very similar to the use of pointers to access an array: the *indirect object* of the head pointer (the thing that it points to, syntactically) is one single object, but it is being used to provide access to several such objects. When the data structure being accessed through head is a stack, we will often use the verbal shorthand of saying that head *is* a stack.

For the time being, we will use an array of four char's as the data portion of each node in the stack.

Throughout this chapter, each structure template will contain one or more pointers to other structures of the same type. Declarations of such structure templates look more uniform if the #define method is used, rather than the typedef method, because the typedef method does not allow us to use the structure's uppercase name inside its own declaration:

```
#define ST_NODE struct st_node
ST_NODE                                 typedef struct st_node
    {                                       {
    ST_NODE *next;                          struct st_node *next;
    char data[4];                           char data[4];
    };                                      } ST_NODE;
```

With the `typedef` method, the name `ST_NODE` is not available for use inside the structure itself, because the name is not seen by the compiler until the end of the declaration. The comparison is aesthetic, not substantive; use whichever form you like. The declaration of the stack node template will go into a `stack.h` header, along with the declaration of some functions to appear shortly.

A new (empty) stack can be created simply by assigning (or initializing) `NULL` to a "head" pointer:

```
ST_NODE *head;

head = NULL;
```

The treatment of different data structures will be made easier, however, if we define a macro `ST_OPEN` which accepts a pointer to the head pointer (a `ST_NODE **` parameter), and assign `NULL` to the head pointer:

```
#define ST_OPEN(headp)    (*(headp) = NULL)
```

Then the "opening" of a stack is accomplished via

```
ST_OPEN(&head);
```

To avoid special cases in the processing of dynamic structures, we will make sure that each node in a structure is well-defined, i.e., all members are well-defined. Thus, no "garbage" values will be found within the structure. The invariant properties of a singly-linked stack can therefore be expressed like this:

0.　If `head == NULL`, the stack is empty, i.e., contains no nodes.

N.　Otherwise, `head` points to a well-defined `ST_NODE`; this is the "first" or "top" node in the stack. Some node, node-N, has a `NULL` next-pointer; this is the "last" or "bottom" node in the stack. The stack accessed through `head` consists of the N nodes reachable via the chain of next-pointers. Every `ST_NODE` in the stack is well-defined.

The basic operations upon a stack are "pushing" a node onto the stack, and "popping" a node off the stack. The simplest implementation is obtained by requiring the user's calling function to allocate the space for a new node before calling the "push" function. And the "pop" function will detach a node from the stack and hand it to the calling function. It is thus up to the calling function to free the node's storage when it is needed no further.

The `head` pointer will also belong to the calling function. This allows the stack functions to be invoked upon several different stacks, but requires that each function must accept the value or the address of the `head` pointer as a parameter of each function. In this example, both the `st_push` and `st_pop` functions must modify the `head` pointer, so they must be passed its address. This is the `st_push` function:

```
st_push:
    /* st_push - install ST_NODE at head of stack */
    #include "stack.h"
    void st_push(headp, p)
        ST_NODE **headp;
        ST_NODE *p;
        {
        p->next = *headp;    /* p->next now points to previous head (or is NULL) */
        *headp = p;          /* *headp now points to p */
        }
```

And this is the `st_pop` function:

```
st_pop:
    /* st_pop - detach top node of stack and return pointer to it */
    #include "stack.h"
    ST_NODE *st_pop(headp)
        ST_NODE **headp;
        {
        ST_NODE *p;

        if (*headp == NULL)
            return (NULL);
        p = *headp;          /* p points to top of stack */
        *headp = p->next;    /* headp now points to next node (or is NULL) */
        p->next = NULL;      /* prevent dangling ptr */
        return (p);
        }
```

Let us pause to examine the types of the pointers and expressions. The parameter `headp` is declared to have the type `ST_NODE **`, i.e., pointer to pointer to `ST_NODE`. The expression `*headp` thus has the type `ST_NODE *`, or pointer to `ST_NODE`. And `p->next` is the `next` member of the node that `p` points to. Its type is also `ST_NODE *`.

Also notice in the `st_pop` function that we assign `NULL` to the `next` member of the popped node, before turning the node over to the calling function. This will ensure that the popped node is not used to provide further access to the stack, whose structure may subsequently be altered by further pushes and pops.

To close a singly-linked stack, we must free any nodes which remain in the stack. We must then assign NULL to its head pointer.

```
st_close:
    /* st_close - close the stack accessed via *headp */
    #include "stack.h"
    void st_close(headp)
        ST_NODE **headp;
        {
        ST_NODE *p;
        ST_NODE *pnext;

        for (p = *headp; p != NULL; p = pnext)
            {
            pnext = p->next;
            free(p);     /* p is (momentarily) undefined */
            }
        *headp = NULL;        /* prevent dangling ptr */
        }
```

A simple for loop can step a pointer over each of the nodes on the stack:

```
for (p = head; p != NULL; p = p->next)
    process *p
```

This operation — looping a pointer over each node in a data structure — will be useful for each data structure, so we will define a macro

```
#define EACH_ST(head, p)  for ((p) = (head); (p) != NULL; (p) = (p)->next)
```

which we can use like this:

```
EACH_ST(head, p)
    process *p
```

Three other macros will be useful: ST_IS_EMPTY(head) produces YES if the stack is empty, NO otherwise; ST_FIRST(head) produces a pointer to the first node on the stack; and ST_NEXT(p) produces a pointer to the ("successor") node that follows the node pointed to by p:

```
#define ST_IS_EMPTY(head) ((head) == NULL)
#define ST_FIRST(head)      (head)
#define ST_NEXT(p)          ((p)->next)
```

This completes the list of operations needed to implement a stack as a singly-linked list. As configured, however, the stack works for only one specific type of node, one in which the data member is an array of four chars. We would prefer for our data structure operations to be more general than this, even at the expense of the simplicity of the implementation. After all, we will create the data structure headers and functions only once but we will use them many different times in different contexts.

The packaging approach that we will show in this chapter will allow the data structure functions and macros to be used upon any structure whose initial members contain the proper pointers. We will, for example, generalize the "stack" package to allow it to be used upon any structure whose first member is a pointer to other such structures, and the name of the first member must be next. The stack.h header will contain a declaration of an ST_NODE that looks like this:

```
#define ST_NODE struct st_node
ST_NODE
    {
    ST_NODE *next;
    /* ... */
    };
```

Suppose, then, that we wish to use the "stack" package with nodes that look like this:

```
#define NAME_NODE struct name_node
NAME_NODE
    {
    NAME_NODE *next;
    char data[4];
    };
NAME_NODE *name_head = NULL;
NAME_NODE *p = NULL;
```

A macro like ST_NEXT will generate the proper code when applied to NAME_NODES: ST_NEXT(name_head) becomes ((name_head)->next) as desired. When calling the functions, such as st_push, there is a type-matching problem to solve. A type-checking environment such as lint will notice that we are passing a pointer to NAME_NODE's to a function that expects pointers to ST_NODES, and will properly complain. Since we know that the two structures are in fact compatible with each other for the uses that are being made within the function, we will add macros to the stack.h which call the function with pointer arguments that have had the proper casts applied to them.

It will also be useful to provide in each data structure header any appropriate "non-NULL" tests for each pointer argument. If the tests are conditional upon NDEBUG they will not slow down the execution version of the system. Since we will make use of the non-NULL tests and the pointer casts in several different data-structure headers, we will make a header, pointer.h, for these useful pointer operations:

```
pointer.h:
    /* pointer.h - concise macros for pointer checking and casting */
    /* PNN(p)      - test that p is not NULL, return p */
    /* PNNC(p, t)  - test that p is not NULL, return p cast to type t */
    #ifndef POINTER_H
    #define POINTER_H
    #ifndef NDEBUG
    #define PNN(p)          ((p) != NULL ? (p) : PNN_BAD(p))
    #define PNNC(p, t)      ((p) != NULL ? (t)(p) : (t)PNN_BAD(p))
    #define PNN_BAD(p)      (fprintf(stderr, "NULL\n"), p)
    #else
    #define PNN(p)          (p)
    #define PNNC(p,t)       ((t)(p))
    #endif
    #endif
```

We can now show the contents of the stack.h header:

```
stack.h:
    /* stack.h - header for stack package */
    #ifndef STACK_H
    #define STACK_H
    #include "local.h"
    #include "pointer.h"
    #define ST_NODE struct st_node
    ST_NODE
        {
        ST_NODE *next;
        /* ... */
        };

    void st_close();        /* PARMS(ST_NODE **headp) */
    ST_NODE *st_pop();      /* PARMS(ST_NODE **headp) */
    void st_push();         /* PARMS(ST_NODE **headp, ST_NODE *p) */

    #define ST_P(p)         PNNC(p, ST_NODE *)
    #define ST_PP(p)        PNNC(p, ST_NODE **)

    #define ST_CLOSE(h)     (st_close(ST_PP(h)))
    #define ST_POP(h)       (st_pop(ST_PP(h)))
    #define ST_PUSH(h, p)   (st_push(ST_PP(h), ST_P(p)))

    #define EACH_ST(head, p)    for ((p) = (head); (p) != NULL; (p) = (p)->next)
    #define ST_FIRST(head)      (head)
    #define ST_IS_EMPTY(head)   ((head) == NULL)
    #define ST_OPEN(headp)      (*(headp) = NULL)
    #define ST_NEXT(p)          ((p)->next)
    #endif
```

Consider the ST_CLOSE macro. It makes use of an auxiliary macro named
ST_PP which ensures that its argument is non-NULL and casts it to the
type ST_NODE ** (pointer to pointer to ST_NODE). The macros ST_POP and
ST_PUSH are similarly implemented.

The end result of all this packaging is that we can use the "stack" package with any structure that has a next pointer as its first member. All the operations are provided as macros that have uniform uppercase names beginning with "ST_."

In order to give a simple demonstration of the stack functions, we will create a small interactive program, st_main.c:

st_main.c:
```
/* st_main - test routine for stack package
 */
#include "local.h"
#include "stack.h"

#define NAME_NODE struct name_node
NAME_NODE
    {
    NAME_NODE *next;
    char data[4];
    };
NAME_NODE *head = NULL;       /* head node of stack */
NAME_NODE *p = NULL;          /* current node */
void show_cmds(), push_name(), pop_name(), dump_names();
```

```
/* st_main (main) */
main()
    {
    char buf[2];                /* buffer for input */

    ST_OPEN(&head);             /* open the stack */
    show_cmds();
    while (getreply("?: ", buf, 2) != EOF)
        {
        switch (buf[0])
            {
        case '+':
            push_name();
            break;
        case '-':
            pop_name();
            break;
        case '=':
            dump_names();
            break;
        case '0':
            ST_CLOSE(&head);
            ST_OPEN(&head);        /* open the stack again */
            break;
        case '?':
            show_cmds();
            break;
        default:
            printf("unknown command: %c\n", buf[0]);
            show_cmds();
            break;
            }
        }
    exit(SUCCEED);
    }
```

```
/* show_cmds -- show legal commands */
void show_cmds()
    {
    printf("Type + to push, - to pop, = to print, 0 to reset:\n");
    }
/* push_name - push new name on stack */
void push_name()
    {
    p = (NAME_NODE *)malloc(sizeof(NAME_NODE));
    if (p == NULL)
        error("out of space", "");
    if (getreply("name: ", p->data, 4) == EOF)
        error("unexpected EOF", "");
    ST_PUSH(&head, p);
    }
/* pop_name - pop a name off stack */
void pop_name()
    {
    p = (NAME_NODE *)ST_POP(&head);
    if (p == NULL)
        printf("EMPTY STACK\n");
    else
        {
        printf("name= %s\n", p->data);
        free(p);
        }
    }
/* dump_names - print the current stack of names */
void dump_names()
    {
    if (ST_IS_EMPTY(head))
        printf("EMPTY STACK\n");
    else
        EACH_ST(head, p)
            printf("name= %s\n", p->data);
    }
```

We are handling the "out-of-heap" condition by simple "diagnose-and-terminate" logic. This is adequate for simple interactive uses.

7.3 Queues

With a small modification to the stack structure, we obtain a data structure that allows insertion at the one end and deletion at the other — a *queue*, that is.

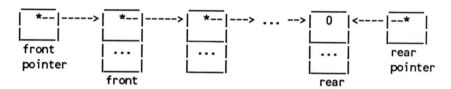

The properties of a queue are similar to those of a stack:

0.   If either front or rear is NULL, both are NULL, and the queue is empty,
      i.e., contains no nodes.

N.   Otherwise, front points to a well-defined node; this is the "first" or
      "front" node in the queue. Some node, node-N, has a NULL next-
      pointer; this is the "last" or "rear" node in the queue, and rear
      points to this node. The queue accessed through front and rear
      contains the N nodes reachable via the chain of next-pointers.
      Every Q_NODE in the queue is well-defined, i.e., all its members are
      well-defined.

      The data structure itself is the same singly-linked list that we used
for the stack; we have just added a second access pointer at the "rear."
The operation of "opening" a queue assigns NULL to both the front and
the rear pointers:

```
#define Q_OPEN(frontp, rearp)  (*(frontp) = *(rearp) = NULL)
```

As with the stack, the "first" and "next" operations are simple macros:

```
#define Q_FIRST(front) (front)
#define Q_NEXT(p)       ((p)->next)
```

A queue can be "popped" just like a stack: simply detach the first node.
(When the single remaining node is popped, the rear pointer must be set
to NULL.)

```
q_pop:
    /* q_pop - detach front node of queue and return pointer to it */
    #include "queue.h"
    Q_NODE *q_pop(frontp, rearp)
        Q_NODE **frontp, **rearp;
        {
        Q_NODE *p;

        if (*frontp == NULL)
            return (NULL);
        p = *frontp;                /* p points to front of queue */
        *frontp = Q_NEXT(p);        /* front now points to next node (or NULL) */
        if (*frontp == NULL)        /* if queue is now empty, */
            *rearp = NULL;          /* then make both ptrs NULL */
        Q_NEXT(p) = NULL;           /* prevent dangling ptr */
        return (p);
        }
```

However, we can define a somewhat more general operation, "detach to the right." Define the *link-in* of a node on a queue as that pointer which points to it. Specifically, the link-in to the first node is the front pointer; the link-in of each other node is the next pointer of the node to its left. Given a pointer to a link-in, we can detach the node to the right of the link-in:

```
q_r_detach:
    /* q_r_detach - detach queue node that *pp links-in and return pointer to it */
    #include "queue.h"
    Q_NODE *q_r_detach(frontp, rearp, pp)
        Q_NODE **frontp, **rearp;
        Q_NODE **pp;
        {
        Q_NODE *p2;                 /* ptr to detached node */

        if (*pp == NULL)
            return (NULL);
        p2 = *pp;                   /* p2 points to node to detach */
        *pp = Q_NEXT(p2);           /* *pp now points to next node (or NULL) */
        if (*frontp == NULL)        /* if queue is now empty, */
            *rearp = NULL;          /* then make both ptrs NULL */
        Q_NEXT(p2) = NULL;          /* prevent dangling ptr */
        return (p2);
        }
```

A node can be "pushed" onto a queue (impolite, but useful sometimes), just as with a stack, except that the rear pointer must be set when the new node is the first arrival onto an empty queue.

```
q_push:
    /* q_push - install Q_NODE at front of queue */
    #include "queue.h"
    void q_push(frontp, rearp, p)
        Q_NODE **frontp, **rearp;
        Q_NODE *p;
        {
        Q_NEXT(p) = *frontp;     /* p points to previous front (or NULL) */
        *frontp = p;             /* *frontp now points to p */
        if (*rearp == NULL)      /* if queue was empty, */
            *rearp = p;          /* *rearp also points to p */
        }
```

As with "pop," the "push" is a special case of inserting a node to the
right of a pointer which becomes the node's link-in:

```
q_r_insert:
    /* q_r_insert - install Q_NODE after *pp */
    #include "queue.h"
    void q_r_insert(frontp, rearp, p, pp)
        Q_NODE **frontp, **rearp;
        Q_NODE *p;
        Q_NODE **pp;
        {
        Q_NEXT(p) = *pp;         /* p points to node following *pp (or NULL) */
        *pp = p;                 /* *pp now points to p */
        if (*rearp == NULL)      /* if queue was empty, */
            *rearp = p;          /* *rearp also points to p */
        }
```

The queue allows an "append" operation, an insertion onto the end of
the queue:

```
q_append:
    /* q_append - install Q_NODE at rear of queue */
    #include "queue.h"
    void q_append(frontp, rearp, p)
        Q_NODE **frontp, **rearp;
        Q_NODE *p;
        {
        Q_NEXT(p) = NULL;        /* new node will be rear of queue */
        if (*frontp == NULL)     /* if queue was empty, */
            *frontp = *rearp = p; /* p becomes front and rear */
        else
            {
            Q_NEXT(*rearp) = p;  /* splice p into queue */
            *rearp = p;          /* p becomes rear of queue */
            }
        }
```

The "close" operation must free all remaining nodes and assign NULL to
both front and rear pointers:

```
q_close:
    /* q_close - close the queue accessed via *frontp and *rearp */
    #include "queue.h"
    void q_close(frontp, rearp)
        Q_NODE **frontp, **rearp;
        {
        Q_NODE *p;
        Q_NODE *pnext;

        for (p = *frontp; p != NULL; p = pnext)
            {
            pnext = Q_NEXT(p);
            free(p);          /* p is (momentarily) undefined */
            }
        *frontp = *rearp = NULL;        /* prevent dangling ptr */
        }
```

The macro EACH_Q behaves the same as the EACH_ST macro did:

```
#define EACH_Q(front, p)  for ((p) = front; (p) != NULL; (p) = (p)->next)
```

A queue is empty if its front pointer is NULL:

```
#define Q_IS_EMPTY(front) ((front) == NULL)
```

A queue can conveniently be used to store an ordered list of nodes; we will soon see a queue of tasks stored in order of the time that they are supposed to be performed. In order for an "ordered insert" function to be general-purpose, it must accept a pointer to a comparison function, just as we saw in the "quicksort" examples:

```
q_insert:
    /* q_insert - install Q_NODE at proper place in queue */
    #include "queue.h"
    void q_insert(frontp, rearp, p, cmpfn)
        Q_NODE **frontp, **rearp;
        Q_NODE *p;
        int (*cmpfn)();                /* function for comparisons */
        {
        Q_NODE *p2;

        if (*frontp == NULL                /* if queue was empty, */
            || (*cmpfn)(p, *frontp) < 0)   /* or if p comes first, */
            Q_PUSH(frontp, rearp, p);      /* push p onto front */
        else
            {
            for (p2 = *frontp; ; p2 = Q_NEXT(p2))
                {
                if (Q_NEXT(p2) == NULL)
                    {                              /* if end of queue, */
                    Q_APPEND(frontp, rearp, p); /* append p at rear of queue */
                    break;
                    }
                else if ((*cmpfn)(p, Q_NEXT(p2)) < 0)
                    {                              /* if p sorts before Q_NEXT(p2) */
                    Q_R_INSERT(frontp, rearp, p, p2);   /* insert after p2 */
                    break;
                    }
                }
            }
        }
```

A "find" function is also easy, given a comparison function pointer. It will, however, be more useful for the "find" operation to produce a pointer to the link-in of the found node, since the link-in is necessary for insertions or deletions inside the queue:

7-18   **RELIABLE DATA STRUCTURES IN C**   **SECTION 7.3**

```
q_lfind:
    /* q_lfind - search queue for equal match to p, return its link-in
     * Return NULL if no match
     */
    #include "queue.h"
    Q_NODE **q_lfind(frontp, rearp, p, cmpfn)
        Q_NODE **frontp, **rearp;
        Q_NODE *p;
        int (*cmpfn)();
        {
        Q_NODE **pp;

        for (pp = frontp; *pp != NULL; pp = &Q_NEXT(*pp))
            if ((*cmpfn)(*pp, p) == 0)
                return (pp);
        return (NULL);
        }
```

Access to all these operations is provided by the header for the queue package:

```
queue.h:
    /* queue.h - header for queue package */
    #ifndef QUEUE_H
    #define QUEUE_H
    #include "local.h"
    #include "pointer.h"
    #define Q_NODE struct q_node
    Q_NODE
        {
        Q_NODE *next;
        /* ... */
        };

    void q_append();      /* PARMS(Q_NODE **frontp, Q_NODE **rearp, Q_NODE *p) */
    void q_close();       /* PARMS(Q_NODE **frontp, Q_NODE **rearp) */
    void q_insert();
        /* PARMS(Q_NODE **frontp, Q_NODE **rearp, Q_NODE *p, int (*cmpfn)()) */
    Q_NODE **q_lfind();
        /* PARMS(Q_NODE **frontp, Q_NODE **rearp, Q_NODE *p, int (*cmpfn)()) */
    Q_NODE *q_pop();      /* PARMS(Q_NODE **frontp, Q_NODE **rearp) */
    void q_push();        /* PARMS(Q_NODE **frontp, Q_NODE **rearp, Q_NODE *p) */
    Q_NODE *q_r_detach();
        /* PARMS(Q_NODE **frontp, Q_NODE **rearp, Q_NODE **pp) */
    void q_r_insert();
        /* PARMS(Q_NODE **frontp, Q_NODE **rearp, Q_NODE *p, Q_NODE **pp) */

    /* (more)
```

```
    */

    #define Q_PP(p)        PNNC(p, Q_NODE **)
    #define Q_P(p)         PNNC(p, Q_NODE *)

    #define Q_APPEND(fp, rp, p)      q_append(Q_PP(fp), Q_PP(rp), Q_P(p))
    #define Q_CLOSE(fp, rp)          q_close(Q_PP(fp), Q_PP(rp))
    #define Q_INSERT(fp, rp, p, fn)  q_insert(Q_PP(fp), Q_PP(rp), Q_P(p), fn)
    #define Q_LFIND(fp, rp, p, fn)   q_lfind(Q_PP(fp), Q_PP(rp), Q_P(p), fn)
    #define Q_POP(fp, rp)            q_pop(Q_PP(fp), Q_PP(rp))
    #define Q_PUSH(fp, rp, p)        q_push(Q_PP(fp), Q_PP(rp), Q_P(p))
    #define Q_R_DETACH(fp, rp, pp)   q_r_detach(Q_PP(fp), Q_PP(rp), Q_PP(pp))
    #define Q_R_INSERT(fp, rp, p, pp) q_r_insert(Q_PP(fp), Q_PP(rp), Q_P(p), Q_PP(pp

    #define Q_IS_EMPTY(front)        ((front) == NULL)
    #define Q_OPEN(frontp, rearp)    (*(frontp) = *(rearp) = NULL)
    #define Q_NEXT(p)                ((p)->next)
    #define EACH_Q(front, p)         for ((p) = front; (p) != NULL; p = (p)->next)
    #endif
```

A queue is a convenient data structure to use for a list of tasks to be performed. Each task has a specified "start time," and can be inserted into the proper chronological position in the queue.

```
task.h:
    /* task.h - header for task package */
    #ifndef TASK_H
    #define TASK_H
    #include "local.h"
    #include "queue.h"
    typedef short TIME;
    #define TASK struct task
    TASK
        {
        TASK *next;
        TIME start;
        char desc[40];
        };
    #endif
```

Here is a program which will accept the following transactions: insert a task into the queue, print the task with the earliest start time and remove it from the queue, print all tasks on the queue.

```
t_main.c:
    /* t_main - manage a queue of tasks */
    #include "local.h"
    #include "queue.h"
    #include "task.h"
    TASK *front = NULL;        /* front node of queue */
    TASK *rear = NULL;         /* rear node of queue */
    TASK *p = NULL;            /* current node */
    void insert_task(), pop_task(), dump_tasks(), show_cmds();
    main()
        {
        char buf[2];                    /* buffer for input */

        show_cmds();
        Q_OPEN(&front, &rear);          /* open the queue */
        while (getreply("?: ", buf, 2) != EOF)
            {
            switch (buf[0])
                {
            case '>':
                insert_task();
                break;
            case '-':
                pop_task();
                break;
            case '=':
                dump_tasks();
                break;
            case '0':
                Q_CLOSE(&front, &rear);
                Q_OPEN(&front, &rear);          /* open the queue */
                break;
            default:
                printf("unknown command: %c\n", buf[0]);
                show_cmds();
                break;
                }
            }
        exit(SUCCEED);
        }
    /* show_cmds -- show legal commands */
    void show_cmds()
        {
        printf("Type > to insert, - to pop, = to print, 0 to reset:\n");
        }
```

```
/* cmptime - compare the start members of two TASKS */
int cmptime(t1, t2)
    TASK *t1, *t2;
    {
    if (t1->start < t2->start)
        return (-1);
    else if (t1->start == t2->start)
        return (0);
    else
        return (1);
    }
/* insert_task - insert new name on queue */
void insert_task()
    {
    char sstart[5];

    p = (TASK *)malloc(sizeof(TASK));
    if (p == NULL)
        error("out of space", "");
    if (getreply("start: ", sstart, sizeof(sstart)) == EOF)
        error("unexpected EOF", "");
    p->start = atoi(sstart);
    if (getreply("desc: ", p->desc, sizeof(p->desc)) == EOF)
        error("unexpected EOF", "");
    Q_INSERT(&front, &rear, p, cmptime);
    }
/* pop_task - pop a name off queue */
void pop_task()
    {
    p = (TASK *)Q_POP(&front, &rear);
    if (p == NULL)
        printf("EMPTY QUEUE\n");
    else
        {
        printf("start=%5d desc=%s\n", p->start, p->desc);
        free(p);
        }
    }
/* dump_tasks - print the current queue of names */
void dump_tasks()
    {
    if (front == NULL)
        printf("EMPTY QUEUE\n");
    else
        EACH_Q(front, p)
            printf("start=%5d desc=%s\n", p->start, p->desc);
    }
```

7.4 Deques: Double-Ended Queues

A "double-ended queue" or *deque* is a data structure in which each node has two pointers, one forward and one backward. Thus, it is also known as a "doubly-linked list."

A deque is often implemented with an extra node which contains no data but serves to make the operations more uniform; we will call this node a *master node*. A picture may help:

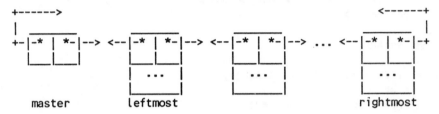

Given a pointer to any node, it is possible to reach all the other nodes by traversing pointers.

A node can be inserted to the right or to the left of any other node; all that is required is a pointer to the new node and a pointer to the insertion point. The following picture shows the insertion of the node d (i.e., the node pointed to by pointer d), to the right of node p, or to the left of node q. (Either p or q is adequate; either can be determined from the other.)

Before insertion:

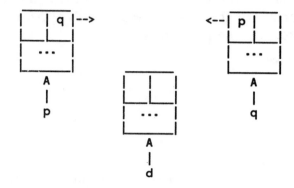

After insertion:

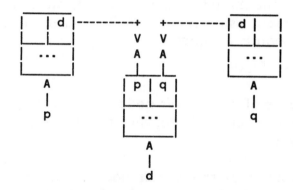

It is possible to remove a node from a deque given nothing more than a pointer to the node itself. Referring to the "after insertion" diagram above, given the pointer d, the nodes to the left and right can be located using information in the node *d. Thus, a deletion is just the exact reversal of an insertion.

An empty deque consists of one node, the master node, whose left and right pointers both point to itself:

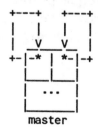

Thus, even in the empty deque, the master node has a left and right node (itself). There are no special cases in the insertion logic. To implement the deletion logic, the only special case is that the master node should not be freed; the manipulation of left and right pointers is the same for the deletion of any node.

Having a master node makes the calling sequence of the deque operations much more uniform. In the header deque.h will appear a type definition for the name DQ_NODE, defined like this:

```
#define DQ_NODE struct dq_node
DQ_NODE
    {
    DQ_NODE *left;
    DQ_NODE *right;
    /* ... */
    };
```

All the nodes in the deque, including the master, conform to this template. Since the master node is not a data node, we can require that the calling program must refer to the master node as a DQ_NODE, rather than as a data node. Thus, any program using the "deque" package must provide a "head" pointer which points to DQ_NODES.

These are the properties of a deque:

0.   If the left or right pointer of the master node contains the address of the master node itself, then both do, and the deque is empty, i.e., contains no data nodes.

N.   Otherwise, the right pointer of the master node points to a well-defined node; this is the "first" node in the deque. Some node, node-N, has a right pointer which points to the master node. The deque consists of the N nodes reachable via the chain of right-pointers, from the first node to node-N. For each node *a* in the deque, the node to the right of node *a* has a left-pointer that points back to *a*. Every node in the deque is well-defined, i.e., all its members are well-defined.

The operations dq_open and dq_close will alter the deque pointer and must be given its address, a "pointer to pointer to DQ_NODE" value. Most of the other operations will take a "pointer to DQ_NODE" first argument. Here are the dq_open and dq_close functions:

```
dq_open:
    /* dq_open - open a deque */
    #include "deque.h"
    void dq_open(pdq)
        DQ_NODE **pdq;
        {
        *pdq = (DQ_NODE *)malloc(sizeof(DQ_NODE));
        if (*pdq == NULL)
            return;
        (*pdq)->left = (*pdq)->right = (*pdq);
        }

dq_close:
    /* dq_close - close a deque  */
    #include "deque.h"
    void dq_close(pdq)
        DQ_NODE **pdq;   /* ptr to ptr to master DQ_NODE */
        {
        DQ_NODE *p;
        DQ_NODE *pnext;

        for (p = (*pdq)->right; p != (*pdq); p = pnext)
            {
            pnext = p->right;
            free(p);
            }
        free(*pdq);
        *pdq = NULL;
        }
```

The dq_close function frees any nodes remaining in the deque, including the master node.

Deques are often used to represent "circular lists," where the first node is considered to be the successor of the last node. The master node is not a data node, so is not to be considered part of the circular list. (As in the other headers, we make use of the macro PNN — "pointer non-NULL" — to provide debugging assistance in preventing NULL pointer bugs.)

```
#define DQ_PRED(dq, d) \
    (DQ_P(d)->left == PNN(dq) ? (dq->left) : (DQ_P(d)->left))
#define DQ_SUCC(dq, d) \
    (DQ_P(d)->right == PNN(dq) ? (dq->right) : (DQ_P(d)->right))
```

Detaching a node requires only a pointer to the node itself. The function does not allow the master node to be detached; a NULL pointer is returned if an attempt is made to detach the master node.

```
dq_detach:
    /* dq_detach - detach node d from deque */
    #include "deque.h"
    DQ_NODE *dq_detach(dq, d)
        DQ_NODE *dq;
        DQ_NODE *d;
        {
        DQ_NODE *p;
        DQ_NODE *q;

        if (d == dq)
            return (NULL);
        q = d->right;
        p = d->left;
        p->right = q;
        q->left = p;
        return (d);
        }
```

The operation "insert to the right of" was shown in the diagrams earlier. Because of the master node, there are no special cases in the insertion logic.

```
dq_r_insert:
    /* dq_r_insert - insert node d to the right of node p */
    #include "deque.h"
    void dq_r_insert(d, p)
        DQ_NODE *d;
        DQ_NODE *p;
        {
        DQ_NODE *q;

        q = p->right;
        d->left = p;
        d->right = q;
        p->right = d;
        q->left = d;
        }
```

Consistent with our adopted packaging, a macro DQ_R_INSERT is provided which verifies that pointers are non-NULL and casts them to the appropriate types:

```
#define DQ_P(p)      PNNC(p, DQ_NODE *)  /* non-NULL, cast to DQ_NODE * */

#define DQ_R_INSERT(d, p)   dq_r_insert(DQ_P(d), DQ_P(p))
```

Insertion to the left of node p is most simply implemented by inserting to the right of node p->left:

```
#define DQ_L_INSERT(d, p)    DQ_R_INSERT((d), (p)->left)
```

The operation DQ_PUSH is trivial; it simply uses DQ_R_INSERT. In other words, to "push" node d onto deque dq, simply insert d after dq:

```
#define DQ_PUSH(dq, d)       DQ_R_INSERT((d), (dq))
```

The dq_pop function returns NULL if the deque is empty (no nodes except the master node). Otherwise, it detaches the node to the right of the master node.

```
dq_pop:
    /* dq_pop - remove leftmost node and return pointer to it
     * Treats deque as a stack to the right of dq master node.
     */
    #include "deque.h"
    DQ_NODE *dq_pop(dq)
        DQ_NODE *dq;
        {
        DQ_NODE *d;

        d = dq->right;
        if (d == dq)
            return (NULL);
        return (DQ_DETACH(dq, d));
        }
```

The work of DQ_APPEND is accomplished by inserting node d to the right of the last node in the deque:

```
#define DQ_APPEND(dq, d)     DQ_R_INSERT(d, (dq)->left)
```

The test for "emptiness" of a deque is whether the node to the right of the master node is the master node itself:

```
#define DQ_IS_EMPTY(dq)      (PNN(dq)->right == PNN(dq))
```

The operations dq_insert and dq_find (which require a cmpfn pointer to provide the ordering function) are similar to the corresponding queue functions, except that the end of the list is marked by reaching the master node instead of reaching a NULL pointer. Another difference is that the dq_find function can simply return a pointer to the found node itself, since that pointer is all that is needed for insertion, deletion, or access to the rest of the deque.

```
dq_insert:
    /* dq_insert - install DQ_NODE at proper place in deque */
    #include "deque.h"
    void dq_insert(dq, p, cmpfn)
        DQ_NODE *dq;
        DQ_NODE *p;
        int (*cmpfn)();        /* function for comparisons: neg, zero, or pos */
        {
        DQ_NODE *p2;

        if (DQ_IS_EMPTY(dq)                    /* if deque was empty, */
            || (*cmpfn)(p, DQ_FIRST(dq)) < 0) /* or if p comes first, */
            DQ_PUSH(dq, p);                    /* push p onto front */
        else                                   /* else, p must sort after p2 */
            {
            EACH_DQ(dq, p2, DQ_NODE)    /* find where p belongs */
                {
                if (p2->right == dq)
                    {                          /* if end of deque, */
                    DQ_APPEND(dq, p);   /* append p at rear of deque */
                    break;
                    }
                else if ((*cmpfn)(p, p2->right) < 0)
                    {                          /* if p sorts before p2->right */
                    DQ_R_INSERT(p, p2); /* insert after p2 */
                    break;
                    }
                }
            }
        }

dq_find:
    /* dq_find - search deque for equal match to d, return ptr to match
     * Return NULL if no match
     */
    #include "deque.h"
    DQ_NODE *dq_find(dq, d, cmpfn)
        DQ_NODE *dq;
        DQ_NODE *d;
        int (*cmpfn)();                         /*function for comparisons */
        {
        DQ_NODE *d2;

        EACH_DQ(dq, d2, DQ_NODE)
            if ((*cmpfn)(d2, d) == 0)
                return (d2);
        return (NULL);
        }
```

```
dq_first:
    /* dq_first - produce ptr to first deque node, otherwise NULL */
    #include "deque.h"
    DQ_NODE *dq_first(dq)
        DQ_NODE *dq;
        {
        if (dq->right == dq)
            return (NULL);
        return (dq->right);
        }
```

The loop macro, EACH_DQ, loops until the pointer reaches the master
node. A third argument is necessary to specify the type of each node:

```
#define EACH_DQ(dq, d, t) \
    for (d = (t *)(dq)->right; (DQ_NODE *)(d) != dq; d = (d)->right)
```

Here is the full deque.h header:

```
deque.h:
    /* deque.h - header for deque package */
    #ifndef DEQUE_H
    #define DEQUE_H
    #include "local.h"
    #include "pointer.h"
    #define DQ_NODE struct dq_node
    DQ_NODE
        {
        DQ_NODE *left;
        DQ_NODE *right;
        /* ... */
        };

    #define DQ_P(p)         PNNC(p, DQ_NODE *)
    #define DQ_PP(p)        PNNC(p, DQ_NODE **)

    void dq_close();        /* PARMS(DQ_NODE **pdq) */
    DQ_NODE *dq_detach();    /* PARMS(DQ_NODE *dq, DQ_NODE *d) */
    DQ_NODE *dq_find();      /* PARMS(DQ_NODE *dq, DQ_NODE *d, int (*cmpfn)()) */
    void dq_insert();        /* PARMS(DQ_NODE *dq, DQ_NODE *d, int (*cmpfn)()) */
    void dq_open();          /* PARMS(DQ_NODE **pdq) */
    DQ_NODE *dq_pop();        /* PARMS(DQ_NODE *dq) */
    void dq_r_insert();      /* PARMS(DQ_NODE *d, DQ_NODE *p) */

    /* (more) */
```

```
/* pure macros */
#define DQ_APPEND(dq, d)      DQ_R_INSERT(d, (dq)->left)
#define DQ_IS_EMPTY(dq)       (PNN(dq)->right == PNN(dq))
#define DQ_L_DETACH(dq, d)    DQ_DETACH(dq, (d)->left)
#define DQ_L_INSERT(d, p)     DQ_R_INSERT((d), (p)->left)
#define DQ_PRED(dq, d) \
    (DQ_P(d)->left == PNN(dq) ? (dq->left) : (DQ_P(d)->left))
#define DQ_PUSH(dq, d)        DQ_R_INSERT((d), (dq))
#define DQ_R_DETACH(dq, d)    DQ_DETACH(dq, (d)->right)
#define DQ_SUCC(dq, d) \
    (DQ_P(d)->right == PNN(dq) ? (dq->right) : (DQ_P(d)->right))
#define EACH_DQ(dq, d, t) \
    for (d = (t *)(dq)->right; (DQ_NODE *)(d) != dq; d = (d)->right)
/* function-interface macros */
#define DQ_CLOSE(pdq)         dq_close(PNN(pdq))
#define DQ_DETACH(dq, d)      dq_detach(DQ_P(dq), DQ_P(d))
#define DQ_FIND(dq, d, fn)    dq_find(PNN(dq), DQ_P(d), fn)
#define DQ_FIRST(dq)          dq_first(PNN(dq))
#define DQ_INSERT(dq, d, fn)  dq_insert(PNN(dq), DQ_P(d), fn)
#define DQ_OPEN(pdq)          dq_open(PNN(pdq))
#define DQ_POP(dq)            dq_pop(PNN(dq))
#define DQ_R_INSERT(d, p)     dq_r_insert(DQ_P(d), DQ_P(p))
#endif
```

A natural example of a circular list is provided by train cars on a circular track. To be specific, consider an airport with four terminals (A, B, C, and D, naturally). An automated system of train cars circulates among the four terminals. Each car remains at each terminal for a small random period of time, and then proceeds on its way. When braking, each car's velocity decreases by one meter per second; when accelerating, velocity increases by one meter per second. A car's stopping distance, then, is a simple function of its velocity:

$$stop\_dist(0) == 0$$
$$stop\_dist(v) == v + stop\_dist(v-1)$$

(In other words, stop_dist is the sum from 0 to v of v.) A car begins braking whenever the distance to the next station or to the car ahead (whichever is closer) is less than or equal to a conservative stopping distance, based on current velocity plus one. When not at rest in the station, each car is either accelerating or braking.

The station is four cars long, to accommodate this vastly over-simple algorithm; the patrons do not seem to mind that cars tend to jerk viciously, both in the station and on the track. And in any event, the track is 1000 meters long, but the display resolution is only 100 positions, so the car appears to stand still in the station. The track layout of the airport is, by a remarkable coincidence, the exact layout that was provided by the plot_trk function in Section 5.5:

```
                    . . . . . . . . . . . . . . . . . . . .
                  .                                           .
                .                         C                     .
              .                                                   .
            .                                                       .
          .                                                           .
        .                                                               .
      .                                                                   .
    . D                                                                   B .
    .                                                                       .
    .                                                                       .
      .                                                                   .
        .                                                               .
          .                                                           .
            .                                                       .
              .                                                   .
                .                         A                     .
                  .                                           .
                    . . . . . . . . . . . . . . . . . . . .
```

The question of interest is, what is the number of cars which provides the greatest number of station stops per hour?

The program models the cars as nodes on a deque. (The "car" structure is a CAR.) The car just ahead of car p is located via

```
psucc = (CAR *)DQ_SUCC(p);
```

This is the program:

```
run_cars.c:
    /* run_cars - simulate airport terminal train cars */
    #include "deque.h"
    #include "screen.h"
    #define TRKSIZE 1000
    #define CAR struct car
    CAR
        {
        CAR *left;        /* pointer to previous deque node; !NULL */
        CAR *right;       /* pointer to next deque node; !NULL */
        short pos;        /* position on track; {0:TRKSIZE-1} */
        short vel;        /* velocity; {0:SHORT_MAX} */
        char ident[2];    /* identifier for this car; {"a":"z"} */
        };
    void init();              /* initialize the simulation */
    void run();               /* run one time step */
    DQ_NODE *cars = NULL;     /* pointer to master deque node */
    CAR *p = NULL;            /* pointer to a CAR */
    short ncars = 0;          /* number of cars on track; {2:26} */
    char idents[] = "abcdefghijklmnopqrstuvwxyz";
    main(ac, av)
        int ac;
        char *av[];
        {
        short t;              /* loop counter */
        SCR_CMDCHAR c;        /* input from keyboard */

        if (ac < 2)
            error("usage: run_cars  #-of-cars", "");
        ncars = atoi(av[1]);
        if (ncars < 2 || ncars > 26)
            error("#-of-cars must be between 2 and 26", "");
        scr_open();
        scr_clear();
        scr_curs(21, 40); scr_putc('A');
        scr_curs(11, 75); scr_putc('B');
        scr_curs( 1, 40); scr_putc('C');
        scr_curs(11,  5); scr_putc('D');
        init();
        do {
            for (t = 0; t < 200; ++t)
                run();
            scr_curs(scr_lins - 1, 0);
            scr_print("More? ");
            scr_refresh();
            c = scr_getkey();
            scr_putc(c);
            } while (c == 'y');
        scr_close();
        exit(SUCCEED);
        }
```

```
/* init - initialize the simulation */
void init()
    {
    short i;             /* loop counter; {0:ncars-1} */

    DQ_OPEN(&cars);
    for (i = 0; i < ncars; ++i)
        {
        p = (CAR *)malloc(sizeof(CAR));
        if (p == NULL)
            error("out of space", "");
        p->pos = i * (TRKSIZE / ncars);
        p->vel = 0;
        p->ident[0] = idents[i];
        p->ident[1] = '\0';
        DQ_APPEND(cars, p);
        }
    }
/* run - run the simulation for one time step */
void run()
    {
    short to_station;    /* distance to next station */
    short to_car;        /* distance to next car */
    short to_stop;       /* safe distance required to stop this car */
    short i;             /* loop counter */
    CAR *psucc;          /* ptr to successor of car p */

    EACH_DQ(cars, p, CAR)
        {
        plot_trk(p->pos / (TRKSIZE/100), ' ');
        p->pos = IMOD(p->pos + p->vel, TRKSIZE);
        plot_trk(p->pos / (TRKSIZE/100), p->ident[0]);
        to_station = IMOD(p->pos, TRKSIZE / 4);
        psucc = (CAR *)DQ_SUCC(cars, p);
        to_car = IMOD(psucc->pos - p->pos, TRKSIZE);
        for (i = 1, to_stop = 0; i <= p->vel+1; ++i)
            to_stop += i;
        if (to_car < 10)
            p->vel = 0;                  /* screeching halt */
        else if (to_station <= 5)
            p->vel = rand() & 0x1;  /* random jerk in station */
        else if (MIN(to_station, to_car) < to_stop && p->vel > 0)
            --p->vel;                    /* slow down */
        else
            ++p->vel;                    /* speed up */
        }
    scr_refresh();
    }
```

7.5 Trees

A binary *tree* is a data structure consisting of *branch nodes* which contain pointers to sub-trees, and *leaf nodes* which do not point to other nodes. In the diagram below, there are two branch nodes (*b* and *d*), and three leaf nodes (*a c*, and *e*).

```
      d
     / \
    b   e
   / \
  a   c
```

The top node is known as the *root node*. A node immediately below a branch node is known as its *child*; the branch immediately above a node is its *parent*.

Referring to the small diagram above, if the node names can be taken as indicative of some ordering of the data, then this tree illustrates the use of a tree for storing data in ordered sequence. Every node in a left subtree compares low to the branch above it, and every node in a right subtree compares high.

One common implementation of trees in C uses two pointers in each node to access the left and right subtrees. In the leaf nodes, the pointers are null. The illustration above might look like this in C structures:

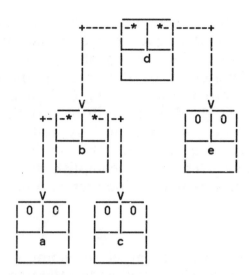

According to the packaging conventions of this chapter, we define a `TR_NODE` ("tree node") like this:

```
#define TR_NODE struct tr_node
TR_NODE
    {
    TR_NODE *right;
    TR_NODE *left;
    /* ... */
    };
```

In the simplest representation, each tree is accessed through a single *root pointer*. In this simple form, "opening a tree" consists of assigning NULL to its root pointer:

```
#define TR_OPEN(ppt) (*(ppt) = NULL)
```

Now we can define the properties of the (binary) tree pointed to by `pt`:

0.   If `pt` is NULL, the tree is empty, i.e., has no nodes.

N.   Otherwise, the node `*pt` is the *root node* of the tree. The pointers `pt->right` and `pt->left` point to trees which are called the *subtrees* of the node `*pt`. None of the `right` and `left` pointers within either subtree of the root node point back to the root node (i.e., there are no "cycles").

Notice that, unlike the other data structures of this chapter, the tree has a recursive definition. The tree consists of its root node and the two (possibly empty) subtrees. And what does a (non-empty) subtree consist of? Its root node and more subtrees of its own.

As with our other data structures, we will assume that each node being installed in a tree has been allocated unique storage by the calling function, and that we will simply splice its existing storage into the structure of the tree. The simplest (and often the only) place to install a node is as a leaf, either as the left subtree of an existing leaf, or as the right subtree of an existing leaf, or as the first node to be installed in the tree. In all three cases, some pointer which is initially null will be assigned the address of the node being installed; this initially-null pointer is the link-in of the new node. Thus, to accomplish the insertion we need a pointer to a pointer to tree nodes ("pointer to link-in of node"):

```
TR_NODE **pln;
```

To get ready for the insertion, pln must be caused to point to the pointer which should receive the address of the new node. Here are the three cases:

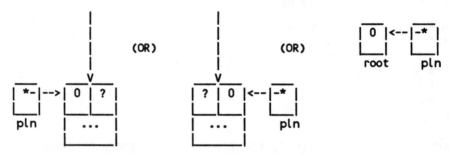

Once pln points to the proper insertion point, and the node to be inserted is pointed to by some pointer d, say, the actual insertion is accomplished by

```
*pln = d;
```

after which the node pointed to by d has become a leaf of the tree.

After the insertion, the new node is part of the tree, and there is some link-in pointer — some node's left pointer, some right pointer, or the root pointer itself — which points to the new node. The link-in is that unique pointer by which the node is made part of the tree, and it will play an important part in the algorithms to follow.

Trees are often processed by recursive algorithms, because their structure naturally lends itself to recursion. For example, given a pointer cmpfn to an ordering function, the tr_insert function involves a simple recursion:

```
tr_insert:
    /* tr_insert - insert a single node in tree (recursive version) */
    #include "tree.h"
    void tr_insert(plt, pn, cmpfn)
        TR_NODE **plt;          /* ptr to link-in of tree or subtree */
        TR_NODE *pn;            /* ptr to node to be inserted */
        int (*cmpfn)();         /* ptr to comparison function */
        {
        TR_NODE *pt;            /* ptr to tree (or subtree) */
        int cmp;                /* result of key comparison; neg, zero, or pos */

        pt = *plt;              /* pt now pts to current tree (if any) */
        if (pt == NULL)         /* if plt pointed to a null pointer, */
            {
            pn->left = pn->right = NULL;    /* has no sub trees yet */
            *plt = pn;          /* then this is the place to install pn; do so */
            }
        else if ((cmp = (*cmpfn)(pn, pt)) == 0) /* if already in tree, */
            return;                              /* then don't install */
        else if (cmp < 0)                   /* if node's key compares low */
            TR_INSERT(&pt->left, pn, cmpfn);    /* then insert in left tree */
        else                                /* otherwise, */
            TR_INSERT(&pt->right, pn, cmpfn);   /* insert in right tree */
        }
```

Searching a tree for a match to a specified key is equally simple, in this recursive form.

```
tr_lfind(#1):
    /* tr_lfind - find node matching a specified key
     * recursive version
     * never returns NULL
     */
    #include "tree.h"
    TR_NODE **tr_lfind(plt, pn, cmpfn)
        TR_NODE **plt;              /* ptr to link-in of tree or subtree */
        TR_NODE *pn;                /* ptr to structure containing key to match */
        int (*cmpfn)();             /* ptr to comparison function */
        {
        TR_NODE *pt;                /* ptr to current tree */
        int cmp;                    /* comparison result: neg, zero, pos */

        pt = *plt;                  /* pt now points to current tree */
        if (pt == NULL)             /* if plt points to a null pointer, */
            return (plt);           /* the data isn't in the tree */
        else if ((cmp = (*cmpfn)(pn, pt)) == 0) /* if key already in tree, */
            return (plt);                        /* return its node's link-in */
        else if (cmp < 0)                   /* if key compares low, */
            return (TR_LFIND(&pt->left, pn, cmpfn));    /* search in left tree */
        else                                /* otherwise, */
            return (TR_LFIND(&pt->right, pn, cmpfn));   /* search in right tree */
        }
```

The recursion can take a lot of stack space and CPU time, so we will look at an equivalent iterative version:

```
tr_lfind(#2):
    /* tr_lfind - find node matching a specified key
     * iterative version
     * never returns NULL
     */
    #include "tree.h"
    TR_NODE **tr_lfind(plt, pn, cmpfn)
        TR_NODE **plt;              /* ptr to link-in of tree or subtree */
        TR_NODE *pn;                /* ptr to structure containing key to match */
        int (*cmpfn)();             /* ptr to comparison function */
        {
        TR_NODE *pt;                /* ptr to current tree */
        int cmp;                    /* comparison result: neg, zero, pos */

        FOREVER
            {
            pt = *plt;              /* pt now points to current tree */
            if (pt == NULL)         /* if plt points to a null pointer, */
                return (plt);       /* the data isn't in the tree */
            else if ((cmp = (*cmpfn)(pn, pt)) == 0) /* if key already in tree, */
                return (plt);       /* return its node's link-in */
            else if (cmp < 0)       /* if key compares low, */
                plt = &pt->left;    /* then search in left tree */
            else                    /* otherwise, */
                plt = &pt->right;   /* search in right tree */
            }
        }
```

A similar function can locate the link-in to the parent of a specified node in the tree:

```
tr_lpfind:
    /* tr_lpfind - find parent of node matching a specified key
     * iterative version
     * never returns NULL; may return addr of null ptr
     */
    #include "tree.h"
    static TR_NODE *nullp = NULL;    /* used to return addr of null ptr */
    TR_NODE **tr_lpfind(plt, pn, cmpfn)
        TR_NODE **plt;              /* ptr to link-in of tree or subtree */
        TR_NODE *pn;                /* ptr to structure containing key to match */
        int (*cmpfn)();             /* ptr to comparison function */
    {
        TR_NODE *pt;                /* ptr to current tree */
        TR_NODE **plp;              /* ptr to link-in of parent of tree */
        int cmp;                    /* comparison result: neg, zero, pos */

        plp = &nullp;                       /* root has no parent */
        FOREVER
            {
            pt = *plt;                      /* pt now points to current tree */
            if (pt == NULL)                 /* if plt points to a null pointer, */
                return (&nullp);            /* the data isn't in the tree */
            else if ((cmp = (*cmpfn)(pn, pt)) == 0) /* if key already in tree, */
                return (plp);               /* return its parent's link-in */
            plp = plt;                  /* before starting subtree, save plt */
            if (cmp < 0)                    /* if key compares low, */
                plt = &pt->left;            /* then search in left tree */
            else                            /* otherwise, */
                plt = &pt->right;   /* search in right tree */
            }
    }
```

Notice that tr_lfind and tr_lpfind return the link-in, not a pointer to the found node itself. The link-in is more generally useful; for example, it will allow us to detach a node without tracing down from the root.

```
tr_detach:
    /* tr_detach - detach node (or subtree) from tree, given link-in
     */
    #include "tree.h"
    TR_NODE *tr_detach(pln)
        TR_NODE **pln;      /* ptr to link-in of node to be detached */
        {
        TR_NODE *p;

        p = *pln;           /* hold the address of the node */
        *pln = NULL;        /* detach the node */
        return (p);         /* return its address */
        }
```

The tr_detach function has entirely detached a single node or a whole subtree and handed its address back to the calling function. It is no longer part of the tree, and when the calling function is finished

with it, its storage must be freed in some fashion. One easy way is to
use a function:

```
tr_close:
    /* tr_close - free a tree or subtree */
    #include "tree.h"
    void tr_close(plt)
        TR_NODE **plt;              /* ptr to link-in of tree */
        {
        TR_NODE *pt;                /* ptr to root of tree */

        pt = *plt;                  /* pt now points to root of tree */
        if (pt == NULL)             /* if link-in is NULL, */
            return;                 /* nothing to do, so return */
        TR_CLOSE(&pt->left);        /* free left subtree */
        TR_CLOSE(&pt->right);       /* free right subtree */
        free(pt);                   /* free the node itself */
        }
```

Assuming that the tree has been built in some ordered sequence,
the "first" node in the tree (the one that compares lowest in the ordering sequence) is the "left-most" node in the tree, i.e., the node that is
found by following the left subtree pointers:

```
tr_lfirst:
    /* tr_lfirst - find first node in tree
     * Returned value is ptr to link-in of first node
     * never returns NULL, and never points to null ptr
     */
    #include "tree.h"
    TR_NODE **tr_lfirst(plt)
        TR_NODE **plt;              /* ptr to (non-null) link-in of tree */
        {
        TR_NODE **pln;              /* ptr to link-in of node */

        for (pln = plt; (*pln)->left != NULL; pln = &(*pln)->left)
            ;
        return (pln);
        }
```

One of the trickiest operations on a sorted tree is to find the successor of a given node, i.e., the node which follows it in sorted
sequence. There are several cases. If the node has a right subtree, the
successor is the "first" node in the right subtree. The successor of *a* is
b, in this diagram:

```
      a
     / \
   ...  d
       / \
      c  ...
     /
    b
```

If the node has no right subtree, and the node is the left subnode of its parent, then its successor is its parent node. (In the diagram, the successor of *c* is *d*.)

Finally, if neither of the above cases applies, the node has no successor; it is the last node in the tree.

```
tr_lnext:
    /* tr_lnext - find the successor of node pn
     * Returned value is ptr to link-in of successor node
     * Never returns NULL; may return addr of a null ptr
     */
    #include "tree.h"
    static TR_NODE *nullp = NULL;   /* used to return addr of null ptr */
    TR_NODE **tr_lnext(plt, pn, cmpfn)
        TR_NODE **plt;              /* ptr to link-in of tree */
        TR_NODE *pn;                /* ptr to specific node of tree */
        int (*cmpfn)();             /* ptr to comparison function */
        {
        TR_NODE **pls;              /* ptr to link-in of successor */
        TR_NODE **pln;              /* ptr to link-in of a TR_NODE */

        if (pn->right != NULL)  /* if node has a right subtree, */
            { /* return ptr to link-in of "leftmost"  node in right subtree */
            return (TR_LFIRST(&pn->right));
            }
        else                            /* if node has no right subtree, */
            {         /* return ptr to link-in of parent of pn */
            pln = TR_LPFIND(plt, pn, cmpfn);
            if (*pln != NULL && (*pln)->left == pn)
                return (pln);           /* node is left subtree of parent */
            else
                return (&nullp);     /* node is rightmost in tree */
            }
        }
```

We can use TR_LFIRST and TR_LNEXT to construct an EACH_TR macro:

```
#define EACH_TR(plt, p, t, fn) \
    for (p = (t *)*TR_LFIRST(plt); (p) != NULL; p = (t *)*TR_LNEXT(plt, p, fn))
```

(The tr_lnext function is rather slow for this purpose. See the exercises below for suggestions for faster methods.)

The final operation that we consider is the deletion of a node in an ordered tree. Simply detaching the node is insufficient; we must be sure that the remaining tree is still ordered. In all cases, we assume that we have a pointer, pln, to the link-in of the node to be deleted, possibly provided by tr_lfind. Three cases must be considered. (1) If the node being deleted is a leaf, we simply detach it which sets its link-in to NULL. The detached node, having no children, is then freed. The deletion of *b* fits this case:

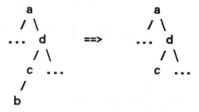

(2) If the node has only one child, we will set the node's link-in to point to the child node, and then free the node itself, as shown by the deletion of *c*:

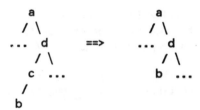

(3) If the node has two children, we need to locate its successor. As we saw earlier, since the node has a right subtree, its successor is the "leftmost" node in that right subtree. Therefore, the successor itself cannot have a left subtree, so the successor's place can be taken by its right subnode, and the successor itself moved into the place of the deleted node. After all this, the node can be freed. This is how *a* would be deleted:

```
    a                  b
   / \                / \
... d      ==>    ... d
   / \                / \
  c ...              c ...
 /
b
```

Expressed in C, here is what it looks like:

```
tr_delete:
    /* tr_delete - delete the node **pln from tree *plt
     */
    #include "tree.h"
    void tr_delete(plt, pln, cmpfn)
        TR_NODE **plt;          /* ptr to link-in of tree */
        TR_NODE **pln;          /* ptr to link-in of node */
        int (*cmpfn)();         /* ptr to comparison function */
        {
        TR_NODE *pn;            /* ptr to specific node of tree */
        TR_NODE *ps;            /* ptr to node's successor */
        TR_NODE **pls;          /* ptr to link-in of successor */

        pn = *pln;                      /* pn pts to the node to delete */
        if (pn->right == NULL)          /* if node has no right subtree, */
            {
            if (pn->left == NULL)   /* if node has no children, */
                *pln = NULL;        /* replacement for pn is NULL */
            else                    /* if node has L subtree, but not R, */
                *pln = pn->left;    /* replacement is pn's L subtree */
            }
        else if (pn->left == NULL)  /* if node has R subtree, but not L */
            *pln = pn->right;       /* replacement is pn's R subtree */
        else                        /* if node has R and L subtrees */
            {
            pls = TR_LNEXT(plt, pn, cmpfn); /* get ptr to link-in of succ */
            ps = *pls;                  /* ps now points to successor */
            *pls = ps->right;           /* succ's R subtree takes succ's place */
            ps->right = pn->right;      /* succ acquires node's R ... */
            ps->left = pn->left;        /* ... and L subtree */
            *pln = ps;                  /* replacement is successor */
            }
        free(pn);
        }
```

The tree.h header summarizes the tree functions from this section:

tree.h:

```
    /* tree.h - header for tree functions
     */
    #ifndef TREE_H
    #define TREE_H
    #include "local.h"
    #include "pointer.h"
    #define TR_NODE struct tr_node
    TR_NODE
        {
        TR_NODE *right;
        TR_NODE *left;
        /* ... */
        };
    void tr_close();        /* PARMS(TR_NODE **plt) */
    void tr_delete();       /* PARMS(TR_NODE **plt, TR_NODE **pln, int (*cmpfn)()) */
    TR_NODE *tr_detach();   /* PARMS(TR_NODE **pln) */
    void tr_insert();       /* PARMS(TR_NODE **plt, TR_NODE *pn, int (*cmpfn)()) */
    TR_NODE **tr_lfind();   /* PARMS(TR_NODE **plt, TR_NODE *pn, int (*cmpfn)()) */
    TR_NODE **tr_lfirst();  /* PARMS(TR_NODE **plt) */
    TR_NODE **tr_lpfind();  /* PARMS(TR_NODE **plt, TR_NODE *pn, int (*cmpfn)()) */
    TR_NODE **tr_lnext();   /* PARMS(TR_NODE **plt, TR_NODE *pn, int (*cmpfn)()) */

    #define TR_RIGHT(p)     ((p)->right)
    #define TR_LEFT(p)      ((p)->left)

    #define TR_P(p)         PNNC(p, TR_NODE *)
    #define TR_PP(p)        PNNC(p, TR_NODE **)

    #define TR_CLOSE(plt)              tr_close(TR_PP(plt))
    #define TR_DELETE(plt, pln, fn)    tr_delete(TR_PP(plt), TR_PP(pln), fn)
    #define TR_DETACH(pln)             tr_detach(TR_PP(pln))
    #define TR_INSERT(plt, pn, fn)     tr_insert(TR_PP(plt), TR_P(pn), fn)
    #define TR_LFIND(plt, pn, fn)      tr_lfind(TR_PP(plt), TR_P(pn), fn)
    #define TR_LFIRST(plt)             tr_lfirst(TR_PP(plt))
    #define TR_LPFIND(plt, pn, fn)     tr_lpfind(TR_PP(plt), TR_P(pn), fn)
    #define TR_LNEXT(plt, pn, fn)      tr_lnext(TR_PP(plt), TR_P(pn), fn)

    /* true macros */
    #define TR_OPEN(plt)               (*(plt) = NULL)
    #define TR_FIRST(plt)              (*TR_LFIRST(plt))
    #define TR_FIND(plt, pn, fn)       (*TR_LFIND(plt, pn, fn))
    #define TR_NEXT(plt, pn, fn)       (*TR_LNEXT(plt, pn, fn))
    #define EACH_TR(plt, p, t, fn) \
        for (p = (t *)*TR_LFIRST(plt); (p) != NULL; p = (t *)*TR_LNEXT(plt, p, fn))
    #endif
```

Exercise 7-1. If a revised version of tr_lfirst and tr_lnext cooperated to create a traversal stack, the time to perform EACH_TR could be drastically reduced. Define a "visit state" for each node: 1 means its left subtree is being visited, 2 means that the node itself is being visited, 3 means that the right subtree is being visited. Here are the five states of the traversal stack while traversing the following tree:

```
    b            1 b      2 b        3 b        3 b        3 b
   / \
  a   d          2 a                 1 d        2 d        3 d
     / \
    c   e                            2 c                   2 e
```

We now have all the functions that we would need to maintain an in-memory "database" of PARTS records, suitable for use with the "parts menu" program from the previous chapter.

part_db_tr.c:

```
/* part_db_tr.c - simulated database access to parts
 * uses binary tree for in-memory storage
 */
#include "tree.h"
#include "part.h"
#define TPART struct tr_part
TPART
    {
    TPART *right;
    TPART *left;
    PART part;
    };
static TPART tpart = {0};
static TPART *parts = NULL;

/* db_cmp_part - comparison function for database access */
static int db_cmp_part(p1, p2)
    TPART *p1, *p2;
    {
    return (strcmp(p1->part.part_no, p2->part.part_no));
    }
/* (more) */
```

```
/* db_add_part - add a part record to database */
bool db_add_part(partp)
    PART *partp;
    {
    TPART *p;

    p = (TPART *)malloc(sizeof(TPART));
    if (p == NULL)
        {
        remark("Part storage is full", "");
        return (NO);
        }
    STRUCTASST(p->part, *partp);
    TR_INSERT(&parts, p, db_cmp_part);
    return (YES);
    }
```

```
/* db_find_part - find a part record in database */
bool db_find_part(partp)
    PART *partp;
    {
    TPART *pn;        /* ptr to part record in tree */

    STRUCTASST(tpart.part, *partp);
    pn = (TPART *)TR_FIND(&parts, &tpart, db_cmp_part);
    if (pn == NULL)
        return (NO);
    STRUCTASST(*partp, pn->part);
    return (YES);
    }
/* db_del_part - delete a part record in database */
bool db_del_part(partp)
    PART *partp;
    {
    TPART **pln;          /* ptr to link-in of part record in tree */

    STRUCTASST(tpart.part, *partp);
    pln = (TPART **)TR_LFIND(&parts, &tpart, db_cmp_part);
    if (*pln == NULL)
        {
        remark("No record for this part", "");
        return (NO);
        }
    TR_DELETE(&parts, pln, db_cmp_part);
    return (YES);
    }
/* db_chg_part - change a part record in database */
bool db_chg_part(partp)
    PART *partp;
    {
    TPART *pn;        /* ptr to part record in tree */

    STRUCTASST(tpart.part, *partp);
    pn = (TPART *)TR_FIND(&parts, &tpart, db_cmp_part);
    if (pn == NULL)       /* validation done in menu should prevent */
        return (NO);    /* non-existent part from reaching here */
    STRUCTASST(pn->part, *partp);
    return (YES);
    }
/* (more) */
```

```
/* db_open_part - open a part record database */
void db_open_part()
    {
    TR_OPEN(&parts);
    }

/* db_close_part - close the part record database */
void db_close_part()
    {
    TR_CLOSE(&parts);
    }
```

CHAPTER 8: FILES

8.1 Standard (Default) Files

One of the virtues that C inherited from UNIX systems is a uniform concept of data transfer through files. A file, to a C program, is a transmission stream of bytes to or from the main memory. The ultimate source or sink for the bytes may be of many forms: disk file, tape, printer, communication channel to other programs, etc. With a few exceptions, the C program can be written independent of the ultimate source or sink.

One important distinction about files is present in most operating systems except for UNIX: the distinction between *binary files* and *text files*.

A binary file is a one-for-one transmission stream of bytes. If a program writes a binary file onto an external medium, that file will read byte-for-byte the same when read back in as a binary file (provided that the same compiler and machine are used both times). However, some implementations may append extra nul characters to conform to binary block-size conventions.

A text file is a mapping between internal machine bytes and external conventions for representation of text. For example, some implementations map the newline ('\n') into a two-character sequence (carriage-return, newline). Some append a ctrl-Z character to mark the end of file. Some systems delete some nonprinting characters from text files.

On UNIX systems, of course, there are no such distinctions. On other systems, binary files might seem simpler to use and understand, but on such systems most of the utility programs that deal with text will expect to see files that conform to the text-file conventions. Therefore, on non-UNIX systems, the default type for files will generally be the text file.

The most portable scheme for accessing files originated with UNIX 7th Edition. Each file is represented by a FILE structure, whose contents are specified by the header <stdio.h>. (A FILE object is, strictly speaking, not required to be a C structure, but most implementations do define it that way.) Such files have generally been implemented with buffers associated with the structure, so they have sometimes been referred to as "buffered" files. Since each operating system may have its own treatment of I/O buffers, we will follow ANSI C in adopting the more neutral term *stream file* to designate the type of file represented by a FILE structure.

8.2 Processing Named Files

To perform I/O on files opened by name, we use the function fopen:

```
FILE *fp;

fp = fopen("input.dat", "r");
```

will open the file input.dat for reading ("r"). The variable fp was declared as a pointer to FILE. After the fopen call, fp will point to a FILE properly initialized for reading. If the open fails, fp will contain a NULL pointer; hence this rule:

Rule 8-1: Always test the returned value from fopen to be sure that the open succeeded.

The reasons why an open might fail are implementation-defined; some possible reasons are that no file exists by the specified name, or the file may exist but be unreadable to the program, or the program has already opened the maximum allowable number of files.

The file-name argument must specify a name in a format acceptable to the host system, and systems differ in their naming rules for files. In general, a name in the form xxxxxx.xxx, where x is a letter or a digit, will be acceptable to most C environments. Name formats such as /tmp/t11111, a:infile, or [70,40]datfil will work only on some systems.

Note that the environment may be allowed some liberty in mapping the name string into a system's format for file names, for example by mapping lower case into upper case, or by mapping the "dot" (.) into some other character.

Note also that the file name may specify a device (terminal, printer, tape drive, etc.) if the host system provides the appropriate name mapping. However, there are no standard names for any devices, so such usage is potentially non-portable.

A file thus opened for reading can be used with functions analogous to the default-input functions shown earlier:

Named-file function	Default-file function
getc(fp)	getchar()
fscanf(fp, fmt, ...)	scanf(fmt, ...)
fgets(s, n, fp)	gets(s)

Note, however, that `fgets` (unlike `getc` and `fscanf`) is not functionally equivalent to its default-file version: `fgets` takes an argument specifying the size of the available storage in `s`, and `fgets` does not delete the newline from the input characters (whereas `gets` does delete the newline).

A file can be opened for output by specifying `"w"` as its usage. If the file existed previously, it will be truncated to zero length. If it did not exist, it is created with zero length. Output functions analogous to the default-file versions are available:

Named-file function	Default-file function
putc(c, fp)	putchar(c)
fprintf(fp, fmt, ...)	printf(fmt, ...)
fputs(s, fp)	puts(s)

As with `gets`, there is a functional difference between `fputs` and `puts`: `fputs` does not tack a newline onto its output, whereas `puts` does.

A third option available from `fopen` is `"a"` ("append") mode. The previous contents of the file (if any) are left undisturbed; each write operation will take place at the end of the file.

Besides the functions above which have default-file analogs, there are a few functions available only in their named-file versions, notably `fread`, and `fwrite`. The call

```
n = fread(s, elt_size, num_elts, fp);
```

will read a designated number of elements (each of a designated size) into the object pointed to by `s`, using the file specified by `fp`. The returned value tells how many elements were successfully read. A return of zero is ambiguous; it might indicate end-of-file, or it might reflect the occurrence of an I/O error before any elements were read.

A call upon feof(fp) will return YES if the file fp is at end-of-file, and NO otherwise. Similarly, ferror(fp) will tell whether any I/O errors have taken place on the file. A program can call clearerr(fp) to clear both the end-of-file and the I/O error indicators for the file.

When fread is called upon to read an array of char's, with elt_size specified as 1, the usage is portable onto any system. If the elements are multi-byte data, the byte-ordering is environment-dependent. Similarly for writing files with fwrite:

```
n = fwrite(s, elt_size, num_elts, fp);
```

will write a designated number of elements (each of a designated size) onto the file specified by fp.

When the program is finished with a file, the file should be closed via fclose(fp).

As mentioned in Section 5.2, the buffering behavior of a file can be changed by calling the setbuf function after opening the file but prior to any file accesses. Calling setbuf(fp, NULL) turns off the buffering; calling setbuf(fp, mybuf) causes the array mybuf (which should be of size BUF-SIZ) to be used as the buffer for file fp. One use for the latter option might be an environment in which dynamic "heap" memory is limited; a statically-declared buffer can be used instead of one that would be dynamically allocated by the I/O functions.

8.3 Direct Access and Fseek

If a stream file is accessing a "seekable" medium (such as a disk or diskette), a certain measure of direct access is provided by the functions fseek and ftell. For now, we will continue to discuss "text" files, which are the type of file that is specified by the "r", "w", and "a" modes of fopen. The number of char's actually read by a C program, or the number of char's written by the program, may be different from the number of bytes recorded in the file (in a non-UNIX environment). For example, some systems record two bytes (carriage-return, newline) at the end of each text line, but the C program will only see the '\n' (newline) character.

During the reading or writing of a file, the program can call

```
position = ftell(fp);
```

which sets `position` to a `long` integer that represents the current position of the file. At some later time, the program could call

```
success = fseek(fp, position, SEEK_SET);
```

which would re-position the file to the same place where the original `ftell` call was performed. A `success` return of zero indicates no errors; anything else is an error. (The name `SEEK_SET` is defined in various places in recent C libraries: `<unistd.h>` for systems conforming to the /usr/group standard, `<stdio.h>` and also `<stddef.h>` according to draft ANSI C. If neither definition is available, put one in your `stddef.h` header. The conventional definition for `SEEK_SET` is zero.)

It is possible to test whether a file is on a "seekable" device by using

```
seekable = (fseek(fp, 0L, SEEK_CUR) == 0);
```

where `SEEK_CUR` is conventionally equal to 1. This call of `fseek` specifies a displacement of zero bytes relative to the current position. In other words, it has no effect except to test the returned value from `fseek`. (If `fp` turns out not to specify a seekable file, its error indicator will be set as a result of the call to `fseek`. Invoking `clearerr(fp)` will clear the error indicator.)

A text file can be positioned to the end of the file, by calling

```
success = fseek(fp, 0L, SEEK_END);
```

where `SEEK_END` is conventionally equal to 2.

And a file can be re-positioned to the very beginning by calling

```
success = fseek(fp, 0L, SEEK_SET);
```

Because of the text-mapping problem, these four usages of `fseek` are the only ones that can be portably used on text files.

It is possible to `fopen` a file for both reading and writing, but because of the text-mapping problem, these read/write modes are difficult to use on text files. It is time to discuss binary I/O.

8.4 Binary I/O

In the library proposed for ANSI C, a trailing b can be appended to the fopen mode string to indicate a binary file. For example,

```
fopen("payroll.dat", "rb")
```

would open the binary file payroll.dat for reading. Here, then, is the complete list of mode options for fopen:

Text	Binary	Action
"r"	"rb"	Open for reading
"w"	"wb"	Truncate or create for writing
"a"	"ab"	Open or create for writing at end
"r+"	"r+b"	Open for reading and writing
"w+"	"w+b"	Truncate or create for reading and writing
"a+"	"a+b"	Open or create for reading and writing at end

The "reading and writing" modes are most generally useful in binary mode, since over-writing a text file can give unpredictable results; the new text may take more or less space than the previous file contents. In binary mode, however, the number of bytes written into the file is exactly the number of characters specified by the program. (Some environments may provide binary treatment for r+, w+, and a+ modes even without the trailing b on the mode.)

We could, for example, treat a binary file as consisting of a number of fixed-size records, each of which can be read, modified in some way, and then written back into its previous space:

```
FILE *fp;

fp = fopen("records.dat", "r+b");
if (fp == NULL)
    error("can't open", "records.dat");
/* ... */
if (fseek(fp, (long)recno * recsize, SEEK_SET) != 0) /* seek the record */
    can't find specified record
if (fread(rec, recsize, 1, fp) != 1)     /* read the record */
    can't read the record
modify the record contents
if (fseek(fp, (long)recno * recsize, SEEK_SET) != 0) /* seek record again */
    can't find record
if (fwrite(rec, recsize, 1, fp) != 1)    /* re-write the record */
    can't rewrite record
```

To allow reasonably efficient treatment of buffered files, it is required that an fseek must be performed when switching from reading to writing, or vice versa.

There are some problems involved with this form of binary I/O. For one, many versions of fread and fwrite do not perform very efficiently when used in this manner. And many existing compilers will complain about the b in a mode string. For these reasons, the next section will present a different approach to binary I/O.

8.5 Record I/O

Most existing implementations of C provide another set of functions for performing record-oriented I/O, namely the functions open, close, read, write, and lseek. (These functions are sometimes known as the "file-descriptor library," because they refer to files by numbers known as file descriptors, rather than by the "pointer to FILE" mechanism provided for stream files.) In many implementations they are the most efficient functions for the purpose. They are, however, implemented with a variety of system-dependent options and behaviors, and they will probably not be part of the ANSI C standard. If we restrict ourselves to the problem of doing record-oriented I/O on seekable devices like disks, we can still make effective use of this type of functions.

Our approach will be to provide a header to give access to a set of functions to be known as bin_open, bin_close, bin_read, bin_write, and bin_lseek. On systems with direct equivalents in the underlying library, these names can simply be mapped into the corresponding library name. On other systems, some new C functions must be provided, possibly making use of the (ANSI-style) stream library. Thus, the actual implementation of bin_open will be system-dependent, but the program that calls bin_open will itself be portable [8-1].

We must define a new header, bin_io.h, which will provide the necessary mappings. This version of the bin_io.h header will work on MS-DOS (with Lattice), Idris, and UNIX systems:

```
bin_io.h:
    /* bin_io.h - header for binary file I/O functions
     * SYSTEM DEPENDENT - MUST BE CONFIGURED FOR EACH TARGET SYSTEM
     */
    #ifndef BIN_IO_H
    #define BIN_IO_H
    #include "local.h"

    #include "fcntl.h"        /* provide your own if not standard on system */

    typedef int bin_fd;       /* "binary file descriptor" {0:BIN_NFILE-1} */

    #define BIN_NFILE 20      /* adjust to local system */

    #define O_RWMODE (O_RDONLY|O_WRONLY|O_RDWR) /* uses symbols from fcntl.h */

    #ifndef IDRIS
    #define bin_open(s, m)      open(s, m)
    #endif
    #define bin_close(f)        close(f)
    #define bin_lseek(f, o, w)  lseek(f, o, w)
    #define bin_read(f, b, n)   read(f, b, n)
    #define bin_write(f, b, n)  write(f, b, n)

    #endif
```

The header bin_io.h includes another header via

```
    #include "fcntl.h"
```

Many systems already have this header in one of the standard places for
headers. If yours does not, you will need to create one that is compatible with the open options on your system, using this model:

```
fcntl.h:
    /* fcntl.h - definitions for binary  open
     * Compatible with UNIX Sys V, ...
     */
    #ifndef FCNTL_H
    #define FCNTL_H
    #define O_RDONLY 0       /* delete or change to conform to local */
    #define O_WRONLY 1       /* delete or change to conform to local */
    #define O_RDWR   2       /* delete or change to conform to local */
    #define O_NDELAY 4       /* NOT USED BY bin_io FUNCTIONS */
    #define O_APPEND 8       /* delete or change to conform to local */
    #define O_CREAT  0x100   /* delete or change to conform to local */
    #define O_TRUNC  0x200   /* delete or change to conform to local */
    #define O_EXCL   0x400   /* delete or change to conform to local */
    #endif
```

Each of the binary I/O functions sets the global variable errno to a non-
zero value if an error is encountered, and then returns an error indication in the returned value. Here are the descriptions of the binary I/O

functions:

```
int bin_open(fname, mode)
char fname[];            /* : string */
int mode;                /* as described in fcntl.h */
```

opens the file specified by the string fname, according to the specified mode (which is OR'ed together from "fcntl.h " options). The
returned value is an int file descriptor if successful; otherwise, -1
is returned. For the uses of this chapter, the file should be a seekable disk file.

```
int bin_close(fd)
int fd;          /* : {0:BIN_NFILE-1} */
```

closes the file associated with file descriptor fd. The returned
value is zero if successful, otherwise -1.

```
int bin_read(fd, s, n)
int fd;          /* : {0:BIN_NFILE-1} */
data_ptr s;      /* : !NULL */
int n;           /* : {0:INT_MAX} */
```

reads n bytes into the char array s from the file specified by fd.
The returned value is the number of bytes read, or -1 for an I/O
error, or 0 for end-of-file.

```
int bin_write(fd, s, n)
int fd;          /* : {0:BIN_NFILE-1} */
data_ptr s;      /* : !NULL */
int n;           /* : {0:INT_MAX} */
```

writes n bytes from the char array s onto the file specified by fd.
The returned value is the number of bytes written; anything less
than n indicates an error.

```
long bin_lseek(fd, n, whence)
int fd;          /* : {0:BIN_NFILE-1} */
long n;
int whence;      /* : {SEEK_SET, SEEK_CUR, SEEK_END} */
```

seeks n bytes relative to beginning-of-file, current position, or
end-of-file, according to this scheme:

```
SEEK_SET      relative to beginning-of-file   (usually 0)
SEEK_CUR      relative to current position    (usually 1)
SEEK_END      relative to end-of-file         (usually 2)
```

The returned value is the new file position, relative to beginning-of-file, or -1 if any error occurred. Seeking past end-of-file is not portable, and gives different results on different systems. Note that, unlike the stream file functions, the binary I/O functions allow alternation between reading and writing with no intervening seeks.

Now we need to take note of an important problem about binary I/O on some systems. Sometimes, binary files are padded with nul characters at the end of the file, to make the file conform to a local fixed block-size. If we want to have record files that can grow at the end, the only portable approach is to record the file size at the start of the file. To keep this detail out of the application program, and to make access to fixed-size records easier, we can make up a second level of functions, the "record I/O" functions.

The header rec_io.h defines a rec_fd as an int. (In early printings of this book, it was a short integer, but int gives more consistent calling sequences for these functions.) The following functions are provided for record I/O:

```
rec_fd rec_open(fname, mode, recsize)
char fname[];          /* : string */
int mode;              /* as specified in fcntl.h */
int recsize;           /* : {0:SHORT_MAX} */
```

opens the file named by fname for mode (as in fcntl.h), with the record size specified by recsize. Note that the record size is limited to SHORT_MAX, for maximum portability of the functions.

```
int rec_close(fd)
rec_fd fd;             /* : {0:REC_NFILE-1} */
```

closes the file specified by fd. The return values are 0 for success and -1 for errors.

```
bool rec_get(fd, rec, recno)
rec_fd fd;              /* : {0:REC_NFILE-1} */
data_ptr rec;           /* : !NULL */
long recno;             /* : {REC_NEXT,0:rec_nrecs(fd)-1} */
```

reads from fd into rec the record whose record number is recno. If
recno is specified to be REC_NEXT, the next sequential record is read.
The return is YES for success and NO for failure. More detailed (but
system-dependent) error information is available in errno.

```
bool rec_put(fd, rec, recno)
rec_fd fd;              /* : {0:REC_NFILE-1} */
data_ptr rec;           /* : !NULL */
long recno;             /* : {REC_W_END,REC_NEXT,0:rec_nrecs(fd)} */
```

writes onto file fd the contents of rec in the position specified by
recno. If recno is specified as REC_NEXT, the record is written in the
current file position; if it is specified as REC_W_END, the record is
appended at the end of the file, thus extending the file by one
record. The return is YES if success, NO if failure.

```
long rec_nrecs(fd)
rec_fd fd;              /* : {0:REC_NFILE-1} */
```

returns the current number of records in file fd.

```
int rec_recsize(fd)
rec_fd fd;              /* : {0:REC_NFILE-1} */
```

returns the record size associated with file fd.

Here are the listings of the header and the functions in the rec_io
package.

```
rec_io.h:
    /* rec_io.h - header for record file I/O functions */
    #ifndef REC_IO_H
    #define REC_IO_H
    #include "local.h"
    #include "bin_io.h"

    #define REC_NFILE        BIN_NFILE    /* adjust to local system */
    #define REC_NEXT         (-1L)
    #define REC_W_END        (-2L)
    #define REC_NOT_FOUND    (-3L)   /* codes for hashed file access */
    #define REC_FULL         (-4L)   /* codes for hashed file access */
    #define REC_ERROR        (-5L)   /* codes for hashed file access */
    #define REC_AVAIL        'a'     /* codes for hashed file access */
    #define REC_OCCUP        'o'     /* codes for hashed file access */
    #define REC_DELET        'd'     /* codes for hashed file access */
    #define REC_FILE struct rec_file
    REC_FILE
        {
        short _byte0;               /* offset of the first data byte in file */
        short _recsize;             /* size (in bytes) of each record */
        long _nrecs;                /* size (in records) of current file */
        bits _status;               /* open-modes of file */
        };
    #define REC_BYTE0 BUFSIZ
    #define rec_nrecs(fd)   (rec_files[fd]._nrecs + 0)
    #define rec_recsize(fd) (rec_files[fd]._recsize + 0)

    typedef int rec_fd;

    extern int errno;
    extern REC_FILE rec_files[REC_NFILE];

    int rec_close();      /* PARMS(rec_fd fd) */
    rec_fd rec_open();    /* PARMS(char fname[], int type, int recsize) */
    bool rec_get();       /* PARMS(rec_fd fd, data_ptr buf, long i) */
    bool rec_put();       /* PARMS(rec_fd fd, data_ptr buf, long i) */
    long rec_hfind();
    /* PARMS(rec_fd fd, data_ptr keybuf, data_ptr buf, int (*cmp)(), long (*hash)()
    long rec_havail();
    /* PARMS(rec_fd fd, data_ptr keybuf, data_ptr buf, long (*hash)()) */
    #endif
```

The "record file descriptor" (rec_fd) is used as an index into the array
rec_files. The rec_open function gets a file descriptor from bin_open. If
the file existed previously, its REC_FILE information is read. Otherwise,
the REC_FILE information is written out at the head of the new file.

```
rec_open:
    /* rec_open - open a record-binary file */
    #include "rec_io.h"
    REC_FILE rec_files[REC_NFILE] = {0};
    rec_fd rec_open(fname, type, recsize)
        char fname[];
        int type;
        int recsize;
        {
        rec_fd fd;
        REC_FILE *rfp;          /* pointer to a REC_FILE entry */
        int old_errno = errno;  /* save system error indicator */
        short i;                /* counter to clear first record */

        errno = 0;              /* clear error indicator */
        fd = bin_open(fname, type);
        if (fd < 0 || fd >= REC_NFILE)  /* validate fd */
            return (-1);
        rfp = &rec_files[fd];
        bin_lseek(fd, (long)0, SEEK_SET);   /* seek to initial byte of file */
        if ((type & O_RWMODE) == O_WRONLY ||    /* new file: opened write-only, or */
            bin_read(fd, rfp, sizeof(*rfp)) != sizeof(*rfp))    /* can't be read */
            {
            bin_lseek(fd, (long)0, SEEK_SET);
            rfp->_byte0 = REC_BYTE0;
            rfp->_recsize = recsize;
            rfp->_nrecs = 0;
            bin_write(fd, rfp, sizeof(*rfp));
            for (i = 1; i <= REC_BYTE0 - sizeof(*rfp); ++i)
                bin_write(fd, "\0", 1);
            }
        else if (recsize != rfp->_recsize)  /* file exists, but bad recsize */
            {
            bin_close(fd);
            return (-1);
            }
        if (errno == 0)
            {
            errno = old_errno;              /* restore saved value */
            bin_lseek(fd, (long)rfp->_byte0, 0);
            rfp->_status = type;            /* save the open-mode of file */
            return (fd);
            }
        else /* error was returned from some bin_io function */
            {
            bin_close(fd);
            return (-1);
            }
        }
```

```
rec_close:
    /* rec_close - close the REC_FILE fd */
    #include "rec_io.h"
    int rec_close(fd)
        rec_fd fd;
        {
        REC_FILE *rfp;
        int old_errno = errno;

        errno = 0;
        if (fd < 0 || fd >= REC_NFILE)        /* validate fd */
            return (-1);
        rfp = &rec_files[fd];
        if ((rfp->_status & O_RWMODE) == O_RDONLY)
            return (bin_close(fd));           /* if read-only, all done */
        bin_lseek(fd, (long)0, SEEK_SET);
        bin_write(fd, rfp, sizeof(*rfp));     /* write new REC_FILE info */
        bin_close(fd);
        if (errno == 0)
            {
            errno = old_errno;
            return (0);
            }
        else
            {
            return (-1);
            }
        }
```

If the file was opened read-only, rec_close needs only to close the file.
Otherwise, the rec_close function has to write the REC_FILE information
back to the disk. If any errors took place in the low-level I/O functions,
rec_close returns -1.

```
rec_get:
    /* rec_get - read one record from record-binary file */
    #include "rec_io.h"
    bool rec_get(fd, buf, recno)
        rec_fd fd;        /* which file */
        data_ptr buf;     /* where to put the data */
        long recno;       /* {REC_NEXT,0:rec_nrecs(fd)-1} */
        {
        REC_FILE *rfp;
        short n;          /* size of each record */

        if (fd < 0 || fd >= REC_NFILE)  /* validate fd */
            return (NO);
        rfp = &rec_files[fd];
        n = rfp->_recsize;
        if (recno != REC_NEXT && recno < 0 || recno >= rfp->_nrecs)
            return (NO);
        else if (recno == REC_NEXT)
            ;   /* no seek, ready for next record */
        else if (bin_lseek(fd, rfp->_byte0 + recno * n, SEEK_SET) < 0)
            return (NO);
        return (bin_read(fd, buf, n) == n);
        }
```

Aside from the necessary validation of fd and recno, all that rec_get needs
to do is seek to the proper byte and read the record. If either the seek
or the read fails, rec_get returns NO.

```
rec_put:
    /* rec_put - write one record to record-binary file
     */
    #include "rec_io.h"
    bool rec_put(fd, buf, recno)
        rec_fd fd;
        data_ptr buf;    /* where to get the data */
        long recno;      /* {REC_W_END,REC_NEXT,0:rec_nrecs(fd)} */
        {
        REC_FILE *rfp;
        short n;         /* size of each record */

        if (fd < 0 || fd >= REC_NFILE)
            return (NO);
        rfp = &rec_files[fd];
        n = rfp->_recsize;
        if (recno != REC_NEXT && recno != REC_W_END && recno < 0 ||
            recno > rfp->_nrecs)
            return (NO);
        else if (recno == REC_W_END || recno == rfp->_nrecs)
            {
            recno = rfp->_nrecs;    /* block will be added at end */
            ++rfp->_nrecs;          /* extend the file size */
            }
        if (bin_lseek(fd, rfp->_byte0 + recno * n, SEEK_SET) < 0)
            return (NO);
        return (bin_write(fd, buf, n) == n);
        }
```

The parameter recno can be a proper record number, or the coded value REC_W_END (requesting to write onto the end of the file), or the coded value REC_NEXT (requesting to write the next sequential record). After validating fd and recno, rec_put seeks to the appropriate record and writes the new record. The return is YES if success, NO if failure.

The following demonstration program (rec_main) writes a record file consisting of ten records, each containing one long integer. Then it reads the entire file sequentially and prints each number to the standard output. Next it opens the file for reading and writing, and writes new data into the records, using direct access by record numbers. Finally it reads the file with direct access by record numbers and prints each number to the standard output.

rec_main.c:

```
    /* rec_main - simple test harness for rec_io */
    #include "local.h"
    #include "rec_io.h"

    main()
        {
        long lnum;
        long rec_no;
        rec_fd rfd;

        rfd = rec_open("lnum.dat", O_WRONLY|O_CREAT|O_TRUNC, sizeof(lnum));
        if (rfd < 0)
            error("can't open (output)", "lnum.dat");
        for (lnum = 0; lnum <= 9; ++lnum)
            if (!rec_put(rfd, (data_ptr)&lnum, REC_W_END))
                error("rec_put (END) error", "");
        rec_close(rfd);

        rfd = rec_open("lnum.dat", O_RDONLY, sizeof(lnum));
        if (rfd < 0)
            error("can't open (input)", "lnum.dat");
        while (rec_get(rfd, (data_ptr)&lnum, REC_NEXT))
            printf("%4ld\n", lnum);
        rec_close(rfd);

        rfd = rec_open("lnum.dat", O_RDWR, sizeof(lnum));
        if (rfd < 0)
            error("can't open (update-output)", "lnum.dat");
        for (lnum = 109; lnum >= 100; --lnum)
            if (!rec_put(rfd, (data_ptr)&lnum, lnum - 100))
                error("rec_put (direct) error", "");
        rec_close(rfd);

        rfd = rec_open("lnum.dat", O_RDWR, sizeof(lnum));
        if (rfd < 0)
            error("can't open (update-input)", "lnum.dat");
        for (rec_no = 0; rec_no <= 9; ++rec_no)
            {
            if (!rec_get(rfd, (data_ptr)&lnum, rec_no))
                error("rec_get (direct) error", "");
            else if (lnum != rec_no + 100)
                error("bad data on re-read", "");
            else
                printf("%4ld %4ld\n", rec_no, lnum);
            }
        rec_close(rfd);
        exit(SUCCEED);
        }
```

8.6 A Record File with Hashed Access

The simple scheme of integer-numbered records is convenient only when there is an easy mapping from the data to be stored and an integer record number. Very few databases are keyed with such simple integer keys. One way to use record-numbered files with arbitrary keys is to "hash" each key into an integer:

```
for (p = part.part_no; *p != '\0'; ++p)
    sum += *p;
rec_no = IMOD(sum, rec_nrecs(fd));
```

Here the bytes of a "part-number" string are simply being added together to form a "hash-sum." Taking the remainder upon division by the number of records in the file produces a record-number specifying the place to start looking for this particular record.

Each record on the file contains an extra byte to indicate its status. The possible statuses are "available," "occupied," or "deleted."

When creating a hashed file for the first time, all the records must be marked as "available." The program crhash ("create hash file") will create a file of a specified number of records of specified size.

```
crhash.c:
    /* crhash -- create and initialize an empty hash file
     *       used to hold part database records
     */
    #include "local.h"
    #include "part.h"
    #include "rec_io.h"

    main(ac, av)
        int ac;
        char *av[];
        {
        rec_fd fd;          /* record file descriptor */
        short size;         /* size of one record in created file */
        long nrecs;         /* maximum numbers of records in created file */
        char *buf;          /* data to init. each record */
        long i;             /* counter to write records in created file */

        if (ac != 4)
            error("usage: crhash filename nrecs recsize", "");

        nrecs = atol(av[2]);
        size = atoi(av[3]);
        fd = rec_open(av[1], O_RDONLY, size);
        if (fd > 0)
            {
            rec_close(fd);
            error("file already exists:", av[1]);
            }

        fd = rec_open(av[1], O_RDWR|O_CREAT, size);
        if (fd < 0)
            error("can't create file", av[1]);

        buf = (char *)calloc(size, 1);
        if (buf == NULL)
            error("Need more heap space to allow size =", av[3]);
        *buf = REC_AVAIL;
        /* file was created ok, initialize file */
        for (i = 0; i < nrecs; ++i)
            {
            if (!rec_put(fd, buf, REC_W_END))
                error("I/O error writing new file", "");
            }
        rec_close(fd);
        exit(SUCCEED);
        }
```

The function rec_hfind starts reading at a specified record-number. If the record contains the desired key, the search is finished. Otherwise, successive records are read (wrapping from end-of-file to beginning-of-file if necessary) until the desired record is found or an unoccupied record space is found. rec_hfind needs two pointer-to-function arguments: one to specify the key-comparison function, and one to specify the hashing function. The keybuf argument points to a record that contains the key being searched for. The buf argument points to the storage into which the record will be read. Here is the rec_hfind function:

```
rec_hfind:
    /* rec_hfind.c -- find a record in a hashed file */
    #include "rec_io.h"

    long rec_hfind(fd, keybuf, buf, cmpfn, hashfn)
        rec_fd fd;              /* hashed file */
        data_ptr keybuf;        /* record key to find */
        data_ptr buf;           /* buffer for found record */
        int (*cmpfn)();         /* record key comparison function */
        long (*hashfn)();       /* hash lookup function */
    {
        long nrecs;             /* number of records in file */
        long ntry;
        long i;

        nrecs = rec_nrecs(fd);
        i = (*hashfn)(keybuf);
        for (ntry = 0; ntry < nrecs; ++ntry)
            {
            if (!rec_get(fd, buf, i))
                return (REC_ERROR);         /* i/o error during rec_get */
            if (*(char *)buf == REC_AVAIL)  /* examine first byte of buf */
                return (REC_NOT_FOUND);
            if (*(char *)buf == REC_OCCUP)
                {
                if ((*cmpfn)(keybuf, buf) == 0)
                        return (i);
                }
            i = IMOD(i + 1, nrecs);
            }
        return (REC_FULL);
    }
```

When a new record is to be added to the file, a different function (rec_havail) must be used to search for an available space to store the record. This function requires that the new record's key not be present in the file already, so rec_hfind must have been called first. The rec_hfind function skips over deleted records, because the record it is searching for might still be found further down in the file. On the other hand, rec_havail can stop when it sees the deleted record (or an "available" record), because a new record could be added here.

rec_havail:

```
/* rec_havail.c -- find where a record belongs in a hashed file */
#include "rec_io.h"

long rec_havail(fd, keybuf, buf, hashfn)
    rec_fd fd;              /* hashed file */
    data_ptr keybuf;        /* record key to find */
    data_ptr buf;           /* buffer for found record */
    long (*hashfn)();       /* hash lookup function */
    {
    long nrecs;             /* number of records in file */
    long ntry;
    long i;

    nrecs = rec_nrecs(fd);
    i = (*hashfn)(keybuf);
    for (ntry = 0; ntry < nrecs; ++ntry)
        {
        if (!rec_get(fd, buf, i))
            return (REC_ERROR);
        if (*(char *)buf == REC_AVAIL || *(char *)buf == REC_DELET)
            return (i);
        i = IMOD(i + 1, nrecs);
        }
    return (REC_FULL);
    }
```

Now we have all we need to implement a simple database such as the "parts" file. Each of the "part database" functions now makes use of the "hash file" functions to find, add, change, and delete records.

```
part_hash.c:
    /* part_hash.c -- hash file database access to parts */
    #include "rec_io.h"
    #include "part.h"
    #define HPART struct hash_part
    HPART
        {
        char hcode;
        PART part;
        };
    static HPART hpart = {0};
    static HPART kpart = {0};
    static rec_fd part_fd = 0;

    /* db_cmp_part - compare function for database access */
    static int db_cmp_part(p1, p2)
        HPART *p1, *p2;
        {
        return (strcmp(p1->part.part_no, p2->part.part_no));
        }

    /* db_hash_part - hash the part_no field */
    static long db_hash_part(p1)
        HPART *p1;
        {
        char *p;
        long sum = 0;

        for (p = p1->part.part_no; *p != '\0'; ++p)
            sum += *p;
        return (IMOD(sum, rec_nrecs(part_fd)));
        }

    /* db_open_part - open the parts database */
    void db_open_part()
        {
        part_fd = rec_open("part.dat", O_RDWR, sizeof(HPART));
        if (part_fd < 0)
            error("can't open ", "part.dat");
        }

    /* db_close_part - close the parts database */
    void db_close_part()
        {
        if (rec_close(part_fd) < 0)
            error("can't close ", "part.dat");
        }
```

```
/* db_add_part - add a part to the database */
bool db_add_part(partp)
    PART *partp;
    {
    long i;

    STRUCTASST(hpart.part, *partp);
    hpart.hcode = REC_OCCUP;
    i = rec_havail(part_fd, &hpart, &kpart, db_hash_part);
    if (i == REC_FULL)
        {
        remark("Part storage is full", "");
        return (NO);
        }
    else if (i == REC_ERROR || !rec_put(part_fd, &hpart, i))
        {
        remark("I/O error", "");
        return (NO);
        }
    return (YES);
    }

/* db_chg_part - change a part record on database */
bool db_chg_part(partp)
    PART *partp;
    {
    long this_rec;

    STRUCTASST(kpart.part, *partp);
    this_rec = rec_hfind(part_fd, &kpart, &hpart, db_cmp_part, db_hash_part);
    kpart.hcode = REC_OCCUP;
    return (rec_put(part_fd, &kpart, this_rec));
    }

/* db_del_part - delete a part record on database */
bool db_del_part(partp)
    PART *partp;
    {
    long this_rec;

    STRUCTASST(kpart.part, *partp);
    this_rec = rec_hfind(part_fd, &kpart, &hpart, db_cmp_part, db_hash_part);
    kpart.hcode = REC_DELET;
    return (rec_put(part_fd, &kpart, this_rec));
    }
```

```
/* db_find_part - find a part on the database */
bool db_find_part(partp)
    PART *partp;
    {
    long i;

    STRUCTASST(kpart.part, *partp);
    this_rec = rec_hfind(fd, &kpart, &hpart, db_cmp_part, db_hash_part);
    if (this_rec >= 0)
        {
        STRUCTASST(*partp, hpart.part);
        return (YES);
        }
    else if (this_rec == REC_ERROR)
        {
        remark("I/O error", "");
        return (NO);
        }
    else
        return (NO);
    }
```

This simple database concludes our discussion of file handling. The "hash file" is adequate for very simple applications, with only one key field and a generous amount of disk available for the record storage. Its handling of deleted records is rudimentary. It lacks the ability to find records sequentially. For more sophisticated requirements, there are now numerous database and file management packages available for use with C.

My main purpose throughout the book has been to introduce you to the use of C for programming reliable data structures. Wherever possible, I have tried to show examples which may also be useful in their own right, but ultimately the techniques are the most important thing. You now have all the tools of C language at your disposal, and the necessary concepts to use them reliably.

APPENDIX

[1-1] List of Reliability Rules

The reliability rules from the text are summarized in this list, with section-number references to the discussion of the rule.

Rule 1-1 (Section 1.1): Any macro definition containing operators needs parentheses around the entire definition. Each appearance of a macro argument in the definition also needs to be parenthesized if an embedded operator in the argument could cause a precedence problem.

Rule 1-2 (Section 1.1): Reliable modification of defined constants requires an environmental capability: there must be a means for ensuring that all files comprising a program have been compiled using the same set of headers. (The UNIX make command is one such capability.)

Rule 1-3 (Section 1.1): If there are limitations on the modifiability of a defined constant, indicate the limitations with a comment:

```
#define EOF (-1)    /* DO NOT MODIFY: ctype.h expects -1 value */
```

Rule 1-4 (Section 1.1): If one definition affects another, embody the relationship in the definition; do not give two independent definitions.

Rule 1-5 (Section 1.1): If a value is given for a #defined name, do not defeat its modifiability by assuming its value in expressions.

Rule 1-6 (Section 1.1): Use limits.h for environment-dependent values.

Rule 1-7 (Section 1.2): Use a consistent set of project-wide defined types.

Rule 1-8 (Section 1.3): Be sure that all functions are declared before use; headers are the most reliable way.

Rule 1-9 (Section 1.3): Create a project-wide "local" header for standard definitions and inclusions.

Rule 1-10 (Section 1.4): Use UPPERCASE names for unsafe macro functions, to emphasize the restrictions on their usage.

Rule 1-11 (Section 1.4): Never invoke an unsafe macro with arguments containing assignment, increment/decrement, or function call.

Rule 1-12 (Section 1.4): Whenever possible, use safe macro functions.

Rule 1-13 (Section 1.6): Use `#if 0` if there is a need to comment-out sections of code.

Rule 1-14 (Section 1.6): Enclose each header in an "inclusion sandwich."

Rule 2-1 (Section 2.1): When exactness counts in converting floating-point to integer, be sure the value being converted is non-negative.

Rule 2-2 (Section 2.1): Test `errno` before using results from the math functions.

Rule 2-3 (Section 2.3): Use the `<ctype.h>` facilities for character tests and upper-lower conversions.

Rule 2-4 (Section 2.4): Make sure that Boolean variables are assigned the values zero and one. This means that the type `tbool` is always adequate, and if this rule is part of local standards, the types `bool` and `tbool` could be made synonymous.

Rule 2-5 (Section 2.4): Make sure that each test condition is Boolean, involving only Boolean types or relational and logical operators.

Rule 2-6 (Section 2.5): An enumeration's constants should all be initialized, or else none of them should be initialized.

Rule 2-7 (Section 2.5): Write programs as if enumeration variables could receive no values other than the associated enumeration constants. Treat the enumeration types as if they were unique types, not for any arithmetic `int` usages. Convert between enumeration variables and integer values only by use of an explicit cast.

Rule 2-8 (Section 2.6): Include "one-too-far" values in the ranges for variables, if they are needed for loop terminations or other testing purposes.

Rule 2-9 (Section 2.6): Function parameters accepting the size of an arbitrarily large object should be declared with size_t type.

Rule 2-10 (Section 2.7): When two unsigned int's are subtracted, convert the result using either (unsigned) or UI_TO_I.

Rule 2-11 (Section 2.7): Use IMOD (or some similar mechanism) to ensure that a non-negative modulo result is produced.

Rule 2-12 (Section 2.8): In (signed) integer arithmetic, assume that overflow is illegal, may be detected (hence should never be programmed), and cannot be trapped or ignored.

Rule 2-13 (Section 2.9): Document the defining properties of declared names in a comment on the declaration, using a convention such as "colon followed by property."

Rule 3-1 (Section 3.1): Storage class (if any) should precede the type specifier.

Rule 3-2 (Section 3.1): If a variable has an initialization, its declaration should have a source line to itself.

Rule 3-3 (Section 3.1): Document the defining property of a data object with a comment on its declaration. Ensure that this defining property remains invariant (unchanging) as much as possible throughout the computation, and document any exceptions.

Rule 3-4 (Section 3.1): A program is easier to write correctly and to understand if all arrays are made complete before the array is used.

Rule 3-5 (Section 3.1): If an array's defining property can be true even if not all elements are defined, indicate the property on the array's declaration. For example,

```
char s[10];     /* : string */
```

Rule 3-6 (Section 3.2): Use executable assertions whenever they are simpler than the code being protected, and when the time to execute the assertions is not much greater than the time required to execute the code.

Rule 4-1 (Section 4.1): In each pointer assignment, the right-hand-side value must have exactly the same ("converted") pointer type as the left-hand-side.

Rule 4-2 (Section 4.2): The default requirement for pointer parameters is that they must point to storage that is entirely defined. Whenever a pointer parameter can accept something else, this should be explicitly stated on that parameter's declaration comment.

Rule 4-3 (Section 4.3): A function in which the address of an automatic variable is assigned to a non-automatic pointer must contain a comment to that effect. In any function with such a comment, each return from the function is an event requiring verification that no dangling pointers are left.

Rule 6-1 (Section 6.1): In portable programming, do not hard-code the numeric values of structure offsets. The values may be different in each environment. Refer to members by their symbolic member names only.

Rule 6-2 (Section 6.2): Names with leading underscore should only appear in code that is privy to the internal details of the associated data structure, not in "user-level" portable code.

Rule 6-3 (Section 6.2): Use the "leading underscore" name format for tag and member names if the internal details of the structure are not to be inspected by functions outside of the package. Conversely, avoid leading underscores if the details of the structure are available for inspection by functions that use the structure.

Rule 6-4 (Section 6.3): If a structure is not well-defined when initialized to zero, document this fact in a comment. (The program will in general be simpler if the members are defined such that the zero-initialized structure is well-defined.)

Rule 6-5 (Section 6.5): In portable code, do not depend upon the allocation order of bit-fields within a word.

Rule 6-6 (Section 6.7): Regarding parameters which are pointers to structures, an "out" pointer parameter is assumed to be non-NULL, pointing to the storage for a structure of the specified type. "In" and "in-out" pointer parameters are assumed to point to a well-defined structure of the specified type. Any exceptions should be noted in a comment on the parameter declaration.

Rule 7-1 (Section 7.1): When a pointer p is passed to the free function, the programmer must determine how many pointers are pointing into the freed storage. (This number is known as the "reference count" of the storage.) Steps must be taken (such as assigning NULL) to ensure that none of these pointers are subsequently used to access the freed storage.

Rule 7-2 (Section 7.1): For every instance in which a program allocates storage, there should be an easily identifiable instance in which that storage is later freed.

Rule 8-1 (Section 8.2): Always test the returned value from fopen to be sure that the open succeeded.

[1-2] Declaring Function Parameters

The headers shown in this book show function parameters in comments associated with each function declaration, in this style:

```
double atof();        /* PARMS(char *s) */
```

In this form, the comments serve purely for documentation purposes. However, the ANSI C draft envisions a style of function declaration called a "prototype," in which the function parameters are actually stated in the declaration, like this:

```
double atof(char *s);
```

When the compiler has seen a prototype declaration, it can then perform type-checking of the arguments, much as the lint checker does. More than this, prototypes can also cause the conversion of function arguments. If, for example, the header <math.h> declares sqrt as

```
double sqrt(double x);
```

a function call such as

```
int i = 10;
double y;

y = sqrt(i);
```

will cause the conversion of the integer i to the expected double parameter type.

All of this makes it more important than ever that library functions should be properly declared, and the standard headers are the most reliable way to do this.

Some recent C compilers which are incorporating concepts from the ANSI draft have already introduced prototypes; you may be seeing them in your next compiler version. Thus, for some period of time you may be concerned to write programs in such a way that they can be compiled both by the previous generation of compilers and by the new-style compilers as well. To accomplish this, you will want to do two things:

1. During this transition, you must make sure never to depend upon the argument conversions being done by the newer compilers. Your programs must continue to follow the argument-passing restrictions of the older compilers.

2.   You could, if you like, avoid declaring any argument information
     in your function declarations, thus keeping to the old style. You
     could, alternatively, package the argument declarations in a
     fashion which can be targeted either to old or new compilers. To
     do this, you could add a PARMS macro to your local header and use it
     in your function declarations like this:

```
void reverse PARMS((char *s));
```

The definition of PARMS for older compilers would simply discard the
argument (which must be enclosed in a second set of parentheses, to
allow for an arbitrary list of arguments):

```
#define PARMS(x)  ()          /* empty parens */
```

The declaration of reverse as given above would produce

```
void reverse ();
```

The definition of PARMS for newer compilers would simply produce the
argument:

```
#define PARMS(x) x
```

Thus the declaration of reverse would produce

```
void reverse (char *s);
```

If you adopt this transitional approach, you could take the PARMS
information out of the comments, add an extra set of parentheses, and
put the information onto the actual function declaration itself. I
thought that it was somewhat premature to present all my examples this
way in this book, but the translation from my notation should be rather
easy if you want to adopt the approach described here.

[1-3] Side-Effects and Unsafe Macros

A recent compiler innovation opens the way to reliably diagnosing
errors from side-effects on the invocation of unsafe macros. The Whitesmiths 3.0 compiler provides, as an extension, the pseudo-operator
$noside(expr), which causes a compile-time error if the expr contains any
side-effects. In order for the source code to remain portable, one would
add a definition to a header like portdefs.h for an identifier like NOSIDE:

```
#define NOSIDE(expr)  $noside(expr)
```

Then, the definition of unsafe macros could be given in this form:

```
#define ABS(x)  (NOSIDE(x) < 0 ? -(x) : (x))
```

The compiler would then give a diagnostic if x contained side-effects.

In an environment that did not provide this extra checking, the invocation NOSIDE(x) could simply produce (x):

```
#define NOSIDE(x) (x)
```

I have not followed this style in the book, only because the release of the Whitesmiths 3.0 compiler is so recent.

[2-1] Round-off Errors in Math Functions

The output file shown as sqrtx.out was produced by the White-smiths PDP-11/23 compiler (version 2.3). Similar small round-off errors are produced by most other math libraries. Here is a similar output from the Lattice 8088 compiler (version 2.15), which uses the 8087 auxiliary FPP chip:

```
sqrtx86.out:
    2.0    2.00000000000000044   -4.44E-16
    3.0    2.99999999999999955    4.44E-16
    5.0    5.00000000000000088   -8.88E-16
    6.0    5.99999999999999911    8.88E-16
    7.0    7.00000000000000088   -8.88E-16
    8.0    8.00000000000000177   -1.78E-15
   10.0   10.00000000000000176   -1.78E-15
   12.0   11.99999999999999821    1.78E-15
   13.0   12.99999999999999822    1.78E-15
   15.0   15.00000000000000176   -1.78E-15
   18.0   17.99999999999999642    3.55E-15
   19.0   19.00000000000000355   -3.55E-15
   20.0   20.00000000000000353   -3.55E-15
   23.0   22.99999999999999642    3.55E-15
   24.0   23.99999999999999642    3.55E-15
```

[2-2] Floating-to-Integer Truncation

As of June 1985, draft ANSI C requires that floating-to-integer truncation must be toward zero, whether the floating value is positive or negative. Since earlier C compilers may differ in the treatment of the rounding of negative floating values, the conservative course for portability is still to convert only positive values.

[2-3] Error Behavior of Math Functions

Some libraries (e.g., UNIX System V) provide more control over the treatment of errors in the math library. The user can provide a function named matherr which will be invoked if errors occur in a math function. This function could print diagnostics, terminate the execution, or specify the desired return-value.

The matherr function has not been adopted by ANSI C, so its use is not generally portable.

[2-4] Math Functions in ANSI C

These are the math functions that are declared in <math.h> in recent C libraries:

```
double acos(x)       - arc cosine of x
double asin(x)       - arc sine of x
double atan(x)       - arc tangent of x
double atan2(y, x)   - arc tangent of y/x
double ceil(x)       - smallest integer not less than x
double cos(x)        - cosine of x
double cosh(x)       - hyperbolic cosine of x
double exp(x)        - exponential function of x
double fabs(x)       - (floating) absolute value of x
double floor(x)      - largest integer not greater than x
double fmod(x, y)    - (floating) modulo function
double frexp(x, pi)  - normalized fraction
double ldexp(x, n)   - computes x times 2**n
double log(x)        - natural log of x
double log10(x)      - base-10 log of x
double modf(x, pd)   - compute integer and fractional part of x
double pow(x, y)     - raise x to the power y
double sin(x)        - sine of x
double sinh(x)       - hyperbolic tangent of x
double sqrt(x)       - square root of x
double tan(x)        - tangent of x
double tanh(x)       - hyperbolic tangent of x
```

In this tabulation, these are the types of the parameters:

```
double x, y;
double *pd;
int n;
int *pi;
```

[2-5] Character-Test Functions in ANSI C

These are the math functions that are declared in <ctype.h> in recent C libraries:

```
int isalnum(c)  - is c a letter or a digit?
int isalpha(c)  - is c a letter?
int iscntrl(c)  - is c a non-printing character (other than space)?
int isdigit(c)  - is c a digit?
int isgraph(c)  - is c a printing character (other than space)?
int islower(c)  - is c a lower-case letter?
int isprint(c)  - is c a printing character (including space)?
int ispunct(c)  - is c a punctuation character?
int isspace(c)  - is c a whitespace character?
int isupper(c)  - is c an upper-case letter?
int isxdigit(c) - is c a hexadecimal digit?
int tolower(c)  - convert upper-case c to lower case
int toupper(c)  - convert lower-case c to upper case
```

[4-1] Question

Just to be sure that you understand the "sandwich rule," jot down the variable name and type for the following declarations.

DECLARATION	VARIABLE NAME	TYPE ("DECLARED")
short **ap[5];	ap	short ** [5]
long (*pf)[2];	pf	long (*)[2]
double **pps;	pps	double **

[4-2] Printing Pointers

The new format for printing pointers is %p. It will produce a representation that is appropriate for the machine. There is a corresponding %p format for scanf which will read pointer values from a file.

[4-3] Question

Not all of the following "expressions" are valid. For each valid expression, write its value. Write "INVALID" otherwise.

&c	104	c	'1'	*c	INVALID
&pc	112	pc	104	*pc	'1'
&ppc	120	ppc	112	*ppc	104

[4-4] Question

The function call scanf("%c", &c) will read one character into c. What is the value being passed as the second argument to the scanf function?

104

Which of these expressions would accomplish the same result?

N   scanf("%c", c)

Y   scanf("%c", pc)

N   scanf("%c", &pc)

N   scanf("%c", *pc)

Y   scanf("%c", *ppc)

[4-5] Detecting Dangling Pointers

There are two techniques that an interpreter could use to detect dangling pointers. *Reference counts* keep track of the number of pointers that point to an object. *Reverse pointers* encode the "pointed-to" reverse relationship. Such techniques are, of course, diagnostic rather than preventative; a reliable program leaves no dangling pointers, in any environment.

[5-1] Comparison of Printf Versions

ANSI C (as of the June 1985 draft) has added some further refinements to printf. A %p format will print the value of a pointer, in a format appropriate for its machine. The %n format will *store* the number of characters printed so far; the corresponding argument should be a pointer to an *int*. The h modifier is allowed, so that short formats can be more nearly identical for printf and scanf. The L modifier for floating-point formats anticipates the introduction of ("extended precision") long double numbers. And %i is allowed, synonymous with the %d output format. (This is for compatibility with scanf, where %i has a special meaning; see note 5-4 below.)

Letting K stand for the K&R (UNIX Version 7) level of library, U stand for the /usr/group (UNIX System III and System V) level, and A stand for the (draft) ANSI C library, we have the following comparison:

Comparison of printf capabilities

Start:	%	K	U	A	start conversion specifier
Flags:	-	K	U	A	left-adjust
	+		U	A	print '+' or '-' sign
	blank		U	A	print ' ' or '-' sign
	#		U	A	"alternate" forms
Width:	0	K	?	A	leading zeroes
	*		U	A	take width from next arg
	number	K	U	A	minimum output field width
Precis:	*		U	A	take precision from next arg
	number	K	U	A	floating precision or max string width
Conv:	d	K	U	A	decimal int
	o	K	U	A	octal unsigned int
	x	K	U	A	hexadecimal unsigned int
	u	K	U	A	decimal unsigned int
	X		U	A	hexadecimal with caps "ABCDEF"
	i			A	decimal int
	h			A	(with int conv) short
	l	K	U	A	(with int conv) long
	f	K	U	A	"[-]ddd.ddd" fixed-point
	e	K	U	A	"[-]d.ddde÷dd"
	E		U	A	"[-]d.dddE+dd"
	g	K	U	A	smaller of 'e' and 'f'
	G		U	A	smaller of 'E' and 'f'
	L			A	(with floating conv) long double
	c	K	U	A	character
	s	K	U	A	string
	p			A	value of pointer
	n			A	store number of chars printed so far

[5-2] The FILE Defined-Type

In most implementations, FILE designates a particular struct. The tag-name is usually not _file (as suggested in Section 6.2), but more often something like _iob or _iobuf. Portable code cares nothing for all these distinctions, and just uses the FILE without examining its internals.

[5-3] The Fgetsnn Function

The question asked you to convert getsnn into fgetsnn, which takes a FILE * argument. Here is a solution:

```
fgetsnn:
    /* fgetsnn - get one line, omitting the newline (if any)
     * Returns the number of characters stored,
     * which equals size-1 only if no newline was found to that point.
     * Returns EOF at end of file.
     */
    #include "local.h"
    int fgetsnn(s, size, fp)
        char s[];
        int size;
        FILE *fp;
        {
        int i;
        metachar c;

        for (i = 0; i < size-1 && (c = getc(fp)) != EOF && c != '\n'; ++i)
            s[i] = c;
        if (c == EOF)
            return (EOF);
        /* else */
        s[i] = '\0';
        return (i);
        }
```

[5-4] Comparison of Scanf Versions

The full range of formats supported by scanf gets larger with each vendor's release; here is a comparison of the K&R version, the /usr/group version, and the (draft) ANSI version:

Comparison of scanf capabilities

Whitespace:		K			ignored(!)
			U	A	matches whitespace input
Start:	%	K	U	A	start conversion specifier
Flags:	*	K	U	A	suppresses assignment
Width:	number	K	U	A	maximum input field width
Conv:	d	K	U	A	decimal int
	o	K	U	A	octal unsigned int
	x	K	U	A	hexadecimal unsigned int
	u		U	A	decimal unsigned int
	X		U	A	hexadecimal unsigned int
	i			A	int: 0x->hex, 0->octal, else decimal
	h	K			(by itself) decimal short int
	h		U	A	(with int conv) short
	l	K	U	A	(with int conv) long
	f	K	U	A	float
	e	K	U	A	float
	E		U	A	float
	g		U	A	float
	G		?	A	float
	l	K	U	A	(with floating conv) double
	L			A	(with floating conv) long double
	c	K	U	A	character
	s	K	U	A	string (one "word")
	[list]		U	A	string of chars from "list"
	[^list]		U	A	string of chars not in "list"
	p			A	value of pointer
	n			A	store number of chars read so far

The new %n format from ANSI C takes a matching pointer to an int, into which is stored the number of input characters that have been consumed up to this point. This will make it much easier to discover exactly where an error has occurred in the input. Invoking scanf like this

```
getsnn(inputline, sizeof(inputline));
ret = sscanf(inputline, " %n%lf %n%lf", &howfar, &x, &howfar, &y);
if (ret != 2)
    {
    for (i = 0; i < howfar; ++i)
        putchar(' ');   /* space over to offending char */
    putchar('^');        /* print a position marker */
    printf("\nExpected a floating-point number here!\n");
    }
```

will give the user an indication of where the error occurred. (With a little work, you could modify this code to allow for tab characters in the user's entry.)

[6-1] Saving Space with Bit-Fields

As described in the text, a structure with bit-fields must occupy most of a 32-bit integer if its storage is to be economical on a wide range of machines. The (draft) ANSI C standard allows an implementation more freedom in the storage sizes for bit-field structures. If, for example, more compilers became available which would fit a bit-field structure into a short integer, then 16-bit structures would be more economical on 32-bit machines. Only time will tell whether this possibility becomes actualized.

[7-1] Specifying the Amount of Dynamic Memory

Each system has its own method of specifying the dynamic (stack plus heap) size for an executable program. On UNIX systems, the sizes grow dynamically as needed. On Whitesmiths' Idris system, one can use the setb command to set the dynamic size for a program. In the Lattice (MS-DOS) environment, the stack size can be specified by a global variable _stack, or by a command-line option using the "equal sign":

```
PROGNAME =8000
```

[7-2] Undefined Pointers

In the text, I have suggested that undefined pointers should receive some value which will cause an execution error if they are later used for indirection. The assumption here is that some means is available for examining the program state when an execution error occurs. On UNIX systems, for example, if the hardware can detect "out-of-segment" memory accesses, a "core image" file will be produced which can be examined with one of the debuggers. Other systems support various debuggers which will give interactive control to the user on out-of-segment memory accesses. Some interpretive environments will detect indirection through a NULL pointer and suspend execution.

In a number of environments, a NULL pointer will not cause an execution error, but there is some pointer value which will. If one were to add a macro, a_wild_ptr() into portdefs.h, then the macro could be targeted to the capabilities of each system.

A useful companion macro would be is_wild_ptr(p) which returns YES when the pointer argument is definitely invalid.

Not all hardware environments support traps from access-checking, so the approach cannot be universal. The portdefs.h could still follow a lowest-common-denominator approach: use the address of a static object which should otherwise never be referenced. This allows, at least, the is_wild_ptr macro to detect when an explicitly-wild pointer has been used. Not much, but it can help sometimes.

[7-3] Packaging a General-Purpose Library

The functions presented in this chapter have been designed primarily for their teaching value. I have tried to keep each function as simple as possible, while not constraining the applicability unnecessarily. Each function receives pointers to the appropriate type of data structure node, so that the pointer indirections are clear. This necessitated taking liberties with type-checking, in the form of headers which convert the calling program's pointers into the type expected by the function.

The primary constraint imposed by this type of construction is that the nodes declared by the calling program must contain the necessary structural pointers within the node structure itself. Thus, each user-declared node structure must be a stack/queue structure, a deque structure, or a tree structure; it cannot serve more than one purpose. If an already-declared structure is to be incorporated into a dynamic data structure, it must be declared as a sub-member of the node structure.

Execution-time studies of programs with dynamic data structures have often shown that a large percentage of CPU time is spent in the allocation and freeing functions. A more elaborately-designed library could allocate space for a dynamic data structure in larger blocks, and the allocation for each node could be done with a simple macro, to save time. One useful by-product of such allocation is that a development environment could provide assertions to verify that a node being incorporated into a data structure was in fact the appropriate type of node for that data structure.

The main advantage of providing special "allocate" operations for each data structure node is that the all the pointers passed around could be pointers to the actual user data in each node. The structural pointers could precede the data in memory, thus being "invisible" to the application programs that use the data structure. (This is, in fact, how the malloc and calloc functions administer the allocated blocks in several implementations.)

The tricky part is that the allocator mechanism must know about the alignment requirements on the target machine. Here is a set of macros which attempts a portable interface for three capabilities: the data type that has the system's most restrictive alignment; a macro which tells the offset of a member-name m in a structure st, and a macro which tells the alignment requirement of an arbitrary data type. (As of June 1985, ANSI X3J11 has not specified the semantics of structure-member layout sufficiently to guarantee the portability of these macros, which is why they are not in the text. There is even, as of now, no guarantee that portable macros of any sort could be defined with this specification. There are ways of accomplishing these capabilities on most systems, however.)

```
/* structure offsets and bounds; adjust to local system */
#define STRICT_ALIGN int        /* adjust to local alignment requirement */
#define OFFSET(st, m) \
    ((char *)&((st *)&struct_addr)->m - (char *)&struct_addr)
#define BOUNDOF(t) \
    ((char *)(struct {char byte0; t byten; } *)&struct_addr)->byten - \
    (char *)&struct_addr)
static STRICT_ALIGN struct_addr = 0;
```

A general-purpose library could take advantage of the emerging concept of "generic pointer" provided by draft ANSI C, and specify that the relevant pointer parameters of the library functions are generic pointers. We have seen the use of the defined-type data_ptr in this book to prepare for the availability of generic pointers, but in pre-ANSI compiler environments, pointers being passed to generic-pointer parameters must still have an explicit cast each time they are passed. Thus, there is no convenient alternative, for the time being, to the use of a header to automatically apply casts to the appropriate arguments. (Requiring the programmer to apply explicit casts upon every argument is not what I would call convenient.)

The functions provided do, however, provide a resource for program construction which is in general more reliable than hand-coding a new implementation for each specific purpose. I hope that you will find them of use in your work.

[8-1] Implementation of bin_open

The open function, as specified in UNIX manuals and in the /usr/group standard, works fine for the bin_open function. On some other systems, bin_open must be provided explicitly. For example, in the Whitesmiths environments (2.3 and prior), bin_open would be implemented something like this:

```
w_bin_open:
    /* bin_open - open a binary file
     * WSL 2.3 version
     */
    #include "bin_io.h"
    bin_fd bin_open(fname, type)
        char fname[];
        int type;
        {
        int fd;

        if ((type & O_TRUNC) != O_TRUNC)     /* not TRUNC mode */
            {
            fd = open(fname, type & O_RWMODE, 1);        /* attempt open */
            if (fd >= 0)
                {
                if ((type & (O_EXCL|O_CREAT)) == (O_EXCL|O_CREAT))
                    return (-1);             /* not allowed to exist */
                else
                    return (fd);             /* open succeeded */
                }
            else if ((type & O_RWMODE) == O_RDONLY)
                return (fd);                 /* rdonly, open failed */
            }
        if ((type & O_CREAT) != O_CREAT)
            return (-1);                     /* not allowed to create */
        fd = create(fname, type & O_RWMODE, 1);     /* attempt create */
        return (fd);
        }
```

Because the functionality of bin_open is so constrained, it should not be difficult to implement in any environment.

BIBLIOGRAPHY

ANSI Technical Committee X3J11 **[1985]** *C Information Bulletin (Preliminary Draft Proposed ANS).* X3 Secretariat, 311 First Street NW, Suite 500, Washington DC 20001, 1985.

Bentley, Jon Louis **[1982]** *Writing Efficient Programs.* Prentice-Hall, 1982.

Bentley, Jon Louis **[1984]**. "How to Sort." *Communications of the ACM.* Vol 27, No 4, April 1984, Pp 287-291.

Chirlian, Paul. **[1984]** *Introduction To C.* Matrix Publishers, 1984.

Chris DeVoney (Editor) **[1985+]** */c: The Journal for C Users.* Que Corporation, 7999 Knue Road, Indianapolis IN 46250, 1985+.

Feuer, Alan, and Narain Gehani **[1984]** *Comparing And Assessing Programming Languages: Ada, C, Pascal.* Prentice Hall, 1984.

Hancock, Les, and Morris Krieger **[1982]** *The C Primer.* McGraw Hill, 1982.

Harbison, Samuel, and Guy Steele **[1984]** *A C Reference Manual.* Prentice Hall, 1984.

Hunter, Bruce **[1984]** *Understanding C.* Sybex Computer Books, 1984.

Jaeschke, Rex **[1985+]** *The C Journal.* InfoPro Systems, POB 849, Denville NJ 07834, 1985+.

Kelley, Al, and Ira Pohl **[1984]** *A Book On C.* Benjamin Cummmings, 1984.

Kernighan, Brian, and Dennis Ritchie **[1978]** *The C Programming Language.* Prentice Hall, 1978.

Kernighan, Brian, and Rob Pike **[1984]** *The UNIX Programming Environment.* Prentice Hall, 1984.

Kochan, Stephen **[1983]** *Programming in C.* Hayden Book Company, 1983.

Knuth, Donald E. **[1973]** *The Art of Computer Programming: Volume 1: Fundamental Algorithms.* Addison-Wesley, 1973.

Parker, Robert V **[1985].** *A Catskill Eagle.* Delacorte, 1985.

Plum, Thomas **[1983]** *Learning To Program In C.* Plum Hall, 1983.

Plum, Thomas **[1984]** *C Programming Guidelines.* Plum Hall, 1984.

Plum, Thomas, and Jim Brodie **[1985].** *Efficient C.* Plum Hall, 1985.

Pugh, Kenneth **[1985]** *C Language for Programmers.* Scott Foresman Foresman Company, 1985.

Purdum, Jack J., Timothy C Leslie, and Alan L. Stegemoller **[1984]** *C Programmer's Library.* Que, 1984.

Tondo, Clovis, and Scott Gimpel **[1985]** *The C Answer Book.* Prentice Hall, 1985.

Traister, Robert **[1984]** *Programming In C For The Microcomputer User.* Prentice Hall, 1984.

Waite, Mitchell, Stephen Prata, and Donald Martin **[1984]** *C Primer Plus.* Howard W Sams & Company, 1984.

Ward, Terry **[1985]** *Applied Programming Techniques In C.* Scott Foresman & Company, 1985.

Wortman, Leon, and Thomas Sidebottom **[1984]** *The C Programming Tutor.* Robert J Brady Company, 1984.

_____ **[1975]** *A Course in Miracles.* Foundation for Inner Peace, Tiburon, CA, 1975.

INDEX

PLUM HALL

1 Spruce Av Cardiff NJ 08232
609-927-3770

REPLY FORM

Reliable Data Structures in C

Please check all that apply:

_____ I would like to be notified of any revisions to the ANSI standard for C which affect the content of this book, or of any corrections to the book.

_____ I would like to report an error, suggest an improvement, etc:

NAME _____

COMPANY _____

ADDRESS _____

_____

CITY _____ STATE _____ ZIP _____

COUNTRY _____

PHONE _____

86/01/06 ff 7

Plum Hall Inc
1 Spruce Avenue
Cardiff NJ 08232 USA